THE
State
OF THE
Animals III
2 0 0 5

edited by **Deborah J. Salem**
and **Andrew N. Rowan**

Humane Society Press
an affiliate of

Deborah J. Salem is director and editor in chief
of Humane Society Press.

Andrew N. Rowan is executive vice president, Operations,
for The Humane Society of the United States.

Copyright © 2005 by The Humane Society of the United States.
All rights reserved.

First edition
ISBN 0-9748400-5-X

Library of Congress Cataloging-in-Publication Data

Salem, Deborah J.
  The state of the animals, 2001 / edited by Deborah J. Salem and Andrew N. Rowan—1st ed.
(public policy series)
Includes bibliographical references.

ISBN 0965894231

1. Animal welfare—History. 2. Animal welfare—Societies, etc.
3. Animal rights. 4. Human-animal relationships. 5. Animal experimentation.

I. Salem, Deborah J. II. Rowan, Andrew N. III. Humane Society of the United States.
IV. Title. V. Public policy series.
(Humane Society Press)

HV4708.S16 2001
179.3—dc21   2001131096

Printed in the United States of America
Printed on 100 percent post-consumer recycled paper,
processed chlorine free and FSC certified, with soy-based ink.

Ｈ
ＳＰ

Humane Society Press
An affiliate of The Humane Society of the United States
2100 L Street, NW
Washington, D.C. 20037

Other Books in the Humane Society Press Public Policy Series

The Use of Animals in Higher Education:
Problems, Alternatives and Recommendations
by Jonathan Balcombe, Ph.D.

The State of the Animals: 2001
edited by Deborah J. Salem and Andrew N. Rowan

Animal Control Management:
A Guide for Local Governments
by Geoffrey L. Handy
(published by the International City/County Management Association)

Community Approaches to Feral Cats:
Problems, Alternatives, and Recommendations
by Margaret R. Slater

The State of the Animals II: 2003
edited by Deborah J. Salem and Andrew N. Rowan

Humane Wildlife Solutions:
The Role of Immunocontraception
edited by Allen T. Rutberg

Contents

Preface

This volume is the third in a series reviewing the state of animal protection in North America and worldwide. The series is envisioned as the cornerstone of the Public Policy Series of Humane Society Press (HSP), which was founded in 2000 as an affiliate of The Humane Society of the United States (HSUS).

HSP's Public Policy Series is a source of information and informed opinion on current and emerging issues in animal protection. Its audience is policy makers, animal advocates, the academic community, and the media. As of 2005 the series has grown to include seven titles, including this one. The series explores topics in companion animal and wildlife care, control, and management and in general education.

The State of the Animals III: 2005 looks at the unique challenges faced by cats in modern society. It also includes perspectives from outside the United States on legislative, basic animal-control, and international wildlife topics, confirming that the shadow cast by animal-protection issues crosses geographical and political boundaries.

We once again wish to thank Lester Brown and the Worldwatch Institute for providing an excellent model for this volume in the Institute's State of the World series. We also thank all of the contributors for their commitment to the project; perhaps the earliest champion of the State of the Animals concept, HSUS President and CEO Wayne Pacelle; and the editorial and production staff that guided the volume through the production process. Among these last are HSUS Creative Director Paula Jaworski and copyeditor Jean Bernard.

Deborah J. Salem
Andrew N. Rowan

Tracking the "State of the Animals": Challenges and Opportunities in Assessing Change

Randall Lockwood

There is something fascinating about science. One gets such wholesale returns of conjecture out of such a trifling investment of fact.

—Mark Twain
Life on the Mississippi (1874)

The original concept behind the State of the Animals series, as defined by Paul G. Irwin, president emeritus of The Humane Society of the United States (HSUS), in the first edition (2001, 1) was "to evaluate the position of animals in society at the dawn of the twenty-first century." As we embark on the third volume in this series, and as we view the state of the animals from a perspective midway through the first decade of the new century, it is helpful to examine some of the tools we have at our disposal to assess the situation and provide some suggestions for measuring our progress, or lack thereof, in improving the treatment of animals. Careful reflection on what we actually mean by "improving the state of the animals" is an important part of the process for planning and assessing present and future actions.

An increasing demand has been placed on advocacy groups of all kinds to develop ways of planning and evaluating their activities (Wandersman et al. 2000). There has been an erosion of support for well-meaning people engaged in activities that seem to be helpful to animals or people in need, if this support is to be given simply because the activities seemed to be the right thing to do. Advocacy groups of all kinds are seeing more demand for accountability from funders and other sponsors such as United Way (Hatry et al. 1996). Some have described the current situation for nonprofit organizations as a "perfect storm," a collision of a declining economy, reduced government support, and state and local budget crises (Boice 2003). Individual donors, government agencies, foundations, and other supporters of advocates for change want to see meaningful assessments of results. They demand—and deserve—valid and accurate measures of impact before they provide new or continuing support for a program or organization.

We, as animal advocates, also have a basic need to see "how we're doing" and why we are being effective or ineffective. If we are not progressing in the way we had hoped, if we are not improving the state of the animals, then we need to try to identify the social, psychological, cultural, economic, political, and other obstacles to progress and develop new strategies and tactics that may be more effective. We also can benefit from clarification of the "trajectories of change," the processes that lead people and organizations to develop attitudes and behavior that are consistent with those we wish them to adopt and the attitudes or experiences that serve as "entry points" for concern about the issues that are important to us.

In this chapter we:

1. Review some of the measures that have been used in the past to attempt to assess the state of the animals and the extent to which we can continue to apply these measures to track future changes.

2. Review some of the emerging tools and developing technologies that can improve our tracking of the state of the animals and provide some quantitative measures of our progress.

3. Explore some examples of general measures of human interaction with animals that

might prove useful in predicting and tracking changes in how they are treated.

Tools for Assessment

Tools for tracking changes in the state of the animals fall into a few broad categories:

1. Animal Demographic/ Geographic Measures

One important measure is simply the number of animals of a particular kind, or the number kept under certain conditions. The goal of particular actions on behalf of animals may be to increase certain numbers (e.g., the number of individuals of a given species living in protected habitats) or it may be to decrease the numbers (e.g., the number of sows being kept in confinement-rearing situations). These measures may be somewhat different from measures of animal use, described below, since animals kept under similar conditions (e.g., in the laboratory), may be subjected to different treatments with differing effects on their overall welfare.

The most basic demographic measure of the state of the animals that has been applied for decades is the assessment of population levels of threatened or endangered species. Such measures are also closely linked to assessments of the extent of appropriate habitat, for example, number of acres protected in land trusts or measures of acreage of rainforest protected or lost to development. Such population estimates of wildlife numbers are also commonly applied at the national, state, and local levels. However, population estimates of hunted species are frequently the subject of debate since the underlying assumptions behind such estimates are always open to criticism from differing groups. For

example, estimates of black bear populations may be interpreted by some to imply that the population is stable, growing, or even a nuisance and thus is "harvestable," while others may interpret the same data to show that the population is at best "recovering" or potentially fragile.

Demographic measures have frequently been applied to the assessment of farm animal issues. Fraser, Mench, and Millman (2001) and Trent et al. (2003) use worldwide inventories of common farm animals as one significant measure as well as changes in the numbers being kept under different systems or on facilities of different sizes. The same approach has been applied to tracking the state of animals kept in laboratory settings (Rowan and Loew 2001) and the growing proportion of horses being kept primarily for recreational purposes (Houpt and Waran 2003).

Demographic variables have also been key to the assessment of progress on companion animal issues (Clancy and Rowan 2003). Reliable data on the numbers of companion animals sharing the lives of people in different demographic categories (by region, age, family composition, ethnicity, etc.) are important for planning programs that seek to enhance those relationships. Although several groups, including the American Veterinary Medical Association (AVMA 2002) or the American Pet Products Manufacturers Association (APPMA 2004), routinely survey patterns of pet ownership and care, these surveys focus primarily on consumer expenditures or the delivery of veterinary care and do not attempt to specifically track broader aspects of human-animal interactions.

Tracking companion animal issues through demographic analysis of the population of companion animals entering and exiting animal shelters has been difficult. The 1994–1997 Shelter Statistics Sur-

vey conducted by the National Council on Pet Population Study and Policy (NCPPSP 2000) attempted to collect such information via survey cards sent to more than five thousand shelters. Although fewer than 20 percent of shelters responded, information was gathered on the handling of about four million animals for each year of the study. Because the responding shelters could not be assumed to represent a random sampling of facilities, the Council notes that "it is not possible to use these statistics to estimate the number of animals entering animal shelters in the United States, or the numbers euthanized on an annual basis." Other projects undertaken with a smaller number of shelters have attempted to get a clearer picture of the dynamics of the relinquishment of animals to shelters (Salman et al. 1998, 2000; New et al. 1999; Scarlett 1999; New 2000; Kass 2001).

2. Organizational, Individual, and Institutional Measures

Another approach to assessing the state of the animals has been to quantify and describe the number and nature of organizations and individuals involved in or supportive of animal protection. Irwin (2003) offered the number of animal-protection organizations per one million human population as one measure of the relative support for animal-protection causes in a cross section of foreign countries. Such organizations routinely use the number of donors and/or supporters as one of the most significant measures of their success, public support, and potential political strength.

Individual demographics can also be revealing in tracking the changing relationships between people and animals. One important demographic that has frequently been tracked to assess the state of the animals is the proportion of the population holding a hunting license, which has declined from 7.18 percent of the U.S. population in 1980 to 5.35 percent in 2000 (Grandy, Stallman, and Macdonald 2003).

Within any demographic measure, changes in the structure of the demographics can reflect important changes in the nature of support or opposition that should be tracked. Is support for animal-protection ideas and behaviors expanding into demographic groups where it has traditionally been lower (e.g., Hispanic, Asian)? Is the population of those who hold hunting licenses aging? Is the median education level of those employed in animal control rising? Is the purchase of fur by women under thirty years of age rising or falling? Questions like these are important in providing significant dimensions for the assessment of changes in the state of the animals.

In addition to tracking changing demographics of people and organizations, it is meaningful to quantify changes in programs. Recent indicators of progress have included the rising number of law schools offering some instruction in animal law (Davis 2003; Wise 2003); the growing number of communities with "Safe Havens" programs to protect the pets of women leaving situations of domestic violence (Lerner 1999; Lerner and Zorza 1999); and an increasing proportion of animal shelters sponsoring humane education programs (Unti and DeRosa 2003). The existence of such programs is clearly a significant step, but more direct measures of program outcomes are ultimately needed to assess their benefits to animals.

3. Financial Measures

One of the most basic techniques used to assess social, political, or organizational change is to "follow the money." Comparing expenditures, donations, budget allocations, and other monetary measures offers a precise way of comparing different programs over time. Previous *State of the Animals* essays have examined such financial measures as U.S. fur sales (Irwin 2001) and funding from the National Institutes of Health for research involving animal use (Rowan and Loew 2001). The AVMA uses veterinary expenditures for a variety of companion animals as a key measure of trends in the delivery of veterinary care and as a way of understanding the reasons clients give for choosing a veterinarian (AVMA 2002). Because financial expenditures can be adjusted to some standardized unit (e.g., year 2000 dollars), they provide a powerful tool for assessing changes over a relatively long time frame. However, detailed analyses have been used far more often by trade and professional associations like the AVMA and the APPMA than by advocacy groups.

4. Measures of Human-Animal Interaction

Efforts to improve the state of the animals must ultimately rely on assessing changes in how human beliefs and actions affect the lives of animals—how people and animals interact. If we want to improve this interaction and measure the extent to which we are making the desired changes, we need to be able to go beyond the measures we have already outlined and assess the three dimensions of interaction: thoughts, words, and deeds.

Thoughts

Knowing what people think and know about animal issues is an essential component of "social marketing," the use of marketing principles to influence an audience to accept, reject, or modify behaviors for the benefit of others (Kotler, Roberto, and Lee 2002; Ginsberg 2004). Many animal-protection professionals are recognizing the importance of applying the theories, tools, and techniques of marketing science to the social change arena. Green (2004, 1) notes: "Marketing research provides an excellent starting point for identifying effective approaches to animal advocacy." In animal protection, the "commodity" to be marketed is compassion and concern about animal issues. As in any marketing activity, it is essential to assess the attitudes of various segments of the "target audience" toward the product—in this case, concern about animal welfare. The principal tool for this assessment is opinion surveys.

Animal advocates are increasingly recognizing the importance of well-crafted, professional opinion surveys and focus groups to assess public opinion on a variety of issues. Questions on animal issues are now included routinely on a number of professional polls and surveys (see below). At least one professional organization, the Humane Research Council, has begun to apply advanced survey methods to a variety of issues on behalf of The HSUS, The Fund for Animals, and other organizations. Their recent projects have included studies of attitudes and behaviors relating to fur (Humane Research Council 2003) and motives, objections, and barriers to adopting vegetarian and vegan diets.

Animal issues have been the focus of or included in more than 250 polls and surveys since 1948. Summaries of many of these surveys are available through the Tufts University Center for Animals and Public Policy (Kossow n.d.) and the Humane Research Council *(www. humaneresearch.org)*. These studies have been conducted by many different industry, advocacy, and other groups, but few have been conducted in a way that asks the same kinds of questions in the same way over an extended period, thus making comparisons difficult. Most are polls about a single issue or opinion, rather than comprehensive surveys designed to see how attitudes may interact. Future tracking of the state of the animals will require regular, professionally conducted surveys that attempt to trace the development of attitudes and opinions over time. These studies need to be supplemented with smaller focus groups to try to unravel the complexities of the decision-making processes that lead people to develop or resist the attitudes and opinions of concern.

Words

In addition to knowing what people are thinking about animal issues, an important measure of the state of the animals is what people are saying about animals. Public opinion is both shaped and reflected by media coverage. The proliferation of media outlets, from cable stations to satellite radio to websites and Internet "blogs," makes it almost impossible to get systematic and comparative data on the changing depiction of animal issues in the media. Nearly every viewpoint, no matter how extreme, enjoys some representation in today's media universe. However, it is still valuable to track the attention given to animal issues in "mainstream" media (daily newspapers, network and basic cable television and radio, widely distributed movies, etc.) as one measure of the zeitgeist.

Clearly there is a steady stream of progressive media attention given to animal protection, as is recognized each year in the Genesis Awards, formerly presented by the Ark Trust and now coordinated through The HSUS's Hollywood office. A more in-depth analysis of the media picture that is presented will require tracking the content and tone of media coverage over time. Such analysis is time consuming, but it can be useful in detecting important shifts in thinking or obstacles to change. For example, Arluke et al. (2002) examined press reports concerning

cases that involved hoarding large numbers of animals in unsanitary conditions. They identified a variety of themes, ranging from humor to revulsion, that potentially confounded communicating the seriousness of this problem as both an animal protection and human mental health concern. A repeat of this kind of analysis in the future would offer insight into the extent to which humane groups have been able to educate the public and professionals about these issues.

It is difficult to take the pulse of the media and the public even with the most comprehensive quantitative analysis of media coverage and content. Some change in attitudes, opinions, and policy is driven by constant media repetition, even when the problem may not have changed. The widespread attention given to "road rage" by American, Australian, and European media in the late 1990s, for example, was viewed largely as an inappropriate response to extremely rare criminal acts (Elliot 1999). Likewise, the widespread media coverage of dog-bite-related human fatalities attributed to a small number of breeds (mainly pit bulls and Rottweilers) has been criticized as an inappropriate application of an extremely rare event (less than .001 percent of dog attacks) to the formation of public policy (Sacks et al. 2000; AVMA Task Force 2001). Since media in a competitive commercial environment look to each other to get a sense of what they should be covering, any coverage of high-profile issues can quickly escalate, so simple counts of media articles can give very misleading impressions of the depth and breadth of public interest and concern.

Although the sheer volume of coverage of an issue can affect public and professional thinking, major changes can often come about through a timely, well-crafted publication that resonates with public interest and concern. This has clearly been the case with such

influential works as *Animal Liberation* (Singer 1975) and *Dominion* (Scully 2002). Certain issues and approaches strike what media expert Tony Schwartz (1974) describes as "the responsive chord." He notes that some of the most successful political and public information campaigns are those that don't necessarily tell people anything new but rather tell them something they already know in a new and useful way that they are prepared to accept and act on. This has certainly contributed to the success of The HSUS's First Strike™ Campaign, which makes the connection between cruelty to animals and human violence (Ascione and Lockwood 2001). This campaign provided research validation for the generally held concern about individuals who engage in cruelty to animals. It also provided professionals in diverse fields with the tools to apply this information. In 2004 an independently conducted survey (described below) noted that 85 percent of respondents agreed with the statement, "It has been demonstrated that people who repeatedly and intentionally harm animals are more likely to show violence to people." Only 4 percent disagreed with the statement, suggesting that this is an issue that is reaching almost complete public acceptance and agreement and has entered into a phase of shaping public policy and programs.

Deeds

The ultimate goal of social marketing is to change how people behave—the choices they make. Thus the best measure of outcome can be to look not at what people think or say, but at what they actually do. What do people buy? What do they choose to wear? What do they eat? How do they vote? How do they treat the animals in their homes?

This is one of the problems inherent in public opinion research. Thoughts, words, and deeds are not always consistent. For example, Braithwaite and Braithwaite (1982) surveyed college undergraduates about their attitudes and behaviors on many actions that potentially involved animal suffering. They point out a major "disconnect" between opinions and actions. As an example, they note that 73 percent of those surveyed disapproved of force-feeding geese to produce pâté, but only 46 percent disapproved of actually eating pâté produced this way.

Even with sophisticated survey techniques, it is often difficult to reconcile what people do with what they have said they would do or said they have done. The recent controversy surrounding the inaccuracy of exit polls in the 2004 presidential election raised questions about the polling techniques that have been used worldwide. Polling firms for the National Election Pool, which surveyed voters in 1,480 randomly chosen precincts, delivered exit poll results that overstated Sen. John Kerry's support in twenty-six states and President George Bush's in four. In reviewing the errors, they concluded that Kerry supporters were more likely to participate in exit polls for "motivational reasons that were impossible to quantify" (CNN 2005). Freeman (2004), however, notes that the conclusion that Kerry supporters were more likely to participate lacks independent evidence. Such discrepancies illustrate the need for detailed analysis of the many motivational factors that transform ideas and opinions into actions.

For years, many advocacy groups and government agencies measured their productivity in terms of output rather than outcomes. It is usually far easier to measure the number of reports distributed, workshops held, dollars raised or spent, bills introduced, or signatures obtained than it is to demonstrate that efforts have actually proven to be a benefit to those to be helped. Even when the desired

goal is clearly defined and the outcome has clear potential benefits to animals, these benefits may be hard to demonstrate. For example, an important objective of animal advocates is to increase the penalties for serious cruelty to animals to felony level. Although it is essential to have the strongest possible laws available to those who must respond to cruelty to animals, many other variables affect the ultimate impact on animals. Does the public report such crimes? Do police respond and investigate? Do prosecutors move the cases forward? Do judges issue appropriate sentences? For many reasons, simply passing good laws is not necessarily a good predictor that conditions will improve for those protected by the laws (see Rosen and Rowan, this volume).

The gap between action and benefit may exist for other reasons. Popular yet unproductive programs may continue for decades, as illustrated by the persistence of drug abuse prevention programs with no significant effect on drug use among the target audience (Lymen et al. 1999) and Texas abstinence-only sex education programs that resulted in a greater number of participants having sex (Anonymous 2005). Good science is easily obscured by conflicting social and political agendas.

Partly in response to dissatisfaction with conventional evaluation of drug abuse programs, the model for program evaluation adopted by the Substance Abuse and Mental Health Services Administration (SAMHSA) and many other agencies and organizations is the Getting to Outcomes (GTO) approach (Wandersman et al. 2000). This approach stresses accountability for the various elements of successful programming, including:

1. attention to specific needs and resources;
2. clearly defined goals, target populations, and desired outcomes;

3. science-based models for practices and programs that can be useful in reaching those goals;
4. fitting programs to the community context;
5. evaluating specific program outcomes; and
6. planning for sustaining successful programs.

This renewed interest in using well-documented "best practices" to generate desired results for the target audience and sustaining successful programs offers refreshing promise for a wide variety of programs that seek to improve conditions for people and animals.

Tracking and Analyzing Opinions: A Preliminary Study

Tracking and understanding changing attitudes and behaviors will require repeated measures of the same, or at least similar, attitudes. Despite hundreds of surveys and polls, there have been few such repeated measures.

One of the deterrents to effective use of repeated survey or polling techniques has been their high cost. The inclusion of questions on national polls such as the Harris, Gallup, or Roper polls can cost more than one thousand dollars per question. The growth and acceptance of the Internet as a primary means of communication for many activists and private citizens opens the door to Internet survey methods as a potential tool for rapid and inexpensive collection of such information but raises new questions about the applicability of such data to the general public. As Internet use grows, the differences between the universe of Internet-savvy people and the general public will shrink.

The HSUS reviewed data obtained from a July 2004 Internet poll of 1,031 U.S. adults conducted for The HSUS by Edge Research Inc. ("Omnibus Survey"). This was the first HSUS use of an Internet-based polling resource to assess various attitudes and activities regarding animals and animal protection. In addition to a detailed cross-tabulation analysis of the survey results, The HSUS has compared these findings to those generated by an Internet poll of more than 1,600 respondents solicited during April 2004 via invitations posted on the *hsus.org* website (termed "HSUS Website Survey") and a traditional telephone poll of a representative sample of the U.S. population conducted in January of 2003 by Penn, Schoen, and Berland (termed "PSB Survey"). The HSUS expected the HSUS website survey to be non-representative of the population as a whole, since it sampled a motivated, self-selected population of visitors to the website. However, since one of the goals of this analysis was to determine the characteristics of these highly committed supporters, it was felt that identifying differences between them and the general public would help identify the pathway along which The HSUS would like to move the general public.

In addition to assessing the opinions surveyed, The HSUS was interested in reviewing the utility of Internet polling methods, which can be much faster and less expensive but may have built-in biases due to possible demographic differences among respondents with access to Internet technology, HSUS members and constituents, and the general U.S. population.

These surveys addressed many different issues (see appendix A for a summary of responses and comparisons of the survey population demographics to those of the U.S. population). The HSUS focuses on just a few of them to demonstrate how different approaches vary in what they reveal about the opinions of the general public and animal advocates.

Support for Animal Protection

Protecting animals from cruelty and abuse was clearly a high priority for this representative sample, as it was for all the groups surveyed. These results are identical to those of the PSB phone survey. It is not surprising that the HSUS website survey showed even higher concern for protecting animals, with 97.2 percent considering it "very important" or "important."

It is also not surprising that those rating protecting animals from abuse as a high priority were significantly more likely to have made a contribution to an animal-protection or animal rights group in the last year (Question 22)—88 percent—than were those who rated it a low priority (56 percent). The same was true of the HSUS website survey, in which contributions had been made by 85 percent of those who considered animal protection important, as opposed to contributions by only 33–38 percent of those who consider it only "somewhat important" or "not important." The high proportion of the general population that considers this a significant priority suggests that there is a large and untapped pool of potential financial support for such efforts.

More than half of the respondents in the Omnibus survey said they had reported the cruelty to animals they witnessed. This was comparable to the 60 percent of the PSB survey who reported abuse and significantly less than the 77 percent of the HSUS website survey who said they had reported it. In this survey, reporting was significantly more likely among those who rated animal protection a top priority (77 percent) than those who did not (22 percent). Reporting was also significantly more likely among those with dogs and cats (58 percent vs. 33 percent), those with a favorable opinion of The HSUS (60 percent vs. 42 per-

cent), those who donate to animal protection (66 percent vs. 39 percent), women (64 percent vs. 44 percent in men), and those over age 65 (75 percent vs. 37 percent in those under 35).

Pet Ownership

In the Omnibus sample, 96 percent of those who rated protecting animals as a "top priority" had at least one pet. Those who reported they had no pets in the last ten years were significantly more likely to be unfamiliar with The HSUS or to rate The HSUS unfavorably. Only 5.2 percent of those with no pets in the last ten years were animal-protection donors. Animal protection donors were twice as likely to have had five or more pets as were non-donors (39.2 percent vs. 21.2 percent). The highest levels of past pet ownership (seven pets or more) were significantly associated with having children in the home.

Financial Support of Animal-Protection Efforts

Overall, approximately one-third of the Omnibus sample identified themselves as donors to animal protection or animal rights organizations. It is not surprising that donors were significantly more likely to have rated animal protection as very important and a top or high priority. About 42 percent of donors currently had a dog or cat, but 56 percent of those with a dog or cat were not identified as donors, again suggesting a large potential pool of support. Nearly 95 percent of donors reported having had at least one pet over the last ten years. Of those who did not currently have a dog or cat, 78 percent were non-donors. Of those who had not had any dogs or cats over the previous ten years, only 5 percent had donated to animal protection or animal rights.

Pet—specifically, dog or cat—

ownership is clearly a major driving force of concern about animal issues and making financial contributions. Experience with and caring for companion animals is often the portal for compassion and concern that extends to a wide range of issues involving many different species of animals. These results confirm the notion that the large segment of dog and cat owners in the United States, and even in international populations, represents a significant potential audience for outreach on issues beyond those affecting companion animals.

Donations to Non-Animal Charities

Those ranking animal protection as a low priority (46.4 percent) were significantly more likely to support United Way than were those ranking animal protection highly (36 percent), although this shows that more than a third of animal protection donors support United Way or social service charities. Similarly, those who rated animal protection as a low priority were significantly more likely to make contributions to churches or religious organizations (56.3 percent vs. 46.8 percent), but once again this finding shows that nearly half of animal-protection donors also support religious charities. There were no differences in the likelihood of donations to educational institutions associated with the pattern of giving to animal protection. Donations to health-related charities increased with age (19.5 percent of <35, 25.8 of 35–49; 29.5 percent of 50–64; 47.7 percent of 65+). Obviously, older cohorts are more likely to be concerned about and supportive of health-related issues.

Demographic Variations in Survey Methods

One purpose of this study was to evaluate the effectiveness of the Edge Research Internet polling methodology as a way of generating useful information in a cost effective way. All of our surveys (Omnibus, website, PSB) focused on adult respondents (over age eighteen) in assessing opinions as well as patterns of giving. Some of the differences between survey populations and U.S. population are shown in appendix A.

Age

A large proportion (25 percent) of the U.S. population is under age eighteen and was not included in this survey. The HSUS website sample matched the adult U.S. population surprisingly well for *age* distribution. The Omnibus survey seems to have significantly underrepresented the 65+ age group (<2 percent of the sample and >12 percent of the population), perhaps due to demographic differences in web access that were not reflected in website visitors to The HSUS. Conversely, the PSB telephone survey overrepresented older respondents (21 percent vs. 12 percent), perhaps due to older respondents' greater willingness to participate in a phone survey.

Gender

The Omnibus and PSB surveys closely matched the gender division of the U.S. population. The HSUS website survey was strongly skewed to female respondents (90 percent), reflecting greater support for animal organizations by women. This suggests a need to balance this gender discrepancy if this approach is used for future surveys, since gender strongly affects many of the other attitudinal measures we have assessed.

Race

The Omnibus internet survey undersampled African Americans (2 percent vs. 13 percent in the population) and Hispanic/Latinos (1 percent vs. 13.4 percent). The same was true of the HSUS website survey. The PSB phone survey accurately sampled African Americans, but undersampled Hispanic/Latino populations. If animal protection advocates are seeking detailed attitude and behavior information from these populations, special efforts have to be made to specifically sample these populations. A further confound in the Omnibus survey was that the non-Caucasian group was significantly younger; only 12 percent were over age fifty, compared to 40 percent of the Caucasian segment of the sample.

Income

The Omnibus, HSUS website, and PSB surveys were generally comparable in the income breakdown of those sampled, except that the PSB phone survey methodology was less likely to capture the highest income levels.

The Edge Research Omnibus survey method generated a large amount of data rapidly and in a form that allowed easy access to the kind of detailed analysis presented here. With some minor exceptions noted above, the sample did seem to be representative of the U.S. population. However, since much of the support for animal protection issues seems to be strong in the older (50–64 and 65+) cohorts, special effort should be made to sample this group adequately in future surveys. None of the methods used in the past seems to sample African-American or Hispanic/Latino populations adequately. Any efforts to specifically assess attitudes and opinions as part of outreach to these populations will require special sampling and survey methods.

A "Pet Lover's Index"

Large amounts of attitudinal data can be collected by means of the survey methods described. It will be important to have some standardized approaches for simplifying some of these data in a way that allows more rapid analysis and prediction of attitudes and behavior.

Numerous studies have proposed a variety of scales that would assess the degree of attachment people have to their animal companions. One of the most widely used is the Lexington Attachment to Pets Scale or LAPS (Johnson, Garrity, and Stallones 1992). Most existing scales are theory based and tend to measure emotional responses to pets. Others, such as Poresky's (1989) try to add behavioral dimensions such as "how often do you pet/stroke your companion animal?" Berryman, Howells, and Lloyd-Evans (1985) concluded that two types of pet owners emerged from their survey, one in which the pet-owner relationship was most similar to a relationship to the individual's own child and a second in which the relationship was valued for "fun/play" and "relaxation based on absence of demands." Holcomb, Williams, and Richards (1985) used the Pet Attachment Survey (PAS), a twenty-seven-item Likert-type scale with both behavioral and emotional aspects of attachment. Wilson, Netting, and New (1987) advocated the Pet Attachment Index, a fifty-item scale measuring owner characteristics, attachment, and attitudes toward pets. This was used by Kidd and Kidd (1989), who reported that women, children, and childless couples were more attached to their pets than others were.

Few studies examine these attitudes in relation to specific owner behaviors that might benefit the pets. A study is currently underway to analyze the connection between various measures of pet attachment and the well-being of pets (Douglas 2004).

None of the pet attachment studies attempted to relate the level of attachment to the larger issue of attitudes and behaviors in connection with overall support for other animal-related issues. Since the results of the Omnibus survey suggested that pet ownership was significantly correlated with concern for animal protection in general, and concern about a variety of specific issues relating to noncompanion animals, the attempt was made to devise a simplified measure of pet attachment that might be predictive of attitudes and behaviors related to animal welfare (see appendix B for the variables used to create this measure).

This composite score was cross-tabulated with other Omnibus survey measures, including reporting of cruelty to animals, keeping cats indoors, opposing confinement rearing of sows, supporting bans on the use of chimpanzees in research, opposing canned hunts, and donating to animal charities. In every case a high score on the "Pet Lover's Index" was significantly associated with high support for the animal protection position (all chi-square values significant at p<.001). This confirms that caring for and about dogs and cats is a primary portal to compassion and concern about a wide array of animal protection issues.

Conclusions and Recommendations

Efforts to improve the state of the animals can benefit from the systematic application of social marketing approaches that assess existing attitudes and behaviors in different segments of the population, properly design appropriate messages that target well-defined audiences, and apply "Getting to Outcomes"-style assessments that honestly assess the impact of program outcomes.

Future efforts to track these changes should include:

1. Clear definitions of desired goals and appropriate target audiences
2. Baseline information on current demographics, attitudes, and behavior that can be used to assess future trends. These data should be collected both nationally and locally and should carefully examine differences in meaningful subgroups (age, ethnicity, pet ownership, etc.)
3. Tools and techniques for cost-effective, repeated measures of the same attitudes and behaviors and analysis of relationships in the data that may reveal the pathways for change in the desired direction
4. Application of multiple measures of progress (examining people's thoughts, words, and deeds) and multiple techniques (narrowed surveys, focus groups) to clarify uncertain connections when these techniques reveal inconsistencies
5. Careful review of success and failures to better understand the dynamics of changing attitudes and behavior involving animals.

Successful advocacy for animals must combine science, art, empathy, and a passion to improve the lives of others. Greater attention to all of these elements will produce outstanding outcomes. We can hope that the words of Mark Twain that opened this essay will need to be given a slight twist. We can hope that we will get enormous returns of progress out of a small investment of fact.

Literature Cited

Anonymous. 2005. Teen sex increased after abstinence program. Reuters, February 1.

American Pet Products Manufacturers Association (APPMA). 2004. 2003–2004 Pet Owners Survey. Greenwich, Conn.: APPMA.

AVMA Task Force on Canine Aggression and Human-Canine Interactions. 2001. A community approach to dog bite prevention. *Journal of the American Veterinary Medical Association* 218(11): 1732–1749.

American Veterinary Medical Association (AVMA). 2002. *U.S. Pet Ownership and Demographics Sourcebook.* Schaumburg, Ill.: AVMA.

Arluke, A., R. Frost, G. Steketee, G. Patronek, C. Luke, E. Messner, J. Nathanson, and M. Papazian. 2002. Press reports of animal hoarding. *Society and Animals* 10(2): 113–135.

Ascione, F.A., and R. Lockwood. 2001. Cruelty to animals: Changing psychological, social, and legislative perspectives. In *The state of the animals: 2001,* ed. D.J. Salem and A.N. Rowan, 39–53. Washington, D.C.: Humane Society Press.

Berryman, J.C., K. Howells, and M. Lloyd-Evans. 1985. Pet owner attitudes to pets and people: A psychological study. *The Veterinary Record* 21(28): 659–661.

Boice, J.P. 2003. Untapped wealth. *Advancing Philanthropy.* November/December, 16–17.

Braithwaite, J., and V. Braithwaite. 1982. Attitudes toward animal suffering: An exploratory study. *Journal of the Institute for the Study of Animal Problems* 3(1): 42–49.

Clancy, E.A., and A.N. Rowan. 2003. Companion animal demographics in the United States: A historical perspective. In *The state of the animals II: 2003,* ed. D.J. Salem and A.N. Rowan,
9–26. Washington, D.C.: Humane Society Press.

CNN. 2005. Report suggests changes in exit poll methodology. *www.CNN.com.* January 19.

Davis, S. 2003. Demand for animal law courses escalating. *DVM,* October 1.

Douglas, D.K. 2004. Benefits to pets from the human-animal bond: A study of pet owner behaviors and their relation to attachment. Ph.D. diss. proposal, Wichita State University.

Elliot, B.J. 1999. Road rage: Media hype or serious road safety issue? Paper presented at Third International Conference on Injury Prevention and Control, Brisbane, Australia, May 9–12.

Fraser, D., J. Mench, and S. Millman. 2001. Farm animals and their welfare in 2000. In *The state of the animals: 2001,* ed. D.J. Salem and A.N. Rowan, 87–100. Washington, D.C.: Humane Society Press.

Freeman, S.F. 2004. The unexplained exit poll discrepancy. Research report from University of Pennsylvania Center for Organizational Dynamics. Philadelphia: University of Pennsylvania, December 29.

Ginsburg, C. 2004. Marketing social change. Executive update. May. *www.gwsae.org.*

Grandy, J.W., E. Stallman, and D.W. Macdonald. 2003. The science and sociology of hunting: Shifting practices and perceptions in the United States and Great Britain. In *The state of the animals II: 2003,* ed. D.J. Salem and A.N. Rowan, 107–130. Washington, D.C.: Humane Society Press.

Green, C. 2004. How can marketing research help animals? *Humane Research Council Newsletter,* August. *www.humaneresearch.org/whymr.shtml.*

Hatry, H., T.V. Houten, M.C. Plantz, and M. Taylor. 1996. *Measuring program outcomes: A practical approach.* Alexandria, Va.: United Way of America.

Houpt, K.A., and N. Waran. 2003. Horse welfare since 1950. In *The state of the animals II: 2003,* ed. D.J. Salem and A.N. Rowan, 207–215. Washington, D.C.: Humane Society Press.

Holcomb, R., R.C. Williams, and P.S. Richards. 1985. The elements of attachment: Relationship maintenance and intimacy. *Journal of the Delta Society* 2(1): 28–34.

Humane Research Council. 2003. Attitudes and behaviors relating to fur. *www.humaneresearch.org.*

Irwin, P. 2001. Overview: The state of the animals: 2001. In *The state of the animals: 2001,* ed. D.J. Salem and A.N. Rowan, 1–19. Washington, D.C.: Humane Society Press.

———. 2003. A strategic review of internation animal protection. In *The state of the animals II: 2003,* ed. D.J. Salem and A.N. Rowan, 1–8. Washington, D.C.: Humane Society Press.

Johnson, T.P., T.F. Garrity, and L. Stallones. 1992. Psychometric evaluation of the Lexington Attachment to Pets Scale (LAPS). *Anthrozoös* 5(3): 160–175.

Kass, P. 2001. Understanding companion animal surplus in the United States: Relinquishment of nonadoptables to animal shelters for euthanasia. *Journal of Applied Animal Welfare Science* 4(4): 237–248.

Kidd, A.H., and R.M. Kidd. 1989. Factors in adults' attitudes toward pets. *Psychological Reports* 65: 903–910.

Kotler, P., N. Roberto, and N. Lee. 2002. *Social marketing: Improving the quality of life.* Thousand Oaks, Calif.: SAGE Publications.

Kossow, D. n.d. Attitudes towards animals and animal issues: A historical perspective in the U.S. *http://www.tufts.edu/vet/cfa/surveys.html.*

Lerner, M. 1999. From safety to healing: Representing battered women with companion animals. *Domestic Violence Report* 4(2):

17–32.

Lerner, M., and J. Zorza. 1999. What advocates can do for battered women with companion animals. *Domestic Violence Report* 4(3): 35–47.

Lymen, D.R., R. Milich, R. Zimmerman, S.P. Novak, T.K. Logan, C. Martin, C. Leukfeld, and R. Clayton. 1999. Project DARE: No effects at 10-year follow-up. *Journal of Consulting and Clinical Psychology* 67(4): 590–593.

National Council on Pet Population Study and Policy (NCPPSP). 2000. The shelter statistics survey, 1994–97. National Council on Pet Population Study and Policy. *http://www.petpopulation.org/statsurvey.html.*

New, J.C., Jr. 2000. Characteristics of shelter-relinquished animals and their owners compared with animals and their owners in U.S. pet-owning households. *Journal of Applied Animal Welfare Science* 3(3): 179–201.

New, J.C; M.D. Salman, J.M. Scarlett, P.H. Kass, J.A. Vaughn, S. Scherr, and W.K. Kelch. 1999. Moving: Characteristics of dogs and cats and those relinquishing them to 12 U.S. animal shelters. *Journal of Applied Animal Welfare Science* 2(2), 83–96.

Poresky, R.H. 1989. Analyzing human-animal relationship measures. *Anthrozoös* 2(4): 236–244.

Rowan, A.N., and F.M. Loew. 2001. Animal research: A review of developments, 1950–2000. In *The state of the animals: 2001,* ed. D.J. Salem and A.N. Rowan, 111–120. Washington, D.C.: Humane Society Press.

Sacks, J.J., L. Sinclair, J. Gilchrist, G. Golab, and R. Lockwood. 2000. Breeds of dogs involved in fatal human attacks in the United States between 1979 and 1998. *Journal of the American Veterinary Medical Association* 217 (6): 836–840.

Salman, M.D., J. Hutchison, R. Ruch-Gallie, L. Kogan, J.G. New Jr., P. Kass, and J. Scarlett. 2000. Behavioral reasons for relinquishment of dogs and cats to 12 shelters. *Journal of Applied Animal Welfare Science* 3(2): 93–106.

Salman, M.D., J.G. New Jr., J.M. Scarlett, P.H. Kass, R. Ruch-Gallie, and S. Hetts. 1998. Human and animal factors related to the relinquishment of dogs and cats in 12 selected animal shelters in the United States. *Journal of Applied Animal Welfare Science* 1(3): 207–226.

Scarlett, J.M. 1999. Reasons for relinquishment of companion animals in U.S. animal shelters: Selected health and personal issues. *Journal of Applied Animal Welfare Science* 2(1): 41–57.

Schwartz, T. 1974. *The responsive chord.* New York: Doubleday.

Scully, M. 2002. *Dominion.* New York: St. Martin's Press.

Singer, P. 1975. *Animal liberation.* New York: Random House.

Trent, N., P. Ormel, J.L.G. de Siles, G. Heinz, and M. James. 2003. The state of meat production in developing countries: 2002. In *The state of the animals II: 2003,* ed. D.J. Salem and A.N. Rowan, 175–192. Washington, D.C.: Humane Society Press.

Unti, B., and B. DeRosa. 2003. Humane education past, present and future. In *The state of the animals II: 2003,* ed. D.J. Salem and A.N. Rowan, 27–50. Washington, D.C.: Humane Society Press.

Wandersman, A., P. Imm, M. Chinman, and S. Kaftarian. 2000. Getting to outcomes: A results-based approach to accountability. *Evaluation and Program Planning* 23: 389–395.

Wilson, C.C., F.E. Netting, and J.C. New. 1987. The pet attitude inventory. *Anthrozoös* 1(2): 76–84.

Wise, S.M. 2003. The evolution of animal law since 1950. In *The state of the animals II: 2003,* ed. D.J. Salem and A.N. Rowan, 99–106. Washington, D.C.: Humane Society Press.

Number surveyed		U.S. National Sample (NA) Percent	Edge Research Sample (1,031) Percent	HSUS Web Sample (1,341) Percent	PSB 2003 Sample (1,000) Percent
1 Age	<18	25.3			
	18–24		7.0	13.8	11.0
	25–34		19.0	28.8	12.0
	35–49 (18–44 U.S.)	39.3	34.0	37.0	28.0
	50–64 (45–64 U.S.)	23.1	18.8	26.0	25.0
	65 plus	12.3	1.8	11.0	21.0
2 Gender	Male	49.1	52.0	10.0	52.0
	Female	50.9	48.0	90.0	48.0
3 Race	African-American	12.7	2.0	0.8	12.0
	American Indian	1.5	1.0	1.3	NA
	Asian	4.5	3.0	1.8	1.0
	Caucasian	65.2	89.0	84.9	77.0
	Hispanic/Latino	13.4	1.0	3.7	3.0
4 Marital status	Single/Never married	28.1	21.0	36.9	24.0
	Married	54.2	60.0	46.3	55.0
	Widowed	6.4	4.0	1.3	9.0
	Divorced	9.3	11.0	10.5	10.0
5 Area of residence	Northeast	18.8	16.0	not asked	22.0
	South	35.8	35.0	not asked	33.0
	Midwest	22.6	25.0	not asked	20.0
	West	22.8	23.0	not asked	20.0
6 Home ownership	Own	67.9	69.0	not asked	not asked
	Rent	28.1	27.0	not asked	not asked
7 Schooling	College grad and plus	26.7	43.0	47.8	37.0
8 Children under 18		35.7	32.0	22.6	28.0
9 Family income	Under $20,000		12.2	15.9	13.0
	$21,000–50,000		40.0	37.7	37.0
	$51,000–75,000		23.3	20.9	18.0
	$76,000 plus		24.4	24.8	15.0
10 How important is it to you that animals are protected from cruelty and abuse?	Not important		2.0	1.4	2.0
	Somewhat important		13.0	1.3	14.0
	Important		18.0	2.9	18.0
	Very important		67.0	94.3	67.0
	Do not know		1.0	0.1	0
11 Have you seen anyone intentionally inflict pain or suffering on an animal during the last year?	Yes		13.0	21.4	14.0
	No		86.0	76.5	85.0
	Do not know		1.0	2.1	1.0
12 If yes to 11, did you report it?	Yes		53.0	72.1	60.0
	No		45.0	26.3	40.0
	Do not know		2.0	1.7	0
13 I keep a picture of my pet in my wallet or displayed at work.	Yes		32.0	72.0	
	No		68.0	27.0	

APPENDIX A
Comparison of Surveys

No. surveyed		U.S. National Sample (NA) Percent	Edge Research Sample (1,031) Percent	HSUS Web Sample (1,341) Percent	PSB 2003 Sample (1,000) Percent
14 I give the animal gifts on holidays or special events.	Yes No		83.0 16.0	62.0 38.0	
15 The pet sleeps in/on my bed or the bed of a family member.	Yes No		80.0 19.0	69.0 31.0	
16 The pet accompanies me on vacations or overnight trips.	Yes No		59.0 39.0	42.0 58.0	
17 I consider the pet to be an important member of the household.	Yes No		95.0 5.0	98.0 1.0	
18 Please indicate how favorably you view the following organizations (V. Fav. = 2, Fav. = 1, Somewhat Unfav. = -1, V. Unfav. = -2; range is +200 to -200)	HSUS PETA ASPCA NWF WWF AKC PETsMART		127.0 5.0 134.0 111.0 86.0 88.0 90.0		
19 Please indicate how favorably you view... keeping a cat indoors all the time.	Strongly favor Somewhat favor Somewhat oppose Strongly oppose Do not know		47.0 27.0 15.0 5.0 7.0	65.0 21.0 8.0 3.0 4.0	
20 ...Letting a cat outside without supervision	Strongly favor Somewhat favor Somewhat oppose Strongly oppose Do not know		13.0 23.0 23.0 36.0 6.0	5.0 13.0 23.0 54.0 4.0	
21 ...Tethering a dog in the backyard for more than an hour	Strongly favor Somewhat favor Somewhat oppose Strongly oppose Do not know		3.0 16.0 34.0 40.0 7.0	2.0 5.0 19.0 72.0 2.0	
22 ...Keeping a dog outside all day while the owner is at work	Strongly favor Somewhat favor Somewhat oppose Strongly oppose Do not know		9.0 21.0 28.0 36.0 7.0	4.0 13.0 23.0 56.0 4.0	
23 ...Declawing a cat who has damaged drapes or upholstery	Strongly favor Somewhat favor Somewhat oppose Strongly oppose Do not know		24.0 32.0 18.0 19.0 8.0	5.0 13.0 21.0 53.0 7.0	

(continued from previous page)

APPENDIX A
Comparison of Surveys

No. surveyed		U.S. National Sample (NA) Percent	Edge Research Sample (1,031) Percent	HSUS Web Sample (1,341) Percent	PSB 2003 Sample (1,000) Percent
24 ...Euthanizing a dog who has bitten a child without provocation	Strongly favor Somewhat favor Somewhat oppose Strongly oppose Do not know		24.0 32.0 23.0 9.0 12.0	9.0 15.0 27.0 32.0 17.0	
25 If The HSUS issued a report in which it argued that 95 percent of all chickens suffer greatly in agricultural facilities and the USDA then contradicted this assertion, which entity would you trust more?	The HSUS The USDA Trust neither Trust them equally Would not know		28.0 16.0 15.0 11.0 29.0	75.4 2.9 2.4 4.0 15.3	
26 How strongly do you feel about having wildlife such as birds and squirrels in your yard?	Strongly dislike Dislike Neutral Like Strongly like		2.0 4.0 19.0 35.0 41.0	0.5 0.4 5.9 22.6 70.6	
27 How often in the year have you had a conflict with, or damage caused by, wild birds and mammals in your yard or home?	None One to two Three plus I do not have a yard		62.0 18.0 11.0 10.0	69.2 21.4 7.9 1.6	
28 If you had a conflict, did you seek help from someone? Whom?	Yes No Local animal org. Hardware store, etc. Local wildlife rehab The HSUS State/federal agens. Business for wildlife problems		32.0 68.0 38.0 19.0 5.0 5.0 19.0 15.0	37.8 62.2 37.8 20.2 21.8 9.0 9.0 16.0	
29 In the past year, have you made a financial contribution to any animal protection or animal rights organization?	Yes No Do not know		34.0 63.0 3.0	76.0 18.7 5.3	
30 If yes, how much did you give in total?	< $10 $11–$25 $26–$50 Over $51 Not sure		11.0 37.0 20.0 24.0 8.0	3.9 18.9 17.7 50.3 9.2	

APPENDIX B
Components of the "Pet Lover's Index"

The responses to several questions on the Omnibus Survey were recoded and combined into a composite score (POSUM-pet owner summation). This was then cross-tabulated with other responses from the survey to see if those rated high, medium, or low on this composite differed significantly from one another on their attitudes or behaviors relating to animals.

Variable PO1—Any cats? Yes = 1; ELSE = 0

Variable PO2—Any dogs? Yes = 1; ELSE = 0

Variable PO3—Any other pets? Yes = 1; ELSE = 0

Variable PO4—Total 10-year pets? 1–5 = 1; 6+ = 2; ELSE = 0

Variable PO5—Fate of last pet? Died of old age/Euth. = 2, Taken to shelter = 1; ELSE = 0

Variable PO6A—Consider the animal an important member of the household. Yes = 1; ELSE = 0

Variable P06B—Give the animal gifts on holidays or special events. Yes = 1; ELSE = 0

Variable PO6C—The animal accompanies me on some vacations or trips. Yes = 1; ELSE = 0

Variable PO6D—The pet sleeps in or on my bed or the bed of a family member. Yes = 1; ELSE = 0

Variable PO6E—I keep a picture of the animal in my wallet or displayed at work. Yes = 1; ELSE = 0

POSUM—Sum of all variables listed above

Cruelty toward Cats: Changing Perspectives

CHAPTER 2

Randall Lockwood

Some of this content appears in L. Sinclair and R. Lockwood, "Cruelty Towards Cats" (in *Consultations in Feline Internal Medicine*, 5h ed., ed. J.R. August. 2005. Philadelphia: Elsevier Inc.).

Of all the species that have been domesticated, cats have historically been subjected to the widest diversity of treatment by humans. They have been worshipped as gods and reviled as devils, coddled and pampered, but also abandoned and abused. Our treatment of cats has likewise created a range of problems for professionals concerned with their care—from dealing with problems of obesity and overindulgence to tending to the needs of animals who have been neglected, intentionally harmed, or even tortured.

A Brief History of Kindness and Cruelty to Cats

Most authorities consider the cat to be among the most recent animals to be domesticated, with its origins in Egypt (Zeuner 1963; Clutton-Brock 1993). There are no remains of cats from prehistoric Egypt or the Old Kingdom (2686–2181 B.C.). Pictorial representations of cats that are clearly domesticated appear at the time of the fifth dynasty (c. 2600 B.C.), and from the New Kingdom onward (from 1567 B.C.), paintings and statues of cats became increasingly common in Egypt (Beadle 1977).

Recently, remains of a cat found buried in association with a human at a site in Cyprus were dated to approximately 7500 B.C. The rich offerings found in the grave suggested that the person had special social status and a special relationship with the animal. This find could constitute the earliest evidence of taming of the cat (Vigne et al. 2004).

Serpell (1988) notes that the role of cats in the Egyptian pantheon was complex and confusing. Male cats were associated with the sun god Ra. Cats and lionesses were also linked to the warlike goddess Sekmet. The primary association was with the cat goddess Bastet, a symbol of fertility, fecundity, and motherhood who was also associated with the moon and menstrual cycles. The prominence of cat cults did not develop until the twenty-second dynasty (c. 950 B.C.), when the capital became Bubastis, home of the cult of Bastet, and the local cat goddess became the official deity of the kingdom. The modern view of reverence for cats in Egypt comes almost entirely from the writings of Herodotus, about 450 B.C. He describes his visit to the temples in Bubastis and the various practices surrounding the cult, including the harsh penalties for injuring or killing cats (Clutton-Brock 1993, 36): "When a man has killed one of the sacred animals if he did it with malice prepense, he is punished with death, if unwittingly, he has to pay such a fine as the priests choose to impose."

Later in the same volume, Herodotus details the reverence with which deceased cats are embalmed and entombed. Archeologists in the nineteenth century recovered mummified remains of hundreds of thousands of cats from this period. Ironically, it is this collection of remains that provides the first evidence of what might be considered "ritualistic abuse" of cats.

Clutton-Brock (1993) describes findings from the radiological study of fifty-five wrapped cat mummies collected by egyptologist Flinders Petrie in 1907. She notes that "contrary to the general belief that ancient Egyptians never killed their cats, many of these had 'broken necks.' This could be seen in the x-rays as markedly displaced vertebrae in the neck" (38).

15

She notes that the mummies fell into two groups. Twenty were kittens one to four months old when they died or were killed, and seventeen were nine to seventeen months old. Only two were more than two years old. She suggests that the cats were being specially bred to be mummified by the priests for sale as votive offerings, which could explain what appears to have been a mass market in mummified cats. (This market was not without a hint of fraud. Some cat mummies from other sources appear to have been faked by wrapping a cat skull mounted atop fragments of human tibia and fibula.)

The export of cats from Egypt was illegal, so the domestic cat's introduction into Europe and Asia did not begin until several hundred years after the peak period of the cult of Bastet, finally becoming widespread by the tenth century (Zeuner 1963). The spread of Christianity brought with it what Serpell (1986, 155) describes as "extreme ruthlessness in suppressing unorthodox beliefs and in extirpating all traces of earlier pre-Christian religions." Since cats were often central to many of these belief systems, from the cult of Bastet to the worship of the Norse goddess Freya, they became a convenient target for the demonization of all things non-Christian and the focus of myriad forms of abuse intended to drive out and destroy the Devil. Cats also were transformed from a symbol of grace, fertility, and maternal care to one of bewitching sexuality and lasciviousness—an association that continues to affect public interpretation and behavior and serve as a justification for continuing abuse.

In the thirteenth century, Pope Gregory IX (ruling 1227–1241) issued a statement that Cathars, breakaway Christians, were known to be breeding black cats, who were the devil in disguise. In 1489 Pope Innocent VIII issued an official order to persecute all witches and kill all cats within Christian lands.

Similarly, Inquisitor Nicholas Remy, in his 1595 *Daemonolatreiae libri tres,* announced that all cats were demons (Conway 1998).

Darnton (1984) details a variety of forms of widespread institutionalized cat abuse common from the Middle Ages well into the late eighteenth century. Carnival celebrations of deviance came to an end on Shrove Tuesday, or Mardi Gras, when a live cat was incorporated into a straw mannequin, King of Carnival, and given a ritual trial and execution. In Burgundy young men passed around a cat, tearing its fur to make it scream as a form of "rough music." For the cycle of Saint John the Baptist, coinciding with the summer solstice, cats were tied up in bags, suspended from ropes, or burned at the stake. He further notes:

> Parisians liked to incinerate cats by the sackful, while the Courimauds (cour a miaud or cat chasers) of Saint Chamond preferred to chase a flaming cat through the streets. In parts of Burgundy and Lorraine they danced around a kind of burning May pole with a cat tied to it. In the Metz region they burned a dozen cats at a time in a basket on top of a bonfire. The ceremony took place with great pomp in Metz itself, until it was abolished in 1765. (83)

One of the best documented instances of cruelty to cats was the "Great Cat Massacre" of the Rue Saint-Severin, Paris, which took place in the late 1730s (Darnton 1984; Twitchell 1989). The story was obtained from an account by Nicolas Contat, a worker who had witnessed the event. Several young male printer's apprentices systematically slaughtered all the neighborhood cats, starting with a favorite pet of their master's wife. According to Twitchell:

> In fits of laughter they gleefully bashed the heads of cats, snapped the spines of cats, squashed the bodies of cats, twisted cats at the midsection, and suffocated cats. They even improvised a gallows and hung cats by the neck. (1989, 48)

The events were replayed in pantomime many times during the weeks that followed. Darnton puts these events in the context of the social upheaval of the times. Printer's apprentices were among the most exploited workers of the time, while a passion for pet cats was growing among the bourgeois, particularly the masters of the printing trade. Portraits were painted of pampered cats who were fed choice fowl, while the boys in the print shops labored with little hope of promotion to the ranks of journeymen. Cat abuse was already well established in the culture of the time, thus cats were an easy and seemingly appropriate target for this outrage.

Such abuse was also commonplace in England as well. The owners of cats were often suspected of "wickedness" and were killed, along with their cats, under the Witchcraft Act of 1563 (Young 2001). The first person to be tried under this law was Agnes Waterhouse, who was executed in 1566 for owning a cat unfortunately named "Sathan" (Durston 2000).

More conventional abuse of cats at the hands of young offenders flourished in eighteenth-century England. The first illustration in William Hogarth's classic series of woodcuts "The Four Stages of Cruelty" depicts a 1750s street scene in which young boys are tormenting a variety of animals in many ways. Cats are the most abundant victims in this illustration. They are seen being thrown out of windows, hung by their tails from a pole, and set upon by fighting dogs. Hogarth was an astute observer of both animal and human behavior, and it is likely that this illustration was a composite of instances he had witnessed personally. He made these illustrations

[I]n hopes of preventing [to] some degree the cruel treatment of poor Animals which makes the streets of London more disagreeable to the human mind, than anything what ever, the very describing of which gives pain." (Uglow 1997, 500)

Cats did not fare much better in the scientific views of the mid-eighteenth century. The most influential naturalist of the time was Buffon, author of the multivolume *Histoire naturelle* (1749–1788). Kete (1994) notes that, quite simply, "Buffon hated cats," describing them as having a perverse nature and worthy of being kept only to control rodents as "the lesser of two evils."

Conditions seemed to improve for cats in the mid-nineteenth century. In the United Kingdom, cats were not afforded protection under anti-cruelty laws until the 1835 revisions of the 1822 animal welfare legislation protecting livestock, which extended the protections to domestic pets and prohibited bull baiting and cockfighting (Ritvo 1987). The *Annual Report* of the Royal Society for the Prevention of Cruelty to Animals (RSPCA) detailed the animal-cruelty cases investigated and prosecuted under these laws. The majority of cases continued to involve maltreatment of livestock and draft animals, but proponents of companion animal welfare recognized the growing concern about the abuse of dogs and cats. From 1857 to 1860, dogs and cats accounted for only 2 percent of the cruelty convictions, although 13 percent of the RSPCA's reports to the public focused on dog and cat cruelty cases.

In France, the first success of the emerging animal protection movement was the Grammont Law of 1850, prohibiting public abuse of animals. Grammont, a retired cavalry officer, promoted the legislation in part on the basis that "the

spectacle of suffering encourages cruelty....The child accustomed to bloody pastimes or witnessing cruelty will become a dangerous man" (Kete 1994, 5). Such views represented, in part, a continuing concern about the issues raised by the Great Cat Massacre more than a century earlier.

The historical ambivalence of many cultures toward cats continued into the twentieth and twenty-first centuries. In the 1980s cats became the most abundant species (excluding aquarium fish) in American homes, a trend that has continued (AVMA 2002; APPMA 2004). The American Pet Products Manufacturers Association (APPMA) estimates that there are 77.6 million owned cats in the United States, compared to 65 million owned dogs. Although there are more dog-owning homes (40.6 million) than cat-owning homes (35.4 million), there are more cats in the average cat-owning family (average 2.2, compared with 1.6 dogs per dog-owning household). Despite this popularity, cats have not achieved equal status with dogs as true companion animals. The size of feral cat populations is impossible to determine accurately, but it may approach the number of owned cats (Holton and Manzoor 1993; Slater 2002).

Despite the popularity and proliferation of resources on cat care, there is also a continuing stream of material promoting, or at least making light of, cat abuse. This has no parallel in the canine world. Popular books include *The Cat Hater's Handbook or the Ailurophobe's Delight* (1963), *The Official I Hate Cats Book* (1980), *101 Uses for a Dead Cat* (1981), with several sequels, *How to Kill Your Girlfriend's Cat* (1988), and *Cat-Dependent No More!* (1991). Recently there has been a proliferation of video and on-line games allowing simulated cat-killing, such as "Cat Hunter," "Clay Kitten Shooting," and "Cat Blaster," and

other representations in popular culture, including an unaired but widely distributed car commercial making light of the decapitation of a cat by a closing sunroof. A significant proportion of the population continues to express active antipathy toward cats. Kellert and Berry (1980) found that 17.4 percent of people surveyed expressed some dislike of cats, compared with only 2.6 percent who specifically disliked dogs. Holland comments on this discrepancy and associates the differences in American attitudes toward dogs and cats with a degree of xenophobia:

> People who hate cats tend to be proud of that fact, and brag about it as if it proved something honest and straightforward in their natures. Nobody brags about hating dogs. To hate dogs would be mean-spirited and peculiarly unpatriotic; dogs are a very American concept, fraternal, hearty and unpretentious, while cats are inscrutable like the wily oriental and elitist like the European esthete. (1988, 34)

The Psychology and Biology of Cat Abuse

What is it about cats that elicits such paradoxical views? In addition to the long-standing social and cultural factors discussed above that have promoted abuse of cats, certain elements of the animals' biology and ethology have allowed or encouraged their maltreatment.

Sexual and Social Behavior

Cats were associated with femininity, fertility, and sensuality in ancient religions for good reason. Female cats are induced ovulators and are highly promiscuous, inviting the attention and competition of several males, indeed, courting up to twenty males during a single estrus period (Natoli and DeVito 1988). This is an effective reproductive strategy for a solitary hunter who must insure that males contributing to the gene pool of her offspring are capable of repelling their rivals. Many cultures have equated promiscuous sexuality with cats, as seen in slang. As early as 1401 men were warned of chasing "cattis tailis," for example, prostitutes, giving rise to "tail" as slang. Other phrases echoing feline sexuality ("cat house," "pussy") have been in use since before the seventeenth century (Morris 1986).

In addition to being perceived as highly sexual creatures, female cats are frequently aggressive toward their recent mates. As with many solitary hunters, following mating, males are potential competitors for food and may be a threat to kittens, so the females often attack them or drive them off. Individually, cats of both sexes can at one moment exhibit a warm, soft, cuddly demeanor and at the next indicate that they have had sufficient contact by terminating an interaction with a serious bite or scratch. This is often in stark contrast to dogs, who will solicit attention and often continue to invite interaction submissively even when maltreated.

The social independence and resistance to training of most cats, along with their "coy" sensuality, can present a special challenge or threat to those needing to gain a sense of power and control over others as well as over the uncontrollable changes occurring in their own bodies, that is, adolescent boys. It is not surprising that both historically and epidemiologically, the principal abusers of cats have been young males, particularly those seeking to assert their authority. As noted by Serpell (1986, 156), there is "an element of misogyny embedded in this hatred of cats." He further observes

(156) "The unmitigated cruelty cats have received...doubtless speaks volumes about the sexual insecurities of European males."

Resilience

Despite their relatively small size and fragility, cats have a reputation as survivors, perhaps due in part to the speed, agility, quick reflexes, and other adaptations that allow them to survive situations that would be likely to kill a human or dog. Most intriguing have been reports of "high-rise injuries" sustained in falls from tall buildings (Robinson 1976; Whitney and Mehlhaff 1987). One interesting aspect of high-rise injuries in cats is the effect of the distance fallen on the frequency and severity of injuries. The rate of injury is linear up to a fallen distance of approximately seven stories; above this height, injury rates do not increase, and fracture rates decrease, in part because cats falling from greater heights have time to orient themselves to better absorb impact. A cat who free-fell from thirty-two stories onto concrete, the subject of one of the published reports, suffered only mild pneumothorax and a chipped tooth and was released after forty-eight hours of observation.

Although this kind of resilience may have contributed to the perception of the "invulnerability" of cats, Tabor (1983) attributes the specific notion that cats have "nine lives" to distortions of a statement c. 1560 by Baldwin in *Beware the Cat*, who wrote, "it was permitted for a witch to take her cattes body nine times." At the same time, this resilience is to blame for a great deal of feline suffering. Morris (1986, 6) notes, "Because cats can survive when thrown out and abandoned, it makes it easier for people to do just that."

Predatory Behavior

While the hunting behavior of dogs generally is perceived as something that is useful to humans—as a prac-

tical partnership in the pursuit of game—the predatory behavior of cats is often perceived as being "selfish" and unnecessarily cruel. The "game of cat and mouse" has become synonymous with action that is sneaky, malicious, and underhanded. Cats, particularly females with recently weaned kittens, will often wound or maul their prey without killing it quickly, in part as a way of providing the young with disabled prey on which to practice their predatory skills (Turner and Meister 1988). By human standards this adaptation, which potentially prolongs the suffering of the cat's prey, can appear to be cruel, sadistic, and "amoral," and thus, to some, it may seem to justify similar maltreatment of cats, who are often portrayed as enjoying inflicting torment on their victims.

Since many cats that are allowed to hunt will bring dead or maimed prey home to their human "families," the consequences of cat predation can often be obvious and can fuel strong emotional responses against cats. The Mammal Society in the United Kingdom (2001) released a report based on a review of prey killed or captured by 964 owned cats during a five-month period in 1997. The report documented more than 14,000 prey collected by cat owners from their animals. Highly controversial extrapolations to the entire British cat population led to the assertion that "domestic moggies could be killing 275 million creatures a year" in England (BBC 2001). Hartwell (2004) offers a detailed critique of the report and provides details of some of the alarmist reports and anti-cat backlash that followed its release, including a call from a renowned wildlife photographer that cats should be shot.

Patronek (1998) reviewed numerous studies to evaluate the potential impact of free-roaming and feral cats on humans and wild animals. He noted that few studies indicate any long-term effects on songbird or wildlife populations, and many provide evidence to the contrary. This report suggested that humane agencies should continue to urge people to keep cats indoors for their safety and for the safety of potential prey, but they should not see predation as a significant concern in assessing the feasibility of trap-test-vaccinate-neuter-and-release (TTVAR) programs to control feral cats (see Slater and Shain, this volume).

A report released by Defenders of Wildlife (King and Rappole 2003) also questioned the significance of the impact cats have on songbirds, based on review of the North American Breeding Bird Survey and thirty-six other long-term surveys of migratory bird populations. This review notes: "windows, cats, West Nile virus, wind turbines—all those specific causes of death that are apparent in people's backyards—are not, at present, having any known effect on the population size of any continental bird species" (Yakutchik 2003, n.p.). Habitat destruction in both winter and summer habitats of these species was considered a much greater threat to bird populations.

Nocturnal Behavior
Creatures of the night have always been viewed with suspicion and are often equated with occult forces. Nocturnal habits, coupled with the unusual "eyeshine" produced by the reflective tapetum of the cat's eye, helped promote the perception of cats as something alien and suspicious. Such habits, along with the stealth required of a solitary hunter, only reinforce the perception of cats as "occult" (literally "hidden") animals.

Vocalizations
Darnton (1984) notes that the cries of cats subjected to pain or torture have a human-like tone that contributed to the impression that an anthropomorphic demon was being destroyed or driven out when they were tormented during the rituals that were so common in earli-

er centuries. Many of the common abuses in this era seemed designed to elicit such cries from cats, reaching their nadir in the form of "cat organs," musical instruments designed to produce different tones through tormenting cats of different sizes (Barloy 1974).

The "caterwauling" associated with female cats in heat, and the combat between the males they attract, is often used to justify various forms of abuse. The image of a rock or shoe thrown at noisy cats perched on a fence has become a cliché in cartoons and other depictions of cats.

Psychopathology/ Criminology of Cat Abuse
As noted above, cruelty to animals in general has long been associated with an increased risk for involvement in criminal and antisocial behavior (Lockwood and Ascione 1998; Ascione and Arkow 1999; Ascione and Lockwood 2001; Merz-Perez and Heide 2003). Cruelty to cats has been associated specifically with future tendencies toward violence in a number of quantitative and anecdotal accounts. Felthous (1980) reviewed eighteen cases of men admitted to an inpatient psychiatric service who presented a history of repeatedly injuring dogs or cats. These were compared with a group of assaultive patients who did not have a history of animal cruelty. All but one member of the animal abuse group had tortured cats. This group also skewed toward higher levels of reported aggressiveness to people. Over 60 percent of these subjects reported childhood histories that included brutal punishments by father and mother, frequent childhood fights, and school truancy.

Felthous (1984) provides case histories of violent crimes involving prior acts of cruelty to animals, including one in which a man shot

his cat, believing the animal to be gaining control of him, several days before shooting his wife.

Building on these earlier surveys, Felthous and Kellert (1987) provided a systematic review of the choice of animals for abuse based on interviews with 84 prisoners in two penitentiaries. The greatest variety of cruelties had been inflicted on cats (thirty-three different forms of abuse were described), and most subjects who had abused cats used several different methods. Cats were the most frequent targets across all forms of abuse and were the predominant victims in cases involving burning, breaking of bones, or being thrown from a height (Table 1).

They conclude:

> Physical features of cats render them suitable for some specific methods of abuse. Cats have long flexible tails that can be joined together. Fur burns. Their bones are easily broken. Cats are small enough to be carried about and dropped from heights. (231)

They note that these qualities are not unique to cats and suggest that cultural patterns and the sexual symbolism contribute to this selection of cats for abuse by violent offenders. They further note:

> Although none of the subjects identified cats as symbolic of evil women, a "bad mother," or the female genitalia, the possibility of consciously or unconsciously associating cats with women ought to be considered in aggressive men whose sexual and aggressive impulses may be fused at a primitive level, poorly differentiated and poorly modulated. (232)

This view echoes that of Revitch (1965), who suggested that cat abuse was associated with sexually motivated murders of women. This was clearly true in the case of serial murderer Keith Jesperson, who was convicted of three murders but who claimed responsibility for more

Table 1
Self-Reported Patterns of Animal Abuse by Incarcerated Prisoners, by Percentage

Form of Animal Abuse	Reports Involving Dogs	Reports Involving Cats	Reports Involving Other Species
Burning	—	33.3	66.7
Shooting	21.4	7.1	71.4
Breaking Bones	16.7	50.0	33.3
Throwing from Height	30.0	70.0	—
Beating/Stoning	34.5	27.6	37.9
All Abuses	22.5	27.5	50.0

Adapted from Felthous and Kellert (1987)

than one hundred killings, many of which involved prostitutes as victims. In interviews with Jesperson conducted by the author and Jesperson's biographer (Olsen 2002), he has drawn a direct connection from the sense of empowerment he got from childhood killings of animals, usually cats, to the feelings that fueled his murders.

In the trial of Washington, D.C.-area sniper Lee Boyd Malvo, defense psychiatrist Neil Blumberg argued that Malvo's teen history of cat-killing meant that he was "unable to distinguish between right and wrong and was unable to resist the impulse" to commit the sniper killings (Associated Press 2003). Federal Bureau of Investigation (FBI) psychologists who reviewed Malvo's history in detail suggested that his pattern of stalking and shooting cats from a distance was consistent with his actions in his later crimes and served, in some ways, as a rehearsal for those actions (personal communication, FBI Special Agent A. Brantley, June 25, 2004).

It is clear from these and other accounts that the selection of cats as the object of abuse is more than just a result of their availability. Their physical, behavioral, and symbolic attributes often make them the target of choice for those who are or who are destined to become perpetrators of violence against people. This makes detecting, reporting, and responding to acts of cruelty against cats an even more pressing concern.

A Victimological Analysis of Cat and Dog Cruelty

To better understand the nature of cat cruelty cases, The Humane Society of the United States (HSUS) undertook a detailed review of the largest possible sample of such reports. The HSUS receives daily media clips from Cyberalert®, a service tracking more than 13,000 newspapers, magazines, journals, wire services, TV networks, and local TV stations. These clips are drawn from coverage of stories with any mention of animal abuse, cruelty, or neglect. The reports are then reviewed, and data on the specifics of each case are entered into a Microsoft Access® database. The data recorded for each case include offender age and gender, number and species of victims, details of the action against the animal, co-occurrence of other crimes, charges filed, and case outcome. When there are

multiple reports on a case that is covered over a long period (e.g., from the original report of the incident through the prosecution and outcome), all the available information is merged into a single case record. The database in then converted into SPSS® format for more detailed statistical analysis.

For this analysis we reviewed records of reports on 4,695 cases of animal cruelty reported between January 2000 and May 2004. These cases involved 5,225 alleged offenders. Despite the higher incidence of cats in the companion animal population, they were underrepresented in these reports of cruelty. Of these cases, 51.8 percent reportedly involved dogs, 15.1 percent involved cats, 3.7 percent involved both cats and dogs, 3.7 percent involved cats and dogs and one or more other species, and 25.7 percent involved other species only—usually horses, livestock, fighting cocks, and wildlife.

Cruelty to Cats vs. Cruelty to Dogs

Cases were broadly categorized as featuring "intentional cruelty" (e.g., traumatic physical injury), "neglect" (including malnourishment, abandonment, and starvation), or "collecting or hoarding" (i.e., maintaining large numbers of animals in unsanitary conditions without commercial intent, as defined by Patronek [1999]). Overall, 62.7 percent of the cases were characterized as "intentional." This was significantly higher for cats (69.0 percent) than for dogs (60.8 percent, chi-square = 15.43, p<.001). Animals were killed in 47.4 percent of all cases involving cats or dogs. Cats were killed in significantly more cases in which they were victims (56.9 percent) of cruelty than were dogs (44.7 percent, chi-square = 32.39, p<.001). In cases that did not reportedly involve hoarding, there were no significant differences between cats and dogs in the number of animals abused (for cats, mean = 5.29; for dogs, mean = 6.87) or in the number of animals killed (for cats, mean = 3.34; for dogs, mean = 4.98).

Cats were significantly *overrepresented*, when compared to dogs, in incidents involving several specific forms of intentional abuse (Table 2).

There were no statistically significant differences between cat and dog cases in the incidence of hanging, stabbing, shooting, kicking, poisoning, or sexual assault (Table 3).

Animal cruelty often occurs within the context of family violence, particularly domestic violence (DeViney, Dickert, and Lockwood 1983; Ascione 1998; Ponder and Lockwood 2001). Companion animals are frequently threatened, injured, or killed to intimidate or retaliate against a family member. Overall, 4 percent of animal abuse cases included concurrent reports of domestic violence. The incidence rate was not statistically significant for cats vs. dogs (4.4 percent vs. 3.9 percent, chi-square = .28, p>.5). However, children were more likely to witness cases of abuse of cats (5.0 percent) than of dogs (2.7 percent, chi-square = 6.43, p<.05).

Young offenders were more likely to be identified as perpetrators in cases victimizing cats than in those involving dogs. Children under age seventeen accounted for 2.9 percent of intentional cat abuse cases and 1.2 percent of intentional dog abuse cases (chi-square = 6.95, p<.05). Teens (seventeen to twenty-one years of age) accounted for 14.0 percent of all intentional cat abuse cases and 6.9 percent of dog cases (chi-square = 25.3, p<.001). *All* of the fifteen reported cases of cat abuse by children under seventeen years of age involved boys, as did 95 percent of the dog abuse cases. Similarly, 94 percent of the sixty-nine intentional cat abuse

Table 2
Forms of Abuse in 3,488 Reported Cases of Animal Cruelty—Cats Overrepresented, by Percentage

Form of Abuse	Cat Cruelty Cases	Dog Cruelty Cases	Chi Square	Significance
Torture	14.9	6.8	44.3	p<.001
Beating	13.4	10.7	4.0	p<.050
Throwing	11.4	5.3	32.7	p<.001
Mutilation	10.6	5.9	18.6	p<.001
Suffocation	3.4	1.5	10.7	p<.001
Drowning	2.3	.7	11.8	p<.001

Table 3
Forms of Abuse in 3,488 Reported Cases of Animal Cruelty—Cats and Dogs Equally Represented

Form of Abuse	Cat Cruelty Cases	Dog Cruelty Cases	Chi Square	Significance
Shooting	13.4	14.8	.792	p>.30
Poisoning	4.1	3.3	1.060	p>.30
Stabbing	3.3	3.0	.202	p>.60
Kicking	2.7	3.7	1.460	p>.20
Hanging	2.0	1.5	.861	P>.30
Sexual Assault	.3	.6	1.140	P>.28

cases committed by teenagers involved boys, as did 97 percent of the teen dog abuse cases.

Cats were significantly *underrepresented* when compared with dogs in cases reportedly involving *neglect*. Of the 931 companion animal cases characterized as severe neglect of a small number of animals (rather than hoarding), 89.6 percent involved dogs and 10.4 percent involved cats. Looking at it another way, 36.2 percent of all dog-cruelty cases were described as "neglect," vs. 16.6 percent of cat cases (chi-square = 82.7, p<.001).

This reflects the prevailing societal view that cats are self-sufficient and are less likely to suffer if left unattended or not provided for, thus leaving them in this condition is often not perceived as neglect, even when it results in illness or injury.

Virtually all of the dog or cat cases involving "fighting" represented action against dogfighting operations. Cats were listed as victims in two of 224 cases counted as "fighting." In these instances they were being used as bait or training animals. Dogs were significantly overrepresented in the 50 cases in which

Table 4
Victimology of Hoarding and Nonhoarding Cruelty Cases

Type of Case	Mean Number Involved	Mean Number Killed
Dog: Nonhoarding	6.87	3.34
Dog: Hoarding	59.49	19.06
Cat: Nonhoarding	5.29	4.98
Cat: Hoarding	61.48	33.78

animals had been dragged behind a vehicle (96 percent of such cases).

Although a significantly higher proportion of cat cases involved intentional acts of malice, which are often a requirement for a criminal charge of animal abuse, charges were filed in significantly fewer cases involving cats than those involving dogs (56.4 percent of cat cases vs. 65.3 percent of dog cases, chi-square = 18.5, p<.001). This is consistent with the general view that cats tend be less valued than dogs, and that cruelty to cats, however extreme, is seen as less problematic than comparable maltreatment of dogs.

Hoarding Cases

Animal hoarding is a form of animal cruelty that has received growing attention from veterinary, humane, and mental health professionals (Lockwood and Cassidy 1988; Mullen 1993; Lockwood 1994; Patronek 1999; HARC 2000; Davis 2003; Berry, Patronek, and Lockwood 2005) and the media (Arluke et al. 2002). The Hoarding of Animals Research Consortium (HARC) defines an animal hoarder as someone who:

- accumulates large numbers of animals;
- fails to provide minimal standards of nutrition, sanitation, and veterinary care;
- fails to act on the deteriorating condition of the animals;

and

- fails to act on or recognize the negative impact of the collection on his or her own health and well-being.

Overall, 412 cases in the database (9.0 percent) were characterized as animal-hoarding cases. By definition, these cases involved significantly higher numbers of animals than did nonhoarding cases, and, consequently, significantly more animals killed (Table 4). The number of dogs and cats *involved* did not differ significantly in hoarding cases. The mean number of animals *killed* was nearly twice as high in cat-hoarding cases as it was in dog-hoarding cases, but this was not statistically significant due to wide variation across cases and a smaller number of cases for which all of these details were available (62 hoarding cases and 1,382 nonhoarding cases) (t = -.326, p>.5).

In this sample, women were significantly more likely than men to be involved in hoarding cases (62.5 percent vs. 37.5 percent, chi-square = 335, p<.001). This is consistent with other reports of this phenomenon (Worth and Beck 1981; Patronek 1999; HARC 2000). Overall, perpetrators in hoarding cases were older than those in nonhoarding cruelty cases. The mean age for women was 52.6 years in hoarding cases and 38.8 years in all other cases (t = -11.2, p<.001). The mean age for men was 48.7 years

in hoarding cases and 33.3 years in all other cases (t = -9.85, p<.001). The women involved in hoarding cases were significantly older than the men (t = -1.98, p<.05).

There were significant gender differences in the nature of animals who were hoarded (Table 5). Women were overrepresented in cases where cats were hoarded, either exclusively or in connection with dogs or other species. Men were significantly more likely to be involved in cases where dogs alone were victims of hoarding (chi-square = 32.9, p<.001).

Implications for Animal Welfare and Veterinary Professionals

Cruelty to cats is a widespread phenomenon with serious implications not only for animal welfare, but also for potential identification of situations where children, spouses, the elderly, and others may be at risk. It is likely that the incidence of cruelty to cats is underreported significantly. The widespread hostility to cats described above creates an environment in which cat cruelty, even when detected, is more likely to go unreported and/or unprosecuted.

Other characteristics of cat behavior and the human-cat relationship make it likely that much maltreatment of cats is overlooked. Dog owners will usually search for missing and potentially injured dogs if they do not return home when expected. Injured dogs, as highly social creatures, will often solicit care from people if they have been injured. In contrast, cat owners frequently fail to look for cats who do not return home, often assuming they have chosen a life of freedom. Injured cats are more likely to hide from, rather than seek contact with, people, consistent with their basic nature as solitary predators. Fewer than 5 percent of cats entering U.S. shelters as strays are ever reclaimed.

Conclusions and Recommendations

Cruelty to cats, in its many forms, is a serious problem that *dramatically affects* many animals and the people who care about them. It also should raise concerns about perpetrators' potential for other acts of abuse and neglect that might affect other human and non-human victims. Professionals in veterinary medicine, animal behavior, and animal protection, as well as concerned individuals, can take several steps to focus greater attention on this problem.

1. Strengthen and enforce laws protecting cats and other companion animals.

The legal status of cats has undergone some curious changes in the last five hundred years. In the fifteenth and sixteenth centuries, it was not uncommon for a wide variety of animal species, from insects to cattle, to be subjected to criminal prosecution, excommunication, and even execution in a manner almost identical to the treatment of humans (Evans 1906). Although cats often were killed along with their owners who had been accused of witchcraft, Evans found no cases in which a cat was the sole defendant. There were, however, many cases in which cats appeared as "witnesses" at the trials of thieves or murderers.

Most contemporary Western laws trace their origins to the Code Napoleon or English Common Law. The Code Napoleon recognized several kinds of cats. Wild cats were seen as noxious animals whose destruction could be rewarded, but the law declared that "the domestic cat, not being a thing of nought (res nullius) but the property of a master, ought to be protected by law" (Van Vechten 1936). In 1769

William Blackstone provided an early distinction in common law, differentiating between animals raised for food and those kept for "pleasure, curiosity, or whim," which included "dogs, bears, cats, apes, parrots, and singing birds," noting that "their value is not intrinsic, but depending only on the caprice of owners" (in Frasch et al. 2000, 47). Blackstone notes, however, that the ancient Britons viewed cats as "creatures of intrinsic value; and the killing or stealing [of] one was a grievous crime" (47).

For centuries, animal-cruelty laws have continued to view the crime of animal cruelty as a *property crime* that deprives the owner of the property or the use or enjoyment of that property (Favre and Tsang 1993), while society as a whole is increasingly likely to view such acts as a *morals crime*, indicative of poor character, or as a *violent crime* that inflicts suffering and/or death on a fellow sentient creature. Thus the legal response to cat-cruelty cases has often echoed the debates of Napoleonic and common law, centering on the value associated with cats and whether they can be considered "domesticated animals."

Some case law specifically accords cats the status of "domestic animals" (*Thurston v. Carter*, 92 A. 295 [Me. 1914]; cited in Young 2001). One of the more infamous decisions went the other way. In *Commonwealth v. Massini* (188 A. 2d 816, Pa. Super 1963), a man shot and killed his neighbor's cat. The court held that cats did not fit under the state cruelty code's definition of "domestic animal" and thus had "no intrinsic value in the eyes of the law" (Frasch et al. 2000). At the time the statute defined a domestic animal as "any equine animal, bovine animal, sheep, goat or pig." The statute was subsequently amended to "any dog, cat, equine animal, bovine animal, sheep, goat or porcine animal," removing the apparent exemption of cats from coverage in the state's criminal code. Although most states currently define "animal" or "domestic animal" in ways that clearly extend protections to cats, animal advocates should examine existing laws in their areas carefully to ensure that such protection exists.

Even when anti-cruelty laws clearly apply to cats, application of these laws may be hampered by the

Table 5
Species Involved in Animal Hoarding Cases

Species Hoarded	Hoarder's Gender	
	Male	Female
Cats Only	25 (24.0 percent)	79 (76.0 percent)
Dogs Only	52 (56.5 percent)	40 (43.5 percent)
Both Cats and Dogs	11 (19.6 percent)	45 (80.4 percent)
Multiple Species with Cats and Dogs	30 (39.5 percent)	46 (60.5 percent)
Other Species	26 (49.1 percent)	27 (50.9 percent)

perception of the "value" of feline victims. In 1997 three teenage boys broke into an animal shelter in Iowa, bludgeoned sixteen cats and kittens to death, and injured seven others. The three were not charged with animal cruelty, in part because the existing animal-cruelty laws were weak and carried only minimal penalties. They were charged instead with third degree burglary and breaking into an animal facility (ironically, this law was passed with the intent to protect research laboratories from animal activists). These charges could have risen to the level of felony offenses had the damage inflicted on the "property," that is, the cats, been in excess of $500. Despite the fact that the shelter spent in excess of $50 per animal for neutering, vaccination, and other care in preparation for adoption, a jury in the rural community decided that the twenty-three cats were not worth the $500 required to elevate the crimes to the level of felony, and the men were convicted only of misdemeanors (Bollinger 1998).

Laws and policies developed to protect and control cats clearly have not kept pace with their status as America's preferred pet. Even when strong anti-cruelty laws are in place, they may not be enforced vigorously by police, prosecutors, or judges, who may dismiss animal-cruelty cases as being of minor significance. As this study has shown, this is even more likely to be true of cases involving feline victims and young offenders. Cat abuse is not a normal teen pastime, and evidence suggests that ensuring that such behavior has immediate and serious consequences for the offender provides a chance for early intervention at a time when it is more likely to be effective.

There is some indication that the cat's legal status is progressing slowly in other ways, but it still is not on the same level as that granted to dogs. At least a dozen states currently have "lemon" laws that allow compensation to people who obtain companion animals who subsequently are shown to have preexisting diseases or genetic defects. The majority of these are specifically puppy "lemon" laws, but several (New York, Florida, Connecticut, and Arkansas) now include cats as well.

The courts are also evolving in their consideration of the effects of the death or injury of cats on those who care for them. In most court cases seeking redress for the loss of a companion animal, awards, when granted, have been limited to actual monetary value or veterinary costs. This has been changing as some courts consider the emotional significance of animal companions (Wise 1998; Young 2001), and recent decisions have allowed cat owners to sue for mental injuries when a cat was destroyed (*Peloquin v. Calcasieu Parish Police,* Jury S. 2d 1246 [La. Ct. App. 1979]) and for punitive damages in the malicious killing of a cat (*Wilson v. City of Eagan,* 297 N.W.2d 146 Mn. 1980). Still, the movement away from the common law view of cats as property with little or no intrinsic value has been slow.

2. Educate the public and other professionals.

Much cruelty to cats is rooted in long-standing myths and misconceptions about cat behavior and biology. Animal protection and veterinary medicine professionals need to continue to promote efforts to dispel such misinformation and to promote a high standard of care and responsibility in caring for cats. The HSUS initiated a "Safe Cats" campaign to dispel many of these ideas and promote responsible care, including a strong emphasis on the need to keep cats indoors (HSUS 2003).

3. Respond to individuals and organizations promoting abusive practices.

Cruelty to animals, including cats, should never be taken lightly. It causes enormous suffering for the animals and those who care for and about them. Publishers, advertisers, and others who appear to condone or promote such cruelty should be notified of concerns and held accountable for treating cat abuse lightly. This should extend as well to strong opposition to organized and institutional abuse of cats, including the commercial trade in dog and cat fur (HSUS 1999) and use of cats in research involving pain and distress (Spiegel 2003).

4. Promote humane control of "problem" or feral cats.

Historically, communities have responded to cat-related conflicts by using methods that rarely provide long-term solutions. The HSUS believes that community cat care and control programs should include the following (HSUS 2002):

- Mandatory registration or licensing of cats. If a fee is charged, it should be higher for unsterilized cats than for sterilized cats ("differential licensing").
- Mandatory identification of cats. In addition to requiring that cats wear collars and tags, communities should consider implementing a permanent identification system such as microchips.
- Mandatory rabies vaccinations for all cats more than three months of age.
- Mandatory sterilization of all cats adopted from public and private animal shelters and rescue groups.
- Mandatory sterilization of all free-roaming cats.
- A mandatory minimum shelter holding period for stray cats consistent with that established for stray dogs. This policy should allow for euthanasia of suffering animals before the end of the holding period.
- Adequate and appropriate shelter holding space, staffing, and other resources necessary to hold stray felines for the

mandatory minimum holding period.

- An ongoing public education program that promotes responsible cat care.
- Subsidized sterilization services to encourage cat owners to sterilize their animals.

While cats may never again achieve the special status they had in ancient Egypt, they are loved and admired by hundreds of millions of people worldwide. Ensuring that they live safe, healthy, and happy lives is an important part of having a truly humane society.

Literature Cited

American Pet Products Manufacturers Association (APPMA). 2004. *National pet owners survey 2003–2004.* Greenwich, Conn.: APPMA.

American Veterinary Medical Association (AVMA). 2002. *U.S. pet ownership and demographic sourcebook.* Schaumburg, Ill.: AVMA.

Arluke, A., R. Frost, G. Steketee, G. Patronek, C. Luke, E. Messner, J. Nathanson, and M. Papazian. 2002. Press reports of animal hoarding. *Society and Animals* 10 (2): 113–135.

Ascione, F.R. 1998. Battered women's reports of their partners' and their children's cruelty to animals. *Journal of Emotional Abuse* 1: 119–133.

Ascione, F.R., and P. Arkow, eds. 1999. *Child abuse, domestic violence and animal abuse: Linking the circles of compassion for prevention and intervention.* West Lafayette, Ind.: Purdue University Press.

Ascione, F.R., and R. Lockwood. 2001. Animal cruelty: Changing psychological, social, and legislative perspectives. In *The state of the animals: 2001*, ed. D.J. Salem and A.N. Rowan, 39–53. Washington, D.C.: Humane Society Press.

Associated Press. 2003. Psychiatrists: Malvo couldn't tell right from wrong. December 11.

Barloy, J. 1974. *Man and animal.* London: Gordon and Cremonesi.

Beadle. M. 1977. *The cat: History, biology, and behaviour.* London: Collins and Harvill Press.

Berry, C., G. Patronek, and R. Lockwood. In press. Long-term outcomes in animal hoarding cases. *Animal Law.*

Bollinger, V. 1998. One deadly night at Noah's Ark. *HSUS News* 43(2): 36–40.

British Broadcast Corporation. 2001. Purring predator: Pet cats and wildlife. *BBC Wildlife* magazine, February. *www.bbc.co.uk/nature/animals/features/175index.shtml.*

Clutton-Brock, J. 1993. *Cats, ancient and modern.* Cambridge, Mass.: Harvard University Press.

Conway, D.J. 1998. *The mysterious, magical cat.* New York: Grammercy Books.

Darnton, R. 1984. *The great cat massacre.* New York: Basic Books.

Davis, S. 2003. Prosecuting animal hoarders is like herding cats. *California Lawyer.* September.

DeViney, L., J. Dickert, and R. Lockwood. 1983. The care of pets within child abusing families. *International Journal for the Study of Animal Problems* 4(4): 321–336.

Durston, G. 2000. *Witchcraft and witch trials: A history of English witchcraft and its legal perspectives, 1542 to 1736.* Chichester: Barry Rose Law Publishers.

Evans, E.P. 1906. *The criminal prosecution and capital punishment of animals.* London: Heinemann.

Favre, D., and V. Tsang. 1993. The development of anti-cruelty laws during the 1800's. *Detroit College of Law Review,* 1–35.

Felthous, A.R. 1980. Aggression against cats, dogs, and people. *Child Psychiatry and Human Development* 10: 169–177.

———. 1984. Psychotic perception of pet animals in defendants accused of violent crimes. *Behavioral Sciences and the Law* 2: 331–339.

Felthous, A.R., and S.R. Kellert. 1987. Psychosocial aspects of selecting animal species for physical abuse. *Journal of Forensic Sciences* 32: 1713–1723.

Frasch, P., S. Waisman, B. Wagman, and S. Beckstead. 2000. *Animal law.* Durham, N.C.: Carolina Academic Press.

Hartwell, S.L. 2004. Domestic cats: Wildlife enemy number one or convenient scapegoats? *www.messybeast.com/cat-wildlife.htm.*

Hoarding of Animals Research Consortium (HARC). 2000. People who hoard animals. *Psychiatric Times* 17 (4): 25–29.

Holland, B. 1988. *The name of the cat.* New York: Dodd, Mead.

Holton, L., and P. Manzoor. 1993. Managing and controlling feral cat populations: Killing the crisis and not the animal. *Veterinary Forum* March: 100–101.

Humane Society of the United States (HSUS). 1999. *Betrayal of trust.* Washington, D.C.: HSUS.

———. 2002. *Guide to cat law.* Washington, D.C.: HSUS.

———. 2003. *A safe cat is a happy cat.* Washington, D.C.: HSUS.

Kellert, S.R., and J.K. Berry. 1980. Knowledge, affection, and basic attitudes toward animals in American society. Washington, D.C.: U.S. Government Printing Office, #024-010-00-625-1.

Kete, K. 1994. *The beast in the boudoir: Petkeeping in nineteenth century Paris.* Berkeley: University of California Press.

King, D.I., and J.H. Rappole. 2003. Population trends for migrant birds in North America: A summary and critique. Report from Defenders of Wildlife. *www.defenders.org/wildlife/news/birds.html.*

Lockwood, R. 1994. The psychology of animal collectors. *American Animal Hospital Association*

Trends 9(6): 18–21.

Lockwood, R., and F. Ascione, eds. 1998. *Animal cruelty and interpersonal violence: Readings in research and application.* West Lafayette, Ind.: Purdue University Press.

Lockwood, R., and B. Cassidy. 1988. Killing with kindness? *The HSUS News* 33(3): 14–18.

Mammal Society, The. 2001. Look what the cat's brought in! *www.mammal.org.uk/catkills.htm.*

Merz-Perez, L., and K.M. Heide. 2003. *Animal cruelty: Pathway to violence against people.* Walnut Creek, Calif.: Altamira Press.

Morris, D. 1986. *Cat watching.* New York: Crown Publishers.

Mullen, S. 1993. Too many cats. *Cat Fancy.* October: 50–53.

Natoli, E., and E. DeVito. 1988. The mating system of feral cats living in a group. In *The domestic cat,* ed. D. Turner and P. Bateson, 99–108. Cambridge: Cambridge University Press.

Olsen, J. 2002. *I: The creation of a serial killer.* New York: St. Martin's Press.

Patronek, G. 1998. Free-roaming and feral cats: Their impact on wildlife and human beings. *Journal of the American Veterinary Medical Association* 212(2): 218–226.

————. 1999. Hoarding of animals: An under-recognized public health problem in a difficult-to-study population. *Public Health Reports* 114: 81–87.

Ponder, C., and R. Lockwood. 2001. Cruelty to animals and family violence. Training Key #526, Arlington, Va. International Association of Chiefs of Police, 1–6.

Revitch, E. 1965. Sex murder and the potential sex murderer. *Diseases of the Nervous System* 26(10): 640–648.

Robinson, G.W. 1976. The high-rise trauma syndrome in cats. *Feline Practice* 6: 40–43.

Ritvo, H. 1987. *The animal estate.* Cambridge, Mass.: Harvard University Press.

Serpell, J. 1986. *In the company of animals.* New York: Basil Blackwell.

————. 1988. The domestication and history of the cat. In *The domestic cat,* ed. D. Turner and P. Bateson, 151–158. Cambridge: Cambridge University Press.

Slater, M. 2002. *Community approaches to feral cats: Problems, alternatives, and recommendations.* Washington, D.C.: Humane Society Press.

Spiegel, C. 2003. Cat madness: Human research involving cats. *AV Magazine* 111(1): 2–7.

Tabor, R. 1983. *The wildlife of the domestic cat.* London: Arrow Books.

Turner, D., and O. Meister. 1988. Hunting behaviour of the domestic cat. In *The domestic cat,* ed. D. Turner and P. Bateson, 111–121. Cambridge: Cambridge University Press.

Twitchell, J. 1989. *Preposterous violence.* New York: Oxford University Press.

Uglow, J. 1997. *Hogarth: A life and a world.* New York: Farrar, Straus and Giroux.

Van Vechten, C. 1936. *The tiger in the house.* New York: Knopf.

Vigne, J.D., J. Guilaine, K. Debue, L. Haye, and P. Gerard. 2004. Early taming of the cat in Cyprus. *Science* 304: 259.

Whitney, W.O., and C.J. Mehlhaff. 1987. High-rise syndrome in cats. *Journal of the American Veterinary Medical Association* 191: 1399–1403.

Wise, S. 1998. Recovery of common law damages for emotional distress, loss of society, and loss of companionship for the wrongful death of a companion animal. *Animal Law* 4(33): 33–93.

Worth, C., and A. Beck. 1981. Multiple ownership of animals in New York City. *Transactions and Studies of the College of Physicians of Philadelphia* 3: 280–300.

Yakutchik, M. 2003. Plight of the vanishing songbirds. *Defenders* magazine. Spring. *www.defenders.org/defendersmag/issues.spring03/plightsongbird.html.*

Young, S. 2001. The domestic cat and the law: A guide to available resources. Law Library Resource Exchange. *www.llrx.com/features/catlaw.hrm.*

Zeuner, F.E. 1963. *A history of domesticated animals.* London: Hutchinson.

Indoor Cats, Scratching, and the Debate over Declawing: When Normal Pet Behavior Becomes a Problem

CHAPTER 3

Katherine C. (Kasey) Grier and Nancy Peterson

When pet animals share our living spaces, their needs and natural behaviors sometimes are at odds with the varying standards for household appearance, sanitation, and polite social life that Americans have established over time. How pet owners have resolved these issues provides insight into their changing ideas about the role of animals in their households and suggests how much, or how little, people may actually know about the biological behaviors and psychological needs of the creatures they care for. This essay examines one particular issue associated with the problem of sharing spaces: declawing pet cats as a common solution to avoid destructive scratching. This is a volatile issue and has generated much emotional debate. It pits loving cat owners who see such surgery as an act that breaches the trust of responsible pet care for their feline companions against loving cat owners who see the surgery as an act that strengthens their bond with their feline companions. It divides those in the animal welfare and veterinary community as well, where many opinions are believed to be the *right* opinion. The authors wish

to stress that they enjoy the companionship of pet animals in their homes; pointing out the complexities and contradictions in living with pet cats is intended to acknowledge the historical, socially constructed, and changeable character of pet keeping and to encourage people involved in companion animal welfare work to consider why some practices can be promoted or simply tolerated, while others are problematic.

The History of the Cat as a Pet in America

The domestic cat (*Felis catus*) arrived in America with the first permanent European settlers in the seventeenth century. Ships carrying immigrants and supplies almost always carried at least one cat to kill the rats that plagued ships' food supplies. On shore, cats soon played an essential role as predators in the ecology of human-animal communities. Small businesses and government offices relied on resident cats to protect their contents from rats and mice, and, by the mid-1800s, it was even possible for city folk to rent good

mousers. The U.S. Post Office owned what one observer called "quite an army of cats" to protect the mail; postmasters in large cities even had budgets for "cat meat" (this being food *for* cats, not food *from* cats). Around markets and stables and anywhere grain was stored to service livestock, cats were present (Grier, in press).

Although the majority of American cats still worked for a living as late as the 1940s (Jones 2003), some families enjoyed the company of what memoirist Samuel Canby Rumford of Wilmington, Delaware, recalling his childhood in the 1880s, called "just plain cats." While cities were home to many thousands of feral and unowned cats, and even cats with owners were sometimes purely animal workers, ample documentation survives of well-cherished pet cats and of cats who were both workers and well-loved companions. The Quaker diarist Elizabeth Sandwith Drinker cherished her old cat, Puss, so much that, when the cat died from a "disorder among the cats" of Philadelphia in 1800, she arranged a funeral for the animal. The Rumfords had a family pet cemetery with wooden monuments for both cats and dogs dating back to the 1830s. Despite efforts to establish a pet-cat "fancy" with a show circuit beginning in the 1870s, most cat lovers would have scoffed at the idea of buying a "purebred" cat. Pet cats were acquired from friends or neighbors or adopted as strays. At the same time that these lucky cats enjoyed life in the laps of fond owners, in places like the Rumfords' barn, cats who lived on their own ingenuity "multiplied in great numbers" (Grier, in press).

Because cats were expected to hunt, their owners often assumed that they could fend somewhat for themselves. Thus cats occupied an ambiguous position in the household as somehow less tame than dogs, and their quest for prey sometimes put them in conflict with humans. For example, where households kept poultry, cats were a nuisance because they found chicks such easy pickings. In May 1872 cat lover Alice Stone Blackwell, who cared for a small flock at her family's suburban house, found herself marching over to her next-door neighbor to "tell him if he did not keep the cat shut up we should have to kill it" (Grier, in press).

Eventually the problems caused by such ambiguities came to the attention of the animal welfare community. By the early twentieth century, advocates complained about an apparently common practice among city folk of turning out cats for the summer when the family went on vacation, or of keeping cats during the summer at the seaside or country house and leaving them behind when the family returned to the city for the winter.

Also during this time, urban public health professionals in the largest cities turned their attention to remaking cities into orderly, healthier environments with safe water, clean streets, and regular municipal trash pickup. In this context, the ubiquitous urban tramp cat was no longer a joke or even an unpleasant yet acceptable fact of life. Cities had needed them, but now the misery of half-starved feral and unowned cats, and increasing, if misguided, public concern about cats as carriers of diseases, including poliomyelitis, led to new efforts to control their numbers. Whether stray cat populations had increased dramatically in those years, as advocates of control claimed, it is true that hundreds of thousands of cats were captured and killed between 1890 and 1910.

In 1911 the New York Society for the Prevention of Cruelty to Animals (SPCA) killed upwards of three hundred thousand cats, mostly kittens. Philadelphia disposed of fifty thousand and Boston another twenty-five thousand that same year. The author of the *McClure's* magazine article that startled readers with those figures excoriated pet owners who abandoned their cats for the summers or refused to euthanize unwanted kittens:

It does not fit in with the decencies of civilization that so much living and dying should go on casually, in lofts and cellars and drains and coal-pockets and vacant houses. Neither does it accord with a decent humanity that so many sentient and dependent creatures should be left so completely at the mercy of circumstances. (in Grier, in press)

Throughout the nineteenth century, as now, some people were serious cat lovers. Lydia Jackson Emerson, Ralph Waldo Emerson's second wife, was one of these. Her stepdaughter Ellen complained in an 1859 letter to her sister that the family not only tolerated a black kitten, the barn cat, two others named Violet and Kitty Minot, a large black cat, and "Aunty's cat and all mother's pensioners," but that they recently had been "*much* afflicted by the arrival of another cat." Emerson himself joked that the cat came from a nearby town, where she had "met a cat who said 'Why, haven't you heard? There's a Mis' Emerson down Concord-way what's kind to cats.'" While conventional wisdom considered cats to be pets for women and little girls, there were in fact both male and female cat lovers. Samuel Clemens, better known as Mark Twain, was a passionate cat lover (which may surprise readers of *The Adventures of Tom Sawyer,* where Clemens discussed at some length the trading and play value of a dead cat among small boys). This was a trait he shared with his mother, who, he recalled, succored scores of strays in the 1830s and 1840s. Once his own family was established, Clemens indulged his passion for cats freely; one daughter recalled Clemens walking around with a cat named Lazy draped around his neck like a stole (Grier, in press).

In sum, pet cats were more common in eighteenth- and nineteenth-century America than has been suggested previously. Some pet cats had real devotees who loved them and valued them as more than mouse catchers. Even the most beloved pet cats, however, lived lives that were much different from those of their modern counterparts.

For one thing, all cats lived at least part of their lives outdoors. This was a sensible solution given the blunt realities of cat ownership: even pet cats were sexually intact, expressing a range of behaviors (unpleasant to humans) that feline sex lives necessarily engendered. Further, cat owners who confined their animals had to improvise litterboxes with sand, wood shavings, or torn newspaper. Thus, even in big cities, most pet cats were routinely allowed out to wander, and owners expected them to have adventures, including fights with other wanderers. In the early 1890s, teenager John W. Gould of Orange, New Jersey, was pleased when his cat Mike matured enough to have "his experience fighting outside. He has licked all the Tramps but one and I think he will whip that one next time" (Grier, in press). Leaving the house meant that pet cats were exposed to infectious diseases, injury, or death. However, the fact that many cats lived at least part of their lives out of doors also meant that they could express their range of behaviors more fully. Thus, owners were less likely to confront certain behaviors like scratching, and, when they did, they had a handy and inexpensive solution: put the cat outside.

The Changing Experience of Keeping a Cat

Several important changes in the routines of pet keeping made it easier for owners to keep cats as indoor pets. The first was the invention of new products specifically for cat owners. The most important of these was commercial cat litterbox fillers. Kitty Litter™ was bagged and sold in 1947 by Edward Lowe, a Florida salesman who dealt in granulated clay products intended to soak up grease spills. The granulated-clay cat litter business took off rapidly because Lowe and his competitors were actually responding to latent demand in the marketplace; manufacturers of pet supplies had been offering cat "toilets" containing paper pads for some years. There is other circumstantial evidence that increasing numbers of cat owners were interested in considering, or were forced by their living conditions in high-rise apartments or near the busy streets of America's cities, to consider keeping their cats indoors. By the 1930s, commercial scratching posts became available for sale in pet stores; in 1936, the first U.S. patent for a scratching post appeared, and numerous variations followed. By the 1950s, pet stores even offered spray repellants intended to keep cats away from furniture (Grier, in press).

The second important change that made it easier for cat owners

to keep their cats as indoor pets was the growing popularity of spaying and neutering. According to the 2003–2004 National Pet Owners' Survey by the American Pet Products Manufacturers Association (APPMA), 84 percent of cats were spayed or neutered in 2002. Surgically removing the sexual organs of cats eliminates some undesirable behaviors (wandering to find a mate, fighting, noisy heat cycles) and often decreases others (urine spraying to mark territory). Sterilization has become synonymous with responsible pet ownership, thanks to the work of animal welfare organizations, animal shelters, and veterinarians (see appendix A). It signals a dramatic change in human behavior over a relatively short span of time since the 1960s.

Cats seemed to fit well into changing patterns of living in America. They could live comfortably in apartments and small houses and were reputed to make fewer demands on their owners for atten-

(APPMA 2003–2004). In 2002 there were 77.6 million owned cats and 65 million owned dogs in the United States (APPMA 2003–2004). In an informal survey of declawing across the United States, one author (N.P. 2004) found that costs at twenty-five veterinary facilities for the declawing of forefeet range from $50 to $476, or an average of $158 per declaw. Given Patronek's estimate that as many as 25 percent of the owned cat population is declawed (2001), this would represent 19.4 million declawed cats and revenue to veterinarians of more than $3 billion. Any significant lowering of the declawing rate would be a large financial loss to the veterinary community. Declawing opponents argue, however, that addressing behavior problems can enhance the value of a veterinary practice and make up for that loss. By offering pet behavior services and/or recommending outside resources, veterinary practices can maintain

Table 1
Percentage of APPMA Owners with Scratching Posts

	1994	1996	1998	2000	2002
Own a Scratching Post:	28	30	33	37	35

Source: 2003–2004 APPMA National Pet Owners Survey.

tion and care than did dogs. In its first survey of American pet owners in 1978, the APPMA reported that 31.7 million households had dogs and 16.2 million had cats. According to APPMA statistics, the number of cats (62 million) exceeded the number of dogs (53 million) in American households for the first time in 1992. Cats have continued to outpace dogs since then, and the number of households that have a cat increased faster (8 percent) than the number of households with any pet (3 percent)

client loyalty, strengthen their client services, and generate additional revenue from services, products, and referrals (Peterson 2002).

Since 1978, the APPMA has provided a profile of dog owners, but it took another twenty years before the association established a similar profile for cat owners. According to the 1998 cat profile: 68 percent of owners were female; the average age of a cat owner (male or female) was forty-five; and more cat owners were single (36 percent) than were dog owners (27 percent).

Table 2
Demographic Profile of Cat Owners

Female:	68 percent
Age:	40–49 (25 percent)
	50–64 (20 percent)
Marital Status:	married (59 percent)
	single (19 percent) (second largest)

Over the course of their lifetime, 67 percent of cat owners have been pet owners for more than twenty years.

Source: Ralston Purina 2000.

Table 3
Reasons for Removing a Cat from the Household

Eliminating Outside the Litterbox:	33 percent
Biting People:	14 percent
Intolerant of Children:	11 percent
Scratching People:	11 percent
Destroying Household or Personal Items:	8 percent

Source: Ralston Purina 2000.

For the 2002 survey, collected information indicated that 11 percent of cat owners were females living alone and 7 percent were males living alone (Armstrong, Tomasello, and Hunter 2001).

Increasing interest in cats as pets has lead to more intensive patterns of care. In the late 1960s and early 1970s, the growth of the pet-cat population and the demands of cat owners stimulated several veterinary schools to add more information on cats to their curricula, publishers to include cats in their veterinary texts, and pharmaceutical companies to increase the range of products available for cats (Jones 2003). *Cats* Magazine was founded in 1945, a number of popular advice manuals came out after World War II, and many other publications followed.

Commercial cat food had been available since the 1890s, but it was rarely used until the 1930s, and it began to outsell dog food in 1958 (Jones 2003).

Unacceptable Cat Behavior

Pet cats live longer lives thanks to improved health care and nutrition and an indoor lifestyle. From 1987 to 2000, the life span of the average cat increased by more than one-third, according to the American Veterinary Medical Association (AVMA) (2002). This increased life expectancy means that owners are more likely to experience behaviors that they cannot tolerate, such as urination outside the litterbox, which is associated with deteriorating health (conditions such as

arthritis), cats' physical and mental needs being unmet by their caregivers, or the stress caused when cats are expected to adapt to changing human routines.

In 1950 one-person households accounted for 9.5 percent of all households; by 2000, they accounted for 26 percent, an all-time high. Even in multiperson families, however, pets are often left home alone for many hours every day. This situation has prompted the creation of new pet services such as "doggy daycare" and professional dog walkers, but nothing comparable is available for cats in most communities. Because cats are presumed—not without some justification—to be able to occupy themselves indoors just as they used to fend for themselves outdoors, they have become the exemplary urban pet. Yet, reasons given for why cats are surrendered to shelters reveal that behavior problems account for many such relinquishments. Most cats who enter shelters are between six months and three years of age and have lost their homes due to unacceptable behavior (Miller et al. 1996; Patronek et al. 1996; Salman et al. 1998, 2000; Kass et al. 2001). Behavior problems accounted for 14 percent of the reasons owners reported for surrendering a cat; the most commonly reported behavior problem in cats was fearfulness, followed by scratching the furniture, not using the litterbox, and objecting to being held (Miller et al. 1996; Line 1998). Other studies show that destroying household or personal items is among the top five reasons for removing a cat from the household (but not necessarily bringing the pet to a shelter) (Table 3).

It has been estimated that behavior problems are identified in 5 percent of all veterinary visits, account for 20 percent of a veterinarian's time, are the main reason for euthanasia of pets, and cause practitioners to lose 15 percent of their client base annually (Landsberg 1991a). Approximately 97,000 cats are euthanized annually in small animal veterinary practices in the United States because of behavior problems (Patronek and Dodman 1999). Although veterinarians seemed unwilling to euthanize animals for behavior problems solely on the basis of a client's request, many did not inquire routinely about animal behavior and often were not confident enough in their clinical skills to treat behavior problems (Patronek and Dodman 1999).

Keeping Cats Indoors

The human population demographics mentioned previously and the risks of diseases, poisons, attacks by other animals, abuse by humans, or speeding vehicles make the great outdoors a dangerous place for free-roaming animals. When cats are left outside unsupervised, their chance of being injured, becoming ill, or even dying is increased. The estimated average life span of a free-roaming cat, even one who ventures outdoors unsupervised only occasionally, is less than three years, compared to fifteen to eighteen years for the average indoor-only cat (HSUS 2003).

It is important to remember that cats have always lived their lives outdoors; what is different today is that the risks most cat owners were once willing to assume as simply part of the reality of keeping a cat have become less acceptable to many. Two out of three veterinarians now recommend keeping cats indoors, most often citing dangers from vehicles and disease (Jacobs, Jenner, and Kent 2001). Because fewer than 5 percent of "found" cats taken in by animal shelters are reunited with their families, many animal shelters now require potential adopters to promise to keep their cats safely confined. Some com-

munities, such as Aurora, Colorado; Overland Park, Kansas; and Muscle Shoals, Alabama, are adopting ordinances that mandate confinement for cats, a common requirement for dogs (Aurora: Sec. 14-101. Running at large. [a] Prohibited. It shall be unlawful for the owner of any cat to fail to keep the cat from running at large within the city. Code 1979, §7-30; Ord. No. 97-51, §8, 10-13-97).

Animal welfare groups, including The Humane Society of the United States (HSUS), have played an important role in the emphasis on keeping cats indoors. To prevent destruction by indoor cats, the late Phyllis Wright, HSUS director of Companion Animals, recommended that cats' claws be trimmed regularly and carefully with a special nail clipper and that cats be taught to use a scratching post in the first of several articles in The HSUS's

membership magazine urging owners to keep their cats indoors. "Most cats," she added, "will soon get the idea that the scratching post is the perfect outlet for their need to use their claws" (in Dasch 1984, 15). (This was also mentioned in Fox 1987.)

Cats continued to figure prominently in the *HSUS News*, but, while the articles encouraged keeping cats indoors, the majority of cover photographs and internal editorial photographs depicted cats outdoors and without collars (Summer 1985, Spring 1987, Spring 1988, Fall 1991, and Spring 1993 issues) and indoors without collars (Winter 1988 and Winter 1990 issues). According to D.J. Salem, editor of the Massachusetts Society for the Prevention of Cruelty to Animals' *Animals* magazine (1976–1979) and of the *HSUS News* (1981–1999), animal protec-

---

Table 4
Cat Owner Routine, by Percentage

Cat Indoors During the Day		Cat Outdoors During the Day	
1998	56		18
2000	54		11
2002	57		14

Cat Both Indoors and Outdoors During the Day		Cat Outdoors Only During the Night	
1998	34		68
2000	35		63
2002	29		68

Cat Outdoors Only During the Night		Cat Both Indoors and Outdoors During the Night	
1998	16		23
2000	12		25
2002	14		16

Source: APPMA 2003–2004.

tion magazines struggled for decades with the dearth of collared animals in agency-purchased—as well as in unsolicited—photographs (personal communication with N.P., November 2004). Salem believes that the evolution in photographic images came not as a result of increased sensitivity to the issue on the part of magazine staffs but rather with the advent of computer software that allowed the digital "addition" of collars to stock photographs. Commissioned photography, although rarely used by The HSUS because of its cost, depicted both cats and dogs wearing collars, beginning in the mid-1980s (The HSUS's "Until There is None, Adopt One" poster is an example). Salem notes that agency-provided stock photos depict collarless animals to the same extent they always have, but photo retouching can "cure" the problem. She notes that internal discussion on both of these subjects (outdoor cats and collars) and attempts to reconcile policy with available images began soon after her arrival at The HSUS in 1981. By 1996 the cover of the Spring *HSUS News* depicted an indoor cat with collar and ID tag.

Shelter Sense, the HSUS publication for the animal-sheltering community, addressed the issue of indoor cats early in April 1989, August 1990, and March 1994. In 2002 The HSUS launched its Safe Cats campaign to educate owners about the consequences of and solutions to letting owned cats roam unsupervised outdoors.

An unpublished HSUS survey (R. Lockwood, personal communication with N.P., July 22, 2004) indicated that 74 percent of respondents somewhat or strongly favor keeping a cat indoors all the time or under supervision when outdoors. The American Society for the Prevention of Cruelty to Animals (ASPCA) began its transition to a preference for keeping cats indoors about 1989 or 1990 (S.

Zawistowski, personal communication with N.P., August 18, 2004). Zawistowski recalls that the most heated arguments in the education department at that time involved the issue and focused on the impact that cats could have on wildlife populations and the potential dangers to cats. *The ASPCA Complete Cat Care Manual* (Edney 1992) included information on how to build a cat run as a safe outdoor venue. The promotion of indoor cats continued in the more recent *ASPCA Complete Guide to Cats* (Richards 1999).

Indoor-Cat Behavior Problems and the Debate over Declawing

One behavior that figures prominently as distressing to cat owners is scratching. It is second only to climbing in controllable behavior (Table 5).

The top four behavioral problems owners of kittens cited during veterinary office visits were (from most frequent to least frequent) inappropriate elimination, property destruction, aggression toward other animals of the same species,

and aggression toward humans; for adult cats the problems were inappropriate elimination, aggression toward other animals of the same species, aggression toward humans, and property destruction (Patronek and Dodman 1999).

Kittens begin to retract their claws at about twenty-eight days of age and begin to scratch by day thirty-five (Beaver 1992). Thus, eight-week-old kittens are just beginning to scratch when they are adopted into new homes and can be introduced immediately to scratching posts and other acceptable objects to satisfy their need to scratch. Cats scratch to (1) condition their claws by removing old nail sheaths, (2) display dominance in front of subordinate cats, (3) scent mark with the glands on their paws, (4) visually mark by leaving shredded matter as evidence, (5) stretch and exercise their forelegs, and 6) enjoy a pleasant sensation.

A History of Declawing

In the last forty years, an increasing number of indoor cat owners have chosen to deal with clawing at furniture and household textiles through

---

Table 5
The Pros and Cons of Pet Ownership, by Percentage of Respondents

Benefits		Drawbacks	
Companionship, Love, Company:	88	Sadness When They Die:	49
Fun to Watch/ Have in Household:	75		
Convenience, Easy to Maintain:	67	Shedding:	38
Relaxation, Relieves Stress:	65	Climbs on Countertops/ Tabletops:	34
Like Child/Family Member:	62	Damage to Furniture or Carpet:	30

Source: APPMA 2003–2004.

a surgical solution, declawing (feline onychectomy). The last bone of each toe is amputated, with a guillotine-type nail clipper, scalpel blade, or laser, to prevent regrowth of the claw, which is adhered to the bone.

The early history of the procedure remains unclear. A search (by N.P.) of thirty antiquarian veterinary books published between the 1900s to the 1950s uncovered no references to declawing. A search of more recent veterinary medical literature for declawing and onychectomy in cats yielded forty-eight studies from 1973–2002 on the effects of different techniques, anesthesia and pain medications, attitudes of owners, assessment of complications, measurement of pain, and other topics. The earliest citation for declawing was Nagle's *A Technique for Feline Onychectomy* (1976), which describes a technique for declawing cats that Nagle had used for the previous twenty years.

The technique of declawing seems to have entered some small-animal surgical curricula in the 1950s. Class notes on feline surgery from the College of Veterinary Medicine at Iowa State University turned up the first discussion there of declawing in 1955 (George Beran, D.V.M., personal communication with N.P., March 25, 2003). An informal survey (by N.P.) of thirty veterinarians in practice, retired from practice, or in school conducted at the HSUS exhibit booth at the 2004 annual American Veterinary Medical Association conference in Philadelphia indicated that declawing was not taught to those who graduated from Auburn (in 1943); Guelph (1947); Pennsylvania (1951, 1952, 1957); Georgia (1955); Cornell (1961); Ohio (1999); Oklahoma (2003); UC Davis (1970); or Wisconsin (2002). Other veterinarians indicated that declawing was taught when they graduated from Iowa (1949, 1981, 2005); Auburn (1951, 1969, 1984); Cornell (1956, 1965); Georgia (1975); Ohio (1959, 1971); Purdue

(1964); Kansas (1964, 1976, 1984); Pennsylvania (1971, 1994); UC Davis (1977, 1989); and Texas (1972). R. McClure, D.V.M., (personal communication with N.P., February 26, 2003) indicated that he was doing an occasional declawing procedure as early as 1951 in private practice. In 1953 the Merriam-Webster Dictionary first offered a definition of declaw: "to remove the claws of (as a cat) surgically."

One feline veterinarian reports that even early (circa 1968) published discussions of declawing in veterinary journals primarily discussed refinements of technique. She hypothesizes that the first declawings were done on captive lions and tigers and other wild felines (J. Hofve, D.V.M., personal communication with N.P., March 19, 2003). J. Peddie, a 1965 graduate of Cornell in private practice from 1969 to 1991, started to declaw exotic cats in 1969 in Thousand Oaks, California, because of that location's proximity to the movie industry (personal communication with N.P., March 21, 2003). Declawing was standard procedure to satisfy the industry's liability insurance carriers. At the time, a pioneer of exotic animal care, M. Fowler, D.V.M., had developed an exotic declawing technique that involved a total disarticulation of the third phalanx. This technique severed the main tendon that pulls the toes into the paws. The resulting "floppy" toes caused ulceration of the animals' central foot pads, which supported their full weight. Peddie modified Fowler's technique, which he found in Fowler's books on exotic medicine and surgery on cats weighing more than one hundred pounds. Peddie's technique left the extensor process (which enables extension of the claws) intact, thus giving cats toes with which they could grip and on which they could balance.

Many popular books (Simmons 1935; Harman 1948; Schrody 1957; Deutsch and McCoy 1961)

urged owners of indoor cats to provide a suitable object on which to scratch, but none offered declawing as a solution. Then, as now, other, more laissez-faire, attitudes existed: "A special post is not necessary if other suitable provision has been made; the substitute must be something he likes to use, such as a chair a cat has chosen which may be given to him" (Bryant 1969, 44–45). However, Whitney (1953, 262) does include one reference to surgical intervention: "As a last resort, your veterinarian can operate on two toes in each foot and cut a little tendon to prevent a cat from clawing furniture, wallpaper, etc." By the early 1960s, declawing was presented as an option for owners who used veterinary care:

> A comparatively new cat custom, de-clawing an indoor cat, saves endless wear and tear, without making any appreciable difference to the cat. When you take your cat to the hospital for the altering operation, consult with the veterinary surgeon who can de-claw the cat's front paws at the same time and under the same anesthesia. (Schulberg 1961, 128–129)

Although more research remains to be done on the spread of the practice, by the 1970s declawing seems to have become a normal part of feline medical care.

The Financial Component

There are currently 77.6 million owned cats in the United States (American Pet Products Manufacturers Association 2003–2004). In an informal survey undertaken at the American Veterinary Medical Association (AVMA) conference in Philadelphia in 2004, one author (N.P.) found costs for declawing the forefeet at twenty-five U.S. veterinary facilities ranged from $50 to $476, averaging $158 per declaw. (Declawing is commonly combined with spay/neuter surgery, which allows the cat to undergo only one period of anesthesia.) Accepting Patronek's estimate that as much as 25 percent of the owned cat population is declawed (2001) translates into 19.4 million declawed cats, representing more than $3 billion in revenue to veterinarians. Such an amount represents a significant source of income.

The Case Against Declawing

Declawing became controversial soon after it appeared as an elective surgery in small-animal practices. Carr (1963, 113) called it a "drastic remedy" to be confined to "a few problem cats." He reported anecdotally that "occasionally a cat will be taken to a vet to be put to sleep because it has been guilty of so much damage with its claws." Carr added that the practice was already so hotly disputed that

> [T]wo very respected leaders in the cat fancy have offered a reward for the "arrest and conviction" of anyone who has been responsible for declawing a cat. Declawing is not against the law, of course. These people believe sincerely that it should be outlawed. (Carr 1963, 113)

Opponents argued against the surgery because of psychological trauma to cats. Beaver (1992, 81) pointed out

> [C]ats that depend on their claws as weapons or for climbing can become psychologically and physically traumatized if they suddenly discover their lack of claws. Even though there is no evidence of long-term problems as a result of this procedure, there remains a moral controversy about the surgery, and a perception exists that other problems, such as biting and jumping on counters or tables, will develop.

Yet Hetts (1999, 78) argued that, "although it has long been believed that declawing causes cats to become aggressive (to bite), to have litterbox problems, and to

undergo other less defined 'personality changes,' the results of several studies do not support these beliefs." The problem was and remains a lack of hard data. Hetts pointed out that "no prospective studies, in which the frequency of problem behaviors are (sic) measured before as well as after declawing, have been done" (personal communication with N.P., February 11, 2003). Thus, "the most that can be said about adverse behavioral sequelae to onychectomy is that they remain as hard to dismiss as they are to quantify" (Patronek 2001, 936).

In recent years declawing has become a controversial subject outside the veterinary and research communities as well. Cat owners have been urged by some behaviorists, veterinarians, animal welfare groups, cat writers, and others to accept scratching behavior as normal and to seek alternatives to surgical remedies. In 1998 the ASPCA issued a policy statement condemning

> [D]eclawing of cats as a matter of supposed convenience to cat owners. It is a form of mutilation and it does cause pain. The only time the surgery should be considered is when the health and safety of other animals, human beings or the individual cat is involved, and euthanasia or abandonment the only realistic alternative.

Declawing has even become a matter for municipal legislation. In 2003 West Hollywood, California, became the first city in North America to prohibit declawing. The AVMA opposed the bill on the grounds that veterinarians are better suited than are politicians to make medical decisions. The initial attempt to include domestic cats in the state bill was defeated, but a revised bill, A.B. 1857, was introduced in February 2004; signed into law on September 24, 2004; and took effect January 1, 2005. The law added a section to the animal

cruelty statutes in the California Penal Code to make it a misdemeanor for any person to perform, procure, or arrange for surgical claw removal, declawing, onychectomy, or tendonectomy on an exotic or native wild cat species. The AVMA officially opposed declawing of exotic cats in January 2004.

In response to this legislative action, the Cat Fanciers Association (CFA) announced its opposition to any legislative attempts to target veterinary elective surgical procedures. According to the CFA, few declawing procedures are executed on exotic/wild cats in California, and the option to declaw needed to remain available to experienced individuals based on their veterinarian's professional judgment and advice. However, three other California cities—Berkeley, Malibu, and San Francisco—passed resolutions condemning declawing.

There is no consensus on the effects of declawing on the personality or behavior of cats. Some argue that declawing can cause postoperative discomfort or pain (Davis 1993; Estep and Hetts 1994; Pollari and Bonnett 1996; Overall 1997; Jankowski et al. 1998). Others point out that when it is done properly, declawing causes minimal pain, improves the pet-owner relationship (Houpt 1991; Yeon et al. 2001), and is a better alternative to relinquishment or euthanasia (Ames 1968; Landsberg 1991b; Estep and Hetts 1994); Phillips and Phillips 1994).

Small-animal practitioners see all kinds of owner behavior, some of which is less than ideal, and they recognize that even conscientious pet owners have different levels of tolerance for destructive pet behavior. Indeed, one study suggests that furniture clawing is often ignored unless it is performed on some object of high economic value (R. Lockwood, personal communication with N.P., July 22, 2004). In the most extreme cases, owners deciding between euthanasia and declawing will not tolerate the infrequent furniture scratching that might occur (Houpt, Honig, and Reisner 1996). Thus veterinarians tend to frame their observations on the topic in terms of two choices, declawing or relinquishment. They resent the suggestion that they cause unnecessary pain when performing the surgery, arguing that the cats they declaw behave normally soon after the surgery. Many veterinarians point out that the improvement in surgical techniques and analgesics and the more frequent use of analgesics during and following declaw surgery has made what was a potentially traumatic surgery much less so nowadays.[1]

Opponents of declawing cite a study by Kass et al. (2001) that showed that, although 18 percent of the cats specifically presented to shelters for euthanasia were relinquished for behavioral reasons, destructiveness inside or outside the home was, at 14 percent, not even in the top ten objectionable behaviors. Loewenthal (2002) found that relatively few declaws were performed as last-ditch efforts to save a cat from going back to the shelter.

Alternatives to Declawing

Cat owners are now presented with two nonsurgical options for dealing with clawing: nail trimming and the use of plastic nail caps coupled with diversion, through training, the latter using both aversive and positive reinforcement. Nail trimming is much easier for owners to perform when cats have become accustomed to the procedure from kittenhood. Cat behavior experts believe that undesirable scratching can be prevented or eliminated with appropriate behavior modification techniques and urge owners to consider surgical intervention only as a last resort (Lewis 1984; Lands-

berg 1991b; Beaver 1992; Donald 1992; *Shelter Sense* 1994; Houpt, Honig, and Reisner 1996; Lamb 1996; Overall 1997; Lachman and Mickdeit 2000; Christensen and HSUS staff 2002; Horwitz 2003; Thornton 2004). Public education on normal cat behavior seems to be a powerful tool: one study found that the incidence of relinquishment decreased if cat owners had read a book or other educational materials about feline behavior (Salman et al. 1998).

Still, little is known about the success or failure of cat training. In one study on pet keeping (Ralston Purina 2000), the top four cat-behavior problems mentioned by owners were clawing the furniture (20 percent), climbing on furniture or counters (16 percent), eliminating in the house outside the litterbox (10 percent), and bringing birds and/or mice into the house (8 percent), all natural behaviors for a small, agile, predatory animal. Dog owners are encouraged to seek obedience and other forms of training, yet many cat owners seem unwilling to make this same kind of effort with their cats and consider their cats to be untrainable. Cat owners do not seem to be highly successful disciplinarians. Disciplining or scolding their pet is the top method used by cat owners (35 percent) to handle behavior problems; 24 percent of cat owners say they do nothing when their cat misbehaves. Only 30 percent of cat owners have solved their pet's behavior problems completely, although 42 percent of cat owners say they have made some progress (Ralston Purina 2000). Complicating the picture further is evidence that scolding and discipline to discourage cats from scratching without providing an acceptable substitute can actually backfire (Beaver 1992). It can lower the scratching threshold, so that the cat is attempts it even more frequently, and the animal's frustration increases (Beaver

1992). It also teaches the cat to run from the owner (Beaver 1992). Failure at training may also reflect self-selection on the part of owners unable/unwilling to invest the amount of time dog owners must to end up with a comparably obedient animal.

Another approach is to enhance public understanding and tolerance of normal cat behaviors such as scratching. Understanding cats and their behavior was addressed only relatively recently in HSUS publications. Although the *HSUS News* was a report to the members on the activities of The HSUS, the Spring 1995 issue did feature "More than a Meow" and the Winter 1996 issue included "When the Litterbox is a Letterbox," both behavior-oriented articles. The Summer 2001 issue of The HSUS's new members' magazine, *All Animals,* introduced a veterinary column by Debra Horwitz, D.V.M., DACVB, veterinary behaviorist, and subsequent issues featured cats and their behavior (Horowitz 2002, 2003, 2004). Veterinarians who visited HSUS exhibit booths at the AVMA and North American Veterinary Conferences in 2003 and 2004 received a free HSUS *Pets for Life* behavior CD-ROM with behavior tip sheets they could distribute to their clients. Until recently, veterinarians frequently relied on myriad copied journal articles, which were not directed to pet owners, for this purpose.

An Ethical Question with Practical Consequences

Opponents of declawing have strong feelings on the subject. "Declaw? Never. How would you like to have your nails pulled out one by one and be forced to walk around on stumps for the rest of your life?" announce Janik and Rejnis (1996, 95). Declawing is "the worst sort of cosmetic surgery—done entirely for the convenience and benefit of the cat's owners, and almost always to the detriment of the cat. "It's the equivalent of having your fingers cut off at the top joint," according to Christensen (2002, 157). This is a far stronger position than one espoused twenty years previously by Fox:

> With a persistent clawer, it is a simple procedure to trim the claws with a nail trimmer. Some cats will fight being restrained for this, and for some owners the only alternative is euthanasia. A third alternative is declawing, and although it is a controversial subject, I think it is better than getting rid of the pet because it persists in clawing furniture or people. (1974, 147)

Clients and practitioners are beginning to express ethical concerns about onychectomy. These concerns are developing at the same time that attitudes are changing in the United States toward the practices of tail docking and ear cropping in dogs. The AVMA's policy on declawing indicates that the procedure is justifiable, with adherence to appropriate surgical and medical principles, when the cat cannot be trained not to use his or her claws destructively, but it should not be performed solely for cosmetic purposes (Overall 1997).

Internationally, declawing is considered mutilation and is either illegal or considered extremely inhumane and to be performed only under extreme circumstances in Australia, Austria, France, Belgium, Brazil, Denmark, Finland, Germany, Great Britain, Ireland, Italy, Japan, Montenegro, Netherlands, New Zealand, Norway, Portugal, Serbia, Slovenia, Sweden, and Switzerland (The Paw Project, *http://www.pawproject.com/html/faqs.asp*).

Ironically, the debate over declawing is inadvertently at odds with the campaign to keep cats indoors in the United States. (The indoors phenomenon seems to be United States-based. Although 42.73 million cats live in Western Europe, and data on the percentage living indoors have not been published, the proportion of pet cats who are housed indoors is lower in Britain than it is in the United States). The prevalence of declawing in the United States may be due to the fact that many more cats are confined indoors than are confined in Europe (Turner and Bateson 1998).

An unpublished survey indicates that 55.4 percent of the American general public strongly favored or favored declawing. Support for declawing was significantly associated with income, with 42.6 percent of those with incomes under $20,000 and 62 percent of those with incomes over $50,000 favoring the procedure (R. Lockwood, personal communication with N.P., July 22, 2004). Those who favored keeping cats inside were also more likely to support declawing (48 percent) than were those who were opposed to declawing but supported keeping cats inside (31 percent) (R. Lockwood, personal communication with N.P., July 22, 2004). More than 39 percent of those who opposed allowing a cat outside unsupervised still favored declawing, with 23 percent opposing both declawing and allowing cats outside without supervision. This suggests that declawing was not seen as a welfare issue in the same way as were other issues in the survey, which included dogfighting, chaining a dog for extended periods, puppy mills, chimps in research, and canned hunts, but excluded tail and ear docking. Many respondents who opposed other practices did not oppose declawing. Those who reported that they thought protecting animals from cruelty and abuse was "very important" were significantly less likely to favor declawing than were those who said such protec-

tion was not important (51.4 percent vs. 64.4 percent), but more than half of those ranking protecting animals as a high priority still favored declawing, a level of support not seen for any of the other practices surveyed (e.g., 10 percent opposed increased penalties for dogfighting or cockfighting; 10 percent opposed restrictions on sow confinement).

G. Patronek, former director of Tufts Center for Animals and Public Policy, says that animal welfare workers err in basing their opinions on the effects of declawing solely on the animals seen in shelters and without comparison to the general population. He suggests that, when judgments are made without a proper comparison group, a common trait (such as having a full-time job) may appear to be associated with relinquishment just because there are so many owners with that trait (personal communication with N.P., February 2, 2003). The question, he says, is whether it occurs more frequently with animals brought into shelters than with those remaining in their homes. Lack of appreciation of this logic has led to draconian adoption policies (no one who works full time can have a puppy, for example) that are only now becoming recognized as counterproductive (personal communication with N.P., February 2, 2003).

Patronek points out that if declawing procedures using good surgical technique and analgesia caused the large number of neurotic behavior problems alleged by some advocates, shelters would be deluged with spraying, biting cats (2001). This doesn't mean that some cats may not be affected adversely by declawing, but the evidence isn't there yet to support a broad-based problem or to identify which cats are likely to be harmed seriously by the procedure (personal communication with N.P., January 30, 2003).

Patronek offers a possible explanation for shelter workers' perception that inappropriate elimination may be linked to declawing. He sees it as a statistical artifact associated with these observations: owners who declaw their cats are likely to be much more concerned about their furniture and households than owners who don't; therefore, when declawed cats in these households have an inappropriate elimination problem, those owners have a low tolerance for damage and turn the cats in rather than working to resolve or tolerating the problem (Patronek 2001). In contrast, owners of cats with claws are less concerned about furniture, and so forth, so when their cats develop an inappropriate elimination problem, they are much less likely to turn them in and more likely to tolerate or attempt to resolve the problem (Patronek 2001). From the shelter workers' perspective, they encounter the former group, and the latter are invisible to them. Therefore, the logical conclusion is that inappropriate elimination is associated with declawing. Patronek also cautions that, unless one knows how many non-declawed cats in homes exhibit inappropriate elimination behavior, one can't draw that conclusion. Patronek suggests that one reason that declawing looks "protective" against relinquishment in retrospective studies is because it is a marker for other factors (like socioeconomic status and providing veterinary care) that are highly correlated with pet retention. "That doesn't mean," he says, "that if you declaw cats it will reduce their relinquishment across the board" (personal communication with N.P., January 31, 2003).

Further, the success of campaigns for spaying and neutering may have inadvertently normalized the idea of routine surgical intervention to reshape cat behavior. This idea is reinforced by the linkage between the two practices in small-animal veterinary practices,

where declaw/neuter packages are routine. While both the animal welfare community and the majority of pet owners now agree that spaying and neutering should be routine, the fact remains that in both groups, declawing is usually preemptive, anticipating future behavior of pet cats.

What can and should be done about the difference in perception between the animal welfare community and average cat owners? One important first step may be decoupling declawing and neutering in veterinary practice and returning declawing to its former status of last-resort surgery. As Christensen and the staff of The HSUS (2002) note, onychectomy "is almost never medically or behaviorally necessary, and should never be considered routine or done preemptively." Enhancing owner and small-animal veterinary education about cat behavior is an important step. It is also clear that more research on socializing cats and retraining cats with behavior problems is very much needed. This research needs to generate practical options for cat owners, not simply identification of long-term behavioral trauma in declawed cats. Finally, the animal welfare community may need to acknowledge that there are occasions when declawing is appropriate, as in cases where accidental clawing may affect the health of an owner or when the occasional adult cat absolutely resists other kinds of training interventions and the owner wishes to continue keeping the animal indoors. Making otherwise good-enough owners defensive about their care for their animals does not benefit anyone. Should the best position that ordinary cat owners may be expected to take on declawing be much like the position expressed by the author of one recent book on cat care?

Ethically, it's difficult to justify this kind of mutilation simply for an owner's convenience,

especially when it's not difficult to teach a cat to use a scratching post. Instead of declawing your new cat, get her a great scratching post (or two) and teach her how to use it. That said, if the choice is between getting rid of the cat, keeping him outdoors, or declawing, then declawing is the best option. (Thornton 2004, 200)

The question then becomes, is the animal welfare community willing to live with this kind of practical ethics on the part of pet owners?

Since the "last resort" argument is the premise behind so many national recommendations and local policies, it seems there would be data on the likelihood of owners to relinquish cats with claws and on the propensity of potential adopters to reject a shelter that prohibits declawing. But while studies have shown that many owners relinquish cats for scratching furniture and other household items, it's unclear whether a declawing surgery would have prevented those surrenders or whether those cat owners were aware of effective options in the first place. (Lawson 2004, 20)

It behooves all involved in promoting the welfare of cats to educate, educate, educate so that declawing is no longer viewed as a routine preventive surgery but truly becomes a "last resort."

The Future of Declawing

Pet owners turn to veterinarians more often than other sources for pet care advice. Patronek (personal communication with N.P., February 1, 2003) notes that "veterinarians are still the most accepted source of information about pet issues, and when they treat [declawing] as a perfunctory part of owning a cat, then it's no surprise that a lot of owners do not think twice about it."

Patronek suggested that one reason attitudes about declawing are slow to change is that, when the arguments focus on the brutality of the surgery, there are plenty of practices where, when the procedure is performed with good technique and analgesics, the kitten pops up and is running around after surgery with little or no apparent discomfort. It flies in the face of the everyday experience in these practices to suggest that it should not be done because of the pain. When one author (N.P.) contrasted people's reaction to debarking—another surgical intervention designed to solve a behavior problem—with declawing, Patronek agreed that most people look at a debarked dog making hoarse attempts to express normal behavior as obviously grotesque, but they do not feel the same about declawing.

Patronek believes the challenge is to engender the same feeling about creating a disability through declawing, and unless owners report problems or veterinarians actually see something that makes them uncomfortable, or there are well-controlled longitudinal studies to demonstrate some adverse effects, it will be an uphill battle. He acknowledges the possibility that studies would not reveal anything substantial that was not associated with a surgical botch.

He believes that people who want to declaw their cat won't pay any more attention to studies than they do to licensing requirements when they exist. He points out that people do what they please when they take an animal out of a shelter, and, as a 2003 PETsMART study showed, a great percentage of adopters will be unavailable for contact three to six months after the adoption. Patronek asks: does the animal shelter policy on declawing turn away people who refuse to be dishonest on principle? He suggests that a thoughtful

discussion might actually get people thinking about whether they really do need to declaw.

Patronek believes that, short of that, falling back on the ethical issue of animal integrity may be fruitful in convincing cat owners not to declaw. That appeal has worked to some degree with ear cropping, but ears are visible, claws less so.

Declawing cats because they scratch destructively is like debarking dogs. It's a quick fix, but it only treats the symptoms and not the cause. If only cats (and dogs) were provided with more stimulation, perhaps these convenience surgeries wouldn't be necessary. (Personal communication with N.P., January 30, 2003)

Pet keeping inevitably involves human efforts to control natural animal behaviors. Pet owners' desire to preserve their property is valid, and our ideas about what are acceptable behaviors and methods of control change over time. We should be conscious of the historical character of our ideas about acceptable practice on the part of owners, veterinarians, and the animal welfare community and about behaviors on the part of pets.

Note

1 Any significant decrease in the number of declawing procedures performed would translate into a large financial loss to the veterinary profession. Declawing opponents argue, however, that addressing behavior problems can enhance the value of a veterinary practice and make up for that loss. By offering pet behavior services and/or recommending outside resources, practices can maintain client loyalty, strengthen their client services, and generate additional revenue from services, products, and referrals (Peterson 2002).

Appendix

Organizations' Positions on Declawing

The Humane Society of the United States

In 1978 The HSUS issued its policy Cosmetic Surgery on Animals: "The Humane Society of the United States opposes declawing of cats when it is done solely for the convenience of the owner and without benefit to the animal." In the online article (http://www.hsus.org/ace/11789) "Declawing Cats: More Than Just a Manicure," The HSUS says that, "Although new techniques for declawing cats, such as laser surgery and tenectomy, may lessen the pain that typically follows declawing, the surgery is still considered an unnecessary procedure."

The American Veterinary Medical Association

The AVMA believes that authority for decisions regarding the appropriateness of performing declawing should rest within the bounds of a valid veterinarian-client-patient relationship. According to G. Golab, D.V.M., assistant director of the AVMA's Professional Public Affairs Communications Division, the AVMA has always encouraged veterinarians to educate owners concerning any surgical or medical procedure, including declawing (personal communication with N.P., March 17, 2003). The only difference, she says, is that

[I]t has now been formally written into the position statement. The change is related not as much to veterinary education as it is to public education since it's only recently that the public has taken an interest in the AVMA's official positions on issues such as this and, consequently, the AVMA Animal Welfare Committee believes it is prudent to now include information in the position what formerly would have been assumed to be understood.

AVMA Position Statement on Declawing Prior to March 2003:

Declawing of domestic cats is justifiable when the cat cannot be trained to refrain from using its claws destructively.

AVMA Position Statement as of March 2003:

Declawing of domestic cats should be considered only after attempts have been made to prevent the cat from using its claws destructively or when its clawing presents a zoonotic risk for its owner(s).

The AVMA believes it is the obligation of veterinarians to provide cat owners with complete education with regard to feline onychectomy. The following points are the foundation for full understanding and disclosure regarding declawing:

Scratching is a normal feline behavior, is a means for cats to mark their territory both visually and with scent, and is used for claw conditioning ("husk" removal) and stretching activity.

Owners must provide suitable implements for normal scratching behavior. Examples are scratching posts, cardboard boxes, lumber or logs, and carpet or fabric remnants affixed to stationary objects. Implements should be tall or long enough to allow full stretching, and be firmly anchored to provide necessary resistance to scratching. Cats should be positively reinforced in the use of these implements.

Appropriate claw care (consisting of trimming the claws every one to two weeks) should be provided to prevent injury or damage to household items.

Surgical declawing is not a medically necessary procedure for the cat in most cases. While rare in occurrence, there are inherent risks and complications with any surgical procedure including, but not limited to, anesthetic compli-cations, hemorrhage, infection, and pain. If onychectomy is performed, appropriate use of safe and effective anesthetic agents and the use of safe peri-operative analgesics for an appropriate length of time are imperative. The surgical alternative of tendonectomy is not recommended.

Declawed cats should be housed indoors.

Scientific data do indicate that cats that have destructive clawing behavior are more likely to be euthanatized, or more readily relinquished, released, or abandoned, thereby contributing to the homeless cat population. Where scratching behavior is an issue as to whether or not a particular cat can remain as an acceptable household pet in a particular home, surgical onychectomy may be considered.

There is no scientific evidence that declawing leads to behavioral abnormalities when the behavior of declawed cats is compared with that of cats in control groups.

The American Association of Feline Practitioners

The American Association of Feline Practitioners Position Statement on Declawing was passed in September 2002. It maintains that:

Surgical declawing is not a medically necessary procedure for the cat in most cases.

While rare in occurrence, there are inherent risks with any surgical procedure including, but not limited to:

- anesthetic complications
- hemorrhage
- infection
- pain
- side effects of pain medication

The Cat Fanciers' Association (CFA)

The Cat Fanciers' Association (CFA) recently revised its official show rule regarding declawing. Before 1959, the rules required the cat to have all "physical properties" and identified these—"e.g., eyes, ears, legs, tail, etc." Section 10 was changed in 1959 to say, "Cats not having all their physical properties, e.g. eyes, ears, legs, tail, claws, etc., or having any congenital or acquired defects, may not receive any awards." This rule has been in effect ever since. The current show rules (May 1, 2004, to April 30, 2005) cover the claws in section 2.09 (Eligibility for Entry): "A cat or kitten not having all its physical properties—eyes, ears, legs, tail, claws, both descended testicles (adult cat only)—or has had surgery which changes a cat's natural functions (e.g., tendonectomy), is not eligible for entry." And show rule 28.18d says: "A judge will disqualify any entry entered contrary to these rules, including declawed cats or kittens and adult, whole males that do not have two descended testicles...."

The American Animal Hospital Association (AAHA)

The American Animal Hospital Association (AAHA) counts more than 32,000 veterinarians as members. AAHA's newest standards, published in Spring 2003, break ground in six areas of companion animal practice: client services, continuing education, pain management, patient care and compliance, practice leadership, and surgery. The practice leadership area asked, "Is there a moral framework, an ethical definition, for daily practice?" The task force recommended that a practice use written guidelines to outline ethical philosophy regarding commonly encountered ethical issues such as healthy pet euthanasia, cosmetic surgery, devocalization, declawing, client communications regarding errors made within the practice or another practice, and limitation of care for financial reasons.

Literature Cited

American Pet Products Manufacturers Association (APPMA). 1996, 1999–2000, 2001–2002, 2003–2004. National pet owners surveys. Greenwich, Conn.: APPMA.

American Veterinary Medical Association (AVMA). 2002. *U.S. pet ownership and demographics sourcebook*. Schaumburg, Ill.: Center for Information Management.

Ames, F. 1968. *The cat you care for*. New York: The New American Library.

Armstrong, M., S. Tomasello, and C. Hunter. 2001. From pets to companion animals. In *The State of the animals: 200l*, ed. D.J. Salem and A.N. Rowan, 71–85. Washington, D.C.: Humane Society Press.

Beaver, B. 1992. *Feline behavior: A guide for veterinarians*. Philadelphia: W.B. Saunders Co.

Bryant, D. 1969. *Doris Bryant's new cat book*. New York: Ives Washburn Inc.

Carr, W. 1963. *The basic book of the cat*. New York: Charles Scribner's Sons.

Christensen, W., and the Staff of The Humane Society of the United States. 2002. *The Humane Society of the United States complete guide to cat care*. New York: St. Martin's Press.

Davis, L. 1993. Declawing: Delight or despair? The pros, cons, and alternatives. *Cats*: 28–32.

Dasch, D. 1984. Keep your cat indoors! *HSUS News*, Summer, 12–15.

Deutsch, H.J., and J.J. McCoy. 1961. *How to care for your cat*. New York: Cornerstone Library.

Donald, R.L. 1992. All cats should be indoor cats. *Shelter Sense*, August, 1–5.

Edney, A. 1992. *The ASPCA complete cat care manual*. New York: DK Publishing.

Estep, D., and S. Hetts. 1994. Why cats scratch. *Cat Fancy*, March, 26–29.

Fox, M. 1974. *Understanding your cat*. New York: St. Martin's Press.

———. 1987. The responsibilities of cat keeping. *HSUS News*, Winter, 7–9.

Grier, K. In press. *Pets in America: A history*. Chapel Hill: University of North Carolina Press.

Harman, I. 1948. *Cats for pets and show*. London: Williams and Norgate Ltd.

Hetts, S. 1999. *Pet behavior protocols*. Lakewood, Colo.: AAHA Press.

Horwitz, D. 2002. Aggressive behaviors in cats. *All Animals*, Fall, n.p.

———. 2003. The ins and outs of scratching cats. *All Animals*, Fall, n.p.

———. 2004. Handling your scaredy cat. *All Animals*, Winter, n.p.

Houpt, K.A. 1991. Animal behavior and animal welfare. *Journal of the American Veterinary Medical Association* 198(8): 1355–1360.

———. 1996. Breaking the human-companion animal bond. *Journal of the American Veterinary Medical Association* 208(10): 1653–1659.

Humane Society of the United States, The (HSUS). 1994. Every year people who love their cats dearly, kill them. Reproducible. March.

———. 1995. *Close-Up Report: Get the facts on cats*. May. Washington, D.C.: The HSUS.

———. 2003. *A safe cat is a happy cat*. Washington, D.C.: The HSUS.

———. 2000. Pets for life: The HSUS launches an ambitious new campaign to keep pets and their people together. *All Animals*, Spring, 1.

Jacobs, Jenner, and Kent. 2001. HSUS veterinarian study. June.

Janik, C., and Rejnis, R. 1996. *The complete idiot's guide to living with a cat*. New York: Alpha Books.

Jankowski, A., D. Brown, J. Duval, T. Gregor, L. Strine, L. Ksiazekand, and A. Ott. 1998. Comparison of effects of elective tenectomy or onychectomy in cats. *Journal of the American Veterinary Medical Association* 213(3): 370–373.

Jones, S. 2003. *Valuing animals*. Baltimore: Johns Hopkins University Press.

Kass, P., J. New, J. Scarlett, and M. Salman. 2001. Understanding companion animal surplus. *Journal of Applied Animal Welfare Science* 4(4): 246.

Lachman, L., and F. Mickadeit. 2000. *Cats on the counter*. New York: St. Martin's Press.

Landsberg, G. 1991a. Behavior problems in pets: A growing veterinary concern. *Veterinary Medicine*, Oct.: 988.

———. 1991b. Cat owners' attitudes toward declawing. *Anthrozoös* 4(3): 192–197.

Lawson, N. 2004. The declaw dilemma. *Animal Sheltering*, May/June, 15–23.

Lewis, L. 1984. Action research report on the cat's scratching habits. *Cat Fancy*, March, 18–21.

Line, S. 1998. Factors associated with surrender of animals to an urban humane society. *Proceedings of the American Veterinary Medical Association Annual Conference*, 345–348.

Lockwood, R. Unpublished. Omnibus survey. Washington, D.C.: The Humane Society of the United States.

Loewenthal, G. 2002. Why cats need claws. *The Whole Cat Journal*, Sept., 16–20.

Miller, D., S. Staats, C. Partlo, and K. Rada. 1996. Factors associated with the decision to surrender a pet to an animal shelter. *Journal of the American Veterinary Medical Association* 209(4): 738–742.

Nagle, A. 1976. A technique for feline onychectomy. *Veterinary Medicine and Small Animal Clinician* 71(12): 1685–1687.

Overall, K. 1997. *Clinical behavioral*

medicine for small animals. St. Louis: Mosby and Year Book, Inc.

Patronek, G. 2001. Assessment of claims of short- and long-term complications associated with onychectomy in cats. *Journal of the American Veterinary Medical Association* 219(7): 932–937.

Patronek, G., and N. Dodman. 1999. Attitudes, procedures, and delivery of behavior services by veterinarians in small animal practice. *Journal of the American Veterinary Medical Association* 215(11): 1606–1611.

Patronek, G., L. Glickman, A. Beck, G. McCabe, and C. Ecker. 1996. Risk factors for relinquishment of cats to an animal shelter. *Journal of the American Veterinary Medical Association* 209(11): 582–588.

Peterson, N. 2002. Adding behavior services to your practice. *Veterinary Technician* June: 356–359.

Petsmart Charities. 2003. Report on Adoption Forum II. Phoenix, Ariz. January 16–17.

Phillips, B., and D. Phillips. 1994. In awe of the paw. *Cat Fancy*, March, 32–39.

Pollari, F., and B. Bonnett. 1996. Evaluation of postoperative complications following elective surgeries of dogs and cats at private practices using computer records. *Canadian Veterinary Journal* 37: 672–678.

Ralston Purina. 2000. The state of the American pet: A study among pet owners.

Richards, J. 1999. *The ASPCA complete guide to cats*. San Francisco: Chronicle Books.

Salman, M., J. New, J. Scarlett, P. Kass, R. Ruch-Gallie, and S. Hetts. 1998. Human and animal factors related to the relinquishment of dogs and cats in 12 selected animal shelters in the United States. *Journal of Applied Animal Welfare Science* 1(3): 207–226.

Salman, M., J. Hutchison, R. Ruch-Gallie, L. Kogan, J.C. New, Jr., P. Kass, and J. Scarlett. 2000. Behavioral reasons for relinquishment of dogs and cats to 12 shelters. *Journal of Applied Animal Welfare Science* 3(2): 93–106.

Schrody, M. 1957. *Cats*. New York: Galahad Books.

Schulberg, H. 1961. *The care of your cat*. New York: Royal Books.

Shelter Sense. 1994. Shelter Shop. Special offer can help cats keep their claws. *Shelter Sense*, Sept., 14.

Simmons, E.B. 1935. *The care and feeding of cats*. New York: Blue Ribbon Books.

Thornton, K. 2004. *Your new cat*. Sterling, Va.: Capital Books, Inc.

Turner, D., and P. Bateson, eds. 1998. *Declawing the domestic cat*. Cambridge: Cambridge University Press.

Whitney, L.F. 1953. *The complete book of cat care*. Garden City, N.Y.: Doubleday and Company, Inc.

Yeon, S.C., J.A. Flanders, J.M. Scarlett, S. Ayers, and K.A. Houpt. 2001. Attitudes of owners regarding tendonectomy and onychectomy in cats. *Journal of the American Veterinary Medical Association* 218(1): 43–47.

Feral Cats: An Overview

CHAPTER

Margaret R. Slater and Stephanie Shain

Humans and cats have a long and complex history together. Since the nineteenth century, contradictory ideas about the need to protect and care for cats have moved us toward a shift in ideas, values, and behaviors to a more benign perception of cats than was generally the case in previous centuries. In some quarters, but not all, even feral cats have begun to be seen as worthy of our study and humane treatment. In many countries, the welfare of all cats has become a focus of public concern, but nowhere is the shift in values reflected more than in the focus on feral cats—defined as unowned and unsocialized cats. Feral cats likely exist everywhere humans have traveled, whether deliberately introduced to control rodents and other pests, when they accidentally escape the home, or when they have been deliberately abandoned.

Feral Cats in the United States

Scientists in biology, ecology, and wildlife conservation have been publishing work on free-roaming and feral cats since the early 1900s. These early studies in the United States examined free-roaming cat control and licensing, predation on birds and wildlife, and cat territories. Hundreds of scientific articles have been published about the domestic cat's hunting patterns and lifestyles as well as control methods in dozens of countries around the world. Feral cats began to move into the public view in the United States about two decades ago, when the first popular book *Maverick Cats* (Berkeley 1982) was published in hardcover by Walker and Co. (it appeared in paperback from the New England Press in 1987). Cats have exceeded dogs as the most common pet in North America and in most of Europe (Slater 2005). Controlling the "cycle of stray cats" is even a topic of discussion in a popular pet supply catalog *(www.drsfostersmith.com)*. Yet feral cats are still viewed in many quarters as liminal beings existing on the borders of civilization. The existence of these feral cat populations tends to reinforce cats' peripheral status, reminding us of their wildness and separateness. This wildness and separateness makes it easier to see feral, and perhaps all, cats as belonging to the part of nature that humans are responsible for controlling and dominating rather than the part with which humans coexist. If cats are viewed as belonging to nature rather than to civilization, it becomes easier to see them as health threats or nuisances rather than as individuals and companions and to recommend their elimination when they present a "problem" to human society. When problems with feral cats arise, the image of the delightful domestic companion of the hearthside is easily replaced with old stereotypes of cats as evil beings separate from humans and with no place in the civilized world. (This transition from "wild and separate" to part of a unified world is occurring slowly, if the growing use of the term, "nonhuman animal," which deemphasizes the dichotomy between animals and humans, is any indication.)

Perhaps the most remarkable change in the status of feral cats is the fact that they are discussed as a particular population at all. Annabell Washburn of Martha's Vineyard, Massachusetts, is generally credited with bringing the concept of Trap-Neuter-Return (TNR) to feral cat management in the United States in 1980 (Berkeley 1990). Washburn founded the Pet Adoption and Welfare Service (PAWS) on Martha's Vineyard, which practiced TNR on feral cats. In 1986 students and staff from Tufts University's School of Veterinary Medicine worked with PAWS to provide sterilization of feral cats on Virgin Gorda in the British Virgin Islands in one of the earliest partnerships between veterinary medicine and grass-roots organizations to improve the lot of feral cats. In 1987 Washburn spoke about her experiences and elaborated on TNR as a method of controlling feral cats at a pet overpopulation conference in New York City.

The founding of Alley Cat Allies, an organization dedicated to promoting TNR as a nonlethal population control method for feral cats, in 1990 in Washington, D.C., marked the beginning of legitimacy for feral cats and of TNR as a control technique in the United States. Alley Cat Allies provided information, networking, and other resources for individuals and organizations interested in managing feral cat populations. In 2004 its resource pages on the Web (at *www.alleycat.org*) included information for feral cat caregivers, veterinarians, animal care and control and humane society personnel, and government officials. It also provided information on creating new groups, organizing, and advocating on behalf of feral cats. From an initial two-person team, Alley Cat Allies had grown to almost 95,000 donors and supporters as of 2003 (B. Robinson, personal communication with M.S., October 23, 2003).

Several other grass-roots organizations were early pioneers in the TNR movement. The first was the Stanford Cat Network, founded in 1989 (Rosenblatt 1992). This was probably the earliest formal campus program in the United States to manage cats using TNR with adoption of socialized cats and young kittens. Within fifteen years, the approximately five hundred cats present initially on the Stanford University campus in Califor-

nia at the start of the program had been reduced to eighty-five (C. Miller, Stanford Cat Network, personal communication with S.S., August 17, 2004) In recent years most of the cats who joined the feral-cat colony were social, friendly cats and were therefore adopted.

In the past several years, many other campus programs have sprung up around the country. An Internet listserv designed specifically to facilitate communication among these types of programs is hosted by Alley Cat Allies.

In 1989 the San Francisco Society for the Prevention of Cruelty to Animals (SFSPCA) began a major effort to reduce euthanasia in that city. It put in place a full spectrum of programs to that effect, including subsidized or free sterilization of pets, adoption, advice on maintaining pets in the home, and, in 1993, the Feral Cat Assistance Program. This program provides free sterilization, routine medical care, education for feral cat caretakers, assistance in resolving disputes, the loan of traps and free food, and the expertise of Cat Assistance Team members. Within a seven-year period, euthanasia of feral cats dropped by 73 percent, euthanasia of neonatal kittens dropped from more than nine hundred a year to two hundred a year, and more than 47,000 cats were sterilized (Sayres 2000).

Another model grass-roots organizations use in working with feral cats is the high-volume feral cat sterilization program originally developed in 1992 in San Diego by the Feral Cat Coalition (Berkeley 2004). This program was designed to sterilize fifty to two hundred cats in a single day and used a large core of volunteers, including local veterinarians. Since then many similar programs have arisen throughout the country. They have provided manuals and videotapes on how to orchestrate this high-volume approach to sterilization smoothly. Operation Catnip in

North Carolina (founded in 1994) and Florida (founded in 1998) are other good examples of this approach; they also have served as resources for research on feral cat health. A variation on high-volume spay neuter is the mobile clinic approach. A good example is a unit purchased by the Feral Cat Coalition of Oregon (FCCO) in 1998 (Berkeley 2004). In August 2004 the FCCO neutered its twenty thousandth cat (K. Kraus, personal communication with M.S., August 9, 2004).

A more comprehensive approach is a grass-roots program for cats in the community that began as a TNR-only effort. Merrimack River Feline Rescue Society, in Newburyport, Massachusetts, was founded in the early 1990s to manage feral cats on the waterfront in this tourist town. It soon discovered that many of the cats were socialized pets who had been lost or abandoned. This led to the development of a cats-only animal shelter, an extensive education program, and many other cat-related community activities. It has been extremely successful in decreasing the numbers of feral cats in Newburyport because of the broad range of approaches and the widespread geographic application of its work. In ten years, the original two hundred or so cats in the town had decreased to twenty, many of whom were elderly, and, in a few places, there were no feral cats at all (S. LeBaron, personal communication with M.S., July 2, 2002). Neighborhood Cats, founded in 1999, practices TNR in New York City, which few thought was suitable for TNR until this organization demonstrated otherwise (*www.neighborhoodcats.org/about/about_history.htm*). It also is an active advocacy group that networks with other agencies and promotes TNR throughout the area.

Most public or official discussion of feral cats in the field of animal protection in the United States seems to have begun around 1990. The National Animal Control Association began addressing feral-cat issues at its conferences in the early 1990s. Other animal protection agencies, local and national, began considering feral cats seriously in the mid-1990s. Perhaps the most significant turning point was a joint conference, "A Critical Evaluation of Free-roaming/Unowned/Feral Cats in the United States," sponsored by the American Humane Association and the Cat Fanciers' Association in 1996. The convoluted title accurately reflected the confusion about and complexity of the free-roaming cat world. In 1998 The Humane Society of the United States (HSUS) devoted an entire issue (September–October) of its magazine *Animal Sheltering* to free-roaming cats. It laid out a radically new policy statement on free-roaming cats, including a section on managing colonies of feral cats. This section outlined guidelines under which such management might be appropriate and codified the need for ongoing management and care of a colony of cats. Presentations about feral cats and how best to deal with them became a regular part of regional and national humane organization meetings by late in the decade.

In veterinary medical continuing education, feral cats began to appear as a topic in the early and mid-1990s. In 1992 Tufts University's School of Veterinary Medicine sponsored a feral-cat workshop where TNR as a method for control was presented. The American Veterinary Medical Association (AVMA) Animal Welfare Forum in 1995 focused on the welfare of cats and included discussions about feral cats and their management. In 2002 the AVMA annual meeting included a full day on feral cat issues. In 2003 the AVMA Animal Welfare Forum focused solely on feral cat issues and control methods. During 2003 and 2004, the AVMA (*http://www.avma.org/*

policies/animalwelfare.asp#companion) and the American Association of Feline Practitioners (AAFP) worked to update and create, respectively, position statements on free-roaming and feral cats. The balanced AAFP position statement released in mid-2004 provided a brief discussion of the problems associated with free-roaming cats as well as the need to prevent and control free-roaming cats by education, veterinary practice, public policy, and the application of TNR (*www.aafponline.org/positiostate.htm*). A model program was described for TNR recognizing that reducing cat populations was the primary objective.

Only recently has control of cat numbers become the focus of wildlife biologists and conservationists in the United States. In 2003 the Florida Fish and Wildlife Conservation Commission proposed a policy to "protect native wildlife from predation, disease, and other impacts presented by feral and free ranging cats." After much publicity, debate, and a lawsuit, the final policy was modified substantially, and study groups were established to look into the problem. Later that same year, the Pennsylvania Game Commission proposed an amendment to the state game and wildlife code to "make the release of captive held wildlife without a permit or domestic dogs or cats into the wild unlawful." This amendment was removed after public debate with the support of several members of the panel who felt that domestic dogs and cats were outside the scope of their mandate.

Feral Cats in the United Kingdom

Although concern for the control and welfare of feral cats is a very recent phenomenon in the United States, animal welfare organizations in the United Kingdom were

discussing, studying, and publishing scientific work about feral cats as early as the 1960s, '70s and '80s (Universities Federation for Animal Welfare 1981; Neville and Remfry 1984; Berkeley 2004). The first scientific conference on "the ecology and control of feral cats" was held in London in 1980 and its proceedings published by the Universities Federation for Animal Welfare (UFAW). Subsequent UFAW publications in 1982, 1990, and 1995 were the primary scientific references for feral-cat control for many years. Tabor's book (1983) was both scientific and appropriate for the cat-loving public. It included information on predation, cat territories, and feral-cat management, and it set the stage for much of what is known about free-roaming cats in urban areas based on the author's extensive observations on a colony of cats living in London. *Understanding Cats* (Tabor 1997) was a *Reader's Digest* coffee-table book clearly aimed at the general public. It included a chapter on feral cats as well as a discussion on feral-cat colony control that cited work done on TNR in Great Britain in the 1970s.

Feral Cat Populations: What Are the Sources?

Despite the multitude and variety of locations in which feral cats are found, the potential sources of the cats themselves are shared by all. Owned companion cats may become lost or may be abandoned deliberately by their owners. Such animals will become the nucleus of new feral cat colonies, particularly if the cats are intact. Intact cats still in the home may also contribute to the problem, since their unplanned litters may be too wild to be adopted or may be abandoned as well. The relative proportion of each of the sources varies widely among different locations. Relatively little research has been done to document the origins of feral cats in most locations. It is known that stray cats who become pets (the reverse of the owned-cat-becoming-feral phenomenon) account for 21 percent to 33 percent of the owned cat population (Johnson, Lewellen, and Lewellen 1993; Johnson and Lewellen 1995; Patronek, Beck, and Glickman 1997; New et al. 2000).

Feral Cat Issues in the Community

Conflict and confusion surrounding feral cats generally spring from five sources. The first is the variability in human perception about cats in general and feral cats in particular. The public views cats in a wide variety of roles, ranging from surrogate child to vermin. For example, some people find cat footprints on their cars amusing, while others believe cats who leave footprints on their cars should be euthanized. Such a disparity in perception leads to conflict about appropriate ways to treat cats, even among neighbors.

Public health and safety concerns often arise in discussions about feral cats. It is important to remember that these concerns are equally applicable to owned cats in the community who are allowed outdoors.

Public health officials have as their mandate the prevention of the *possibility* of disease in the general human population; therefore, they are interested in zoonotic diseases (Patronek 1998; Slater 2002). The actual magnitude of the risk to the public varies tremendously by disease and specific situation.

Rabies may be the foremost concern among such transmittable diseases. Current recommendations for controlling rabies include understanding the relationships between the residents and animals

and developing culturally appropriate approaches (Beran and Frith 1988). Removal of free-roaming animals is no longer recommended by the World Health Organization (WHO), although it was at one time (WHO Expert Committee 1988, 1994; Meslin, Fishbein, and Matter 1994). Instead, vaccination programs are the cornerstone of prevention. Fortunately, a very effective vaccine for cats exists to protect against rabies. Research in the 1980s indicated that a single early rabies vaccination provides protection for more than three years to cats in a research setting (Soulebot et al. 1981). This supports the idea that rabies vaccines are very effective, and that even one vaccination is likely to be much better than no vaccination at all. TNR programs that include rabies vaccinations can potentially provide a herd immunity against this disease: once a high enough proportion of the population is immune, it is very difficult for the disease to gain entry and establish itself in that population. In addition, vaccinated cats form a barrier between wildlife and humans. If cats are simply rounded up and removed from an area, a few unvaccinated cats will always escape and remain in the colony. New cats, also likely to be unvaccinated, will move in. In a short time the population will have rebounded and none of the cats will be vaccinated. If TNR is practiced, cats are trapped, neutered, and vaccinated for rabies before being returned to the colony, creating a substantial barrier of vaccinated individuals against the disease. When humane caretakers are very diligent, all cats in the colony will have been vaccinated at least once and possibly more frequently.

Another concern, the effects of predation by feral cats on wildlife, may be coupled with concerns about feral cats' competition with native predators and disease transmission. The debate is a collision of three main viewpoints (Slater 2004).

One is philosophical, based on the relative value of cats and wildlife. This view maintains that cats are a domestic species and as such are humans' responsibility. It is, therefore, irresponsible to allow cats to roam freely outdoors and hunt native wildlife, a particular problem since cats often are not regulated in the wild by food supply in the same way other predators are. This argument is not based on numbers of animals killed, but rather on appropriate stewardship of the domestic species. It applies to owned cats allowed to roam, not just to feral cats.

A second view is that cats are an introduced, non-native species that should be removed or prevented from entering native habitats. This view is based on the idea that introduced species have a negative impact on native species and that native species should be valued over introduced ones. In fact, native predators are often killed to protect livestock, and native species are often managed to protect other native species (Cohen 1992). This view assumes that removal of introduced species results in a return to a normal, or pre-introduction, state of the ecosystem. In reality, ecosystems are very complex and are changed in many ways, in addition to the introduction of cats, as a result of human habitation (Terborgh 1992). Cats may integrate into ecosystems such that their predation of other non-native animals like rats and mice can be very beneficial in protecting native species from these predators and competitors (Courchamp, Langlais, and Sugihara 1999; Fitzgerald and Gibb 2001).

The third view is based on the numbers of birds and other wildlife killed by cats, owned as well as unowned ferals. There are many widely cited figures about the extent of cat predation on birds in the United States. Most are based on extrapolation from three to fifteen cats or on estimates made by wildlife biologists that have been taken out of context. Effectiveness of cat predation appears to vary quite a lot, with some cats catching no prey and others catching quite a bit. It is important to remember that cats are opportunistic hunters: they will eat and catch whatever is most readily available. This includes carrion, garbage, and cat food, as well as prey species. Overall, cats are rodent specialists. More than half their diet is composed of rodents, with other species and other sources of food making up a small percentage of the remainder (Fitzgerald and Turner 2000).

Holders of these viewpoints disagree about what to do with feral cats. In some cases, local ordinances about licensing, the numbers of pets allowed per residence, and cat leash laws have been put into place to try to control feral and owned free-roaming cats. Cat licensing is extremely controversial and is sometimes, according to some, used to punish or fine caretakers of feral cats (*www.sfspca.org/figs/pdf_feralcats/licenses.pdf*. The public often views cat licensing as a moneymaking scheme for the benefit of local government, although, in fact, revenues from licensing may support animal-care and -control programs in the community. Licensing efforts for cats are attempts to provide cats with protection similar to that enjoyed by dogs, including mandated holding periods in shelters, intervention by animal-control officers on a cat's behalf, and return to owners. Unfortunately, licensing often is not a constructive approach to controlling feral cat numbers (Slater 2002). Ordinances that require identification rather than licensing are usually more palatable to community residents, and ear tipping of feral cats can be considered a form of identification. A cat identification law in Hawaii took this approach as a way of providing a bigger carrot rather than a stick in trying to convince resi-

dents to put identification on their cats (*http://www.co.honolulu.hi.us/refs/roh/7.htm;* Slater 2002). Identified cats benefit from longer holding periods at the shelter and are much more likely to be returned to their owners.

Another option for communities is differential licensing, in which owners of neutered animals pay a reduced fee—or no fee at all—for licensing as compared to owners of intact animals. This can be made to work for managed feral cat colonies since colony cats are neutered. Some have proposed registration for the colonies themselves as an alternative, but this may be viewed as punitive or as putting cats at risk to be rounded up by animal control.

Defining by law the number of cats that can be owned by a resident or live in a single household (so-called limit laws) can be used against feral cat caretakers since they are usually considered owners of the cats. Many colonies exceed the usual three- to four-cat limit that is common with this type of ordinance. Therefore, caretakers may be in violation and fined. These laws generally are designed to prevent hoarding and to provide leverage or oversight of households that may end up with too many animals. However, they generally do not allow TNR to be practiced legally if the local enforcement agency chooses to include feral cats. Such problems can be avoided with exemptions for managed or managed and registered feral colonies.

Leash laws generally require that animals be kept under the direct control of a person or confined to the owner's property. Leash laws, like the previously described ordinances, are nearly always enforced on complaint: someone has to see free-roaming cats and call the authorities. They will trap cats, who then will be transported to a local shelter or veterinarian. There, feral cats often will be euthanized. Depending on neighbors' tolerance of free-roaming cats, in

some locations trapping may never become necessary because the neighbors never call the authorities. But, in other locations, battles over free-roaming cats can be quite vicious and unrelenting.

An exemption for managed colonies (which may be defined clearly in the ordinance) from any of these laws is a possible option. It allows the law to provide for enforcement where appropriate and gives individuals the option to manage feral colonies. Alternatively, a well-written nuisance law will allow enforcement on complaint if specific feral cats are causing particular problems in an area.

These kinds of punitive laws were designed to protect the people and the animals in the community. Yet, positive rewards for doing the right thing, once people understand what the right thing is, generally will result in a faster and more wholehearted acceptance of the appropriate behavior. There will always be a few people who will not comply even with laws that punish. But is important not to punish those people who are trying to take responsibility for cats no one else wants.

Options

Most individuals and organizations involved in the feral cat debate agree that the ultimate goal is fewer cats. However, the best and most practical method to achieve this is hotly contested and often obscured by fruitless discussions about the number of birds killed, the numbers of cats in a neighborhood, or the exact costs of a particular option. No single approach will work in every location. Each location has a distinct set of problems and available resources as well as a unique public perception. It is critical to remain focused on the idea that there should be fewer feral cats and that practical approaches must be considered. The options for feral cat control have included doing nothing; killing cats on location; or removing cats for euthanasia elsewhere. More recently, TNR with adoption has been advocated as an option (Slater 2004). Trapping and removal, followed by relocation or placement in sanctuaries, has been used as well on a more limited basis (Levy and Crawford 2004).

"Doing Nothing"

The options for feral cat control have historically included doing nothing—or, "letting nature take its course." While still fairly common, this is not a responsible or constructive choice.

Killing Cats on Site

Killing cats on location has been used most commonly on islands and in countries outside the United States, including Australia and New Zealand. Cats are commonly killed by poisoning, shooting, introduction of infectious diseases, hunting by dogs, and trapping (Bester et al. 2002). These are typically components of a complete eradication program in an area with few humans and few other species to worry about. These eradication programs often require years to accomplish and hundreds of hours of work and are only successful in closed populations where no new cats can arrive. Trapping and removal of cats for euthanasia has been used in many communities as a method of handling animal issues. At times, this was justified as a way of providing a humane death for an animal who could not otherwise enjoy a good quality of life. At other times, concerns about cat predation, nuisance problems, or public health were motivating factors. It is appealing to think that removing cats will result in a permanent decrease in the cat population; however, that is almost never the case. It is extremely difficult to remove every cat in a particular location, and most locations are not sufficiently

isolated to prevent migration of new cats into the ecological vacuum created by cat removal. If there is sufficient food and shelter, new cats will move in from nearby areas, and survivors of the removal program will continue to reproduce until the maximum carrying capacity is reached again (Tabor 1983). Local residents may sabotage attempts to remove cats for euthanasia. The result is that, even if half the cats are removed, six months or a year later, the numbers of cats will be increasing quickly, climbing to the same number present before removal.

Relocation

A number of feral cat programs have incorporated a relocation component as part of their efforts. Neutered, vaccinated cats are transported and held for two to four weeks (to acclimate) before being released at their new owners' selected rural properties or farms. This is a time-consuming process complicated by the need to locate suitable release sites, and there are relatively limited data on success of relocation.

Increasingly, wildlife advocates have suggested removal of feral cats with placement in long-term sanctuaries. On the surface, this seems appealing because cats are confined in a selected location where they may receive care for the rest of their lives. While a number of sanctuaries around the country accept feral cats, they fill up rapidly and the quality of care can vary greatly (Levy and Crawford 2004). Overcrowding can be a serious health risk for cats, and feral cats do not always adapt well to confinement in a sanctuary. Unlike socialized cats, the very presence of humans causes feral cats stress. Thus, they need to be housed as essentially "wild" animals. In addition, oversight of this type of facility is highly variable and the quality of care provided is not always adequate or humane. Young cats may

face living ten or twelve years in a sanctuary, and the cost of high-quality care and housing for such animals is often prohibitive, eliminating the ability to expand sanctuary housing for the large numbers of feral cats in the United States.

TNR

The limitations of these options have made TNR increasingly viable as an option for decreasing the numbers of existing feral cats. This approach, at its most basic, includes humane trapping of feral cats, transportation to a veterinarian, surgical sterilization, vaccination for rabies, and ear-tipping or notching. Vaccination for rabies is included in the basic option because, in most parts of the United States, it is a crucial component of addressing public and animal health concerns. Ear tipping is included in the basic package since some form of visual identification of cats who have already been sterilized is critical in preventing re-trapping, re-anesthetizing, and re-operating on already neutered cats.

A variation, explicitly includes testing, managing, and monitoring as part of the TNR program (trap, test, vaccinate, alter, return, manage, and monitor, or TTVARM-M).It is preferred by groups such as The HSUS. The "test" component includes testing for feline leukemia (FeLV) and feline immunodeficiency viruses (FIV). "Managing and monitoring" includes ongoing feeding, housing, and oversight of cats in managed colonies. Ongoing monitoring provides the most effective population control because new, probably unneutered cats, will be identified quickly and trapped before they can reproduce. The cats are looked after so that any illness or injuries can be handled in humane fashion. Very commonly, the shorthand TNR is used to describe these very extensive programs as well as simpler ones.

The advantages of TNR are its ability to (1) stabilize the population through sterilization; (2) increase the proportion of vaccinated cats in a community; (3) decrease nuisance problems, since sterilized cats roam less, fight less, make less noise, and are generally less obtrusive; (4) decrease cat welfare concerns because the cats tend to be healthier when they are not breeding and fighting and no kittens are born; and (5) garner stronger public support than do programs that result in killing cats (Slater 2002; Levy and Crawford 2004).

TNR programs that include aggressive adoption components are the most successful in decreasing the numbers of cats short term. The numbers of young kittens and socialized adults varies but can be upwards of 50–70 percent in some colonies (Levy and Crawford 2004). Removing these animals for adoption results in an immediate and substantial decrease in the numbers of cats at that site.[1]

The Controversy over Testing

Testing for FeLV and FIV is controversial. On the one hand, there is concern about leaving "positive" cats in the environment, because their own health and well-being may be in jeopardy, and they have the potential to transmit disease. When funds are limited, there are cost-benefit considerations since testing costs close to what spay or neuter surgery costs. Testing decreases the number of cats that can be sterilized for the same money. On the other hand, sterilization decreases transmission of these diseases between cats.

The frequency of these and other infectious diseases in feral cat populations is similar to or lower than that of owned-cat populations (Levy and Crawford 2004; Nutter et al. 2004a). Because the frequency of these diseases is so low and the diseases are not spread uniformly throughout the feral cat population, testing a few cats or a

small randomly selected number of cats is unlikely to provide accurate information about the general cat population in the community. Limited testing may prove helpful in specific colonies where there is a high suspicion of disease, particularly of feline leukemia. Animals who test positive for FeLV present another set of problems: for some, euthanasia of positive animals is not acceptable unless the cat is very ill; for others who know that FeLV generally causes a slow death within a few years, euthanasia is a humane option.

FIV is spread through the bite of an infected cat. This disease is much more common in male cats than in females because intact males do most of the fighting. Neutering males decreases their aggression and fighting for mates and disease transmission is nearly eliminated. Many FIV-positive cats will live for many years without any clinical problems, and it is less clear that euthanasia will prevent obvious suffering in the near future.

FeLV is spread from mother to kittens and by prolonged close contact between cats. By spaying the mother cats, disease transmission to kittens is eliminated. FeLV is not a highly contagious disease, and many cats who are exposed will never contract it. By putting the money saved by not testing into spaying more female cats, organizations may prevent many more cases of FeLV.

Ultimately the caregivers and veterinarians involved will have to make a decision about testing and about what to do with positive cats. Some cats who are positive for either of these diseases may be removed for placement into sanctuaries or homes with other disease-positive cats.

There are many different approaches to promoting or offering TNR in a community. Often, it will start with one or two individuals who are feeding cats and realize that they can't continue to feed all

of the cats in the colony if the current population continues to multiply. The feeders discover TNR, often through friends, neighbors, or the internet. Sometimes these individuals will form networks with others who are feeding cats in the same community. This loose network may continue as is or may become an incorporated, nonprofit organization. In other situations, once it realizes there is a problem with feral cats, a group of people may immediately pull together an organization dedicated to helping those animals. Animal-care and -control agencies, humane societies, or veterinary wellness/sterilization clinics also may begin to offer services or programs specifically related to feral cats. These can include trap rental, subsidized or free sterilization and vaccination, provision of education or meeting areas, referral networks, and assistance with adoptions. Sometimes these organizations will partner with existing grass-roots TNR programs. While it may take months (or years) to build the level of trust needed among the parties, these alliances can be extremely productive. Optimally, all interested parties will map out a strategy to work together to decrease the feral cat population and prevent new stray/abandoned cats. The Orange County, Florida, animal-control agency, for example, partnered with a TNR group for an extremely successful program (Hughes, Slater, and Haller 2002).

There is no one best template for introducing TNR in a community. Instead, existing veterinary and sheltering resources should be evaluated and any missing pieces put into place. For example, in a community that already has subsidized or free sterilization for feral cats, a feral cat group might focus on trapping, adoption, and education. In a community without subsidized or free sterilization, a high-volume, feral-cat-only monthly surgery session might be the best use of an organization's resources, since sterilization is a key element in TNR.

In discussing what to do with existing feral cats, communities often do not address the sources of these cats adequately. Generally, irresponsible or ignorant owners are the core problem. Often, there are many different reasons why people choose to allow their cats to roam freely without identification or sterilization or abandon cats altogether. More research needs to be performed to better understand how to identify the problems in each community and how best to intervene. A "safety net" of services for cats and owners could include (1) information on maintaining cats in the home, such as selection of an appropriate kitten or advice on behavior modification; (2) subsidized veterinary care and mechanisms to improve access to care, such as transportation or language translation services; (3) cat identification and sterilization information as well as information on keeping cats safely at home disseminated by local veterinarians, through public schools and community education, and by the animal shelter; (4) programs that assist people in finding new homes for cats they genuinely cannot keep; and (5) better dissemination of information about cats available for adoption at the local shelter. Some central location or referral system to help residents find these existing resources is crucial as well. Local laws or ordinances can have a role in encouraging compliance but should be primarily a mechanism to deal with individuals who do not wish to comply rather than with those who are unable to comply. "Fix-it" tickets can give enforcement officers a means of accomplishing the ultimate goal of the ordinance, for example, having a cat sterilized rather than receiving a fine.

Each community has an existing set of resources that should be evaluated critically so that the missing components of the safety net can be developed and added. All of the diverse constituents who are involved in dealing with cat-related problems should be brought to the table and be involved in creating the solutions.

Guiding Principles

While the specifics on approaches to dealing with feral cat issues in a community will vary, some core principles should be followed in all cases to ensure success.

1. All reputable parties involved with feral cats have as a goal fewer feral cats. The problem is how best to accomplish that goal and to get past other arguments and issues.
2. Each location has a specific set of problems and available resources. While data from other locations can certainly be helpful in guiding decisions, each solution must be tailored to the individual location.
3. Controlling feral cat numbers is really a "herd"-level problem. While each individual cat may (or may not) be seen as having value, it is the population as a whole in a neighborhood, community, or county that must be addressed. Therefore, solutions must work for populations of cats and must be able to be scaled up for the numbers of cats in a given situation.
4. Everyone involved must be guided by concern for the welfare and well-being of the cats, as well as for other species, including humans, but also by what is practical and possible in a specific situation.
5. To reach the goal of fewer cats will require a broad spectrum of programs. No single approach will accomplish this goal. The more diverse the location, the more creative the set of programs must be to result in fewer feral cats.

Example Programs

A published study of feral cats managed on the University of Central Florida campus demonstrates the efficacy of TNR coupled with aggressive adoption in decreasing the numbers of free-roaming cats (Levy, Gale, and Gale 2003). During the eleven years reported in the article, a total of 155 cats were trapped. After five years, only 68 of the original cats remained. At the end of the study, only 23 cats (15 percent) were left, with a median residency duration of seven years. Nearly half the cats were initially or eventually adopted. Eleven percent were euthanized, 15 percent disappeared, 6 percent died, and 6 percent moved to nearby woods. This demonstrates that it is possible to decrease their numbers with time and ongoing monitoring and that adoption is important to ensure this decrease.

Another campus program, at Texas A&M University, had existed for six years as of 2004. The initial two-year startup was published to demonstrate the initial drop in feral cat numbers (Hughes and Slater 2002). In the first six years, 264 cats were trapped, with about half returning to campus and a third being adopted. Cats positive for FeLV (5 percent) or FIV (6 percent) were euthanized. Well over half the cats were trapped and neutered in the first two years of program.

Several animal-control agencies around the country have embraced TNR. Maricopa County (Arizona) Animal Care and Control is the largest animal-control agency in the United States, based on 61,984 animals handled and more than three million people (Anonymous 2002). Its feral cat programs, Operation FELIX and a partnership with AzCats, which began in the fall of 2001, provide high-volume spay/neuter for feral cats as well as mobile spay/neuter programs. These programs are in addition to comprehensive spay/neuter and adoption efforts and have contributed to a drop in euthanasia rate from twenty-five cats per thousand county residents to nine cats per thousand. This agency actively promotes TNR in the community. Recently, county officials proclaimed that TNR was the official management policy for feral cats in Maricopa County. The city of Phoenix, Arizona, planned to allocate $200,000, and Animal Care and Control was to begin to charge $61 per feral cat brought in unless the community it came from actively sponsored a TNR program (Anonymous 2002).

Orange County Animal Care and Control partnered with a nonprofit feral cat organization to facilitate TNR in Orlando, Florida, and the surrounding area (Hughes, Slater, and Haller 2002). As of 1995 the animal-control shelter provided surgeries, rabies vaccination, and ear tipping, while the community feral-cat organization handled complaints and trapping. Despite a growing human population and an expected increase in pet population and related problems, after implementing the program, cat impounds and complaints remained stable, cat euthanasia decreased slightly, and the numbers of spay/neuter cat surgeries exceeded euthanasias for the first time. One six-block residential area had a greater than 50 percent decrease in complaints following implementation of TNR. An additional benefit was a significant improvement in the relationship between animal-control officers and the community and higher morale among the officers.

Creativity is imperative when trying to solve the feral cat problem. The World Society for the Protection of Animals (WSPA) as of 2005 had a program at the Sheraton Rio Hotel in Rio de Janiero, Brazil. Because many cats are attracted to the resort area and many visitors wish to feed them, the cats could have become a problem. The solution was to set up the Cat's Café, an area where cats can be fed and stroked but that is not near restaurants, bars, or swimming pools. Signs assure visitors that cats are vaccinated and provided with veterinary care (E. MacGregor, WSPA, personal communication with S.S., July 1, 2004). This solution provides a humane alternative to trapping and euthanasia while addressing sanitation and health concerns.

An example of an early program to manage feral cats in a prison setting took place in San Quentin State Prison in San Quentin, California, in 1992. Historically, 100 to 250 cats were being euthanized each year (K. White, The HSUS, personal communication with P. Miller, Marin Humane Society, March 13, 1994).

A TNR program was implemented, and approximately 250 cats were trapped. More than 200 were adopted, and approximately 50 neutered and vaccinated feral cats were returned to the prison over an eighteen-month period. Internal prison correspondence indicated benefits to the inmates and staff, such as less violence and tension as well as being able to "model relatedness" to other species and individuals (B. Smythe, R.N., prison employee, personal communication with Warden A. Calderon, n.d.).

What Has Been Achieved with TNR

Many resources are now available around the country to implement TNR programs. Many websites have written materials that can be downloaded and shared. Others have videotapes, links to other useful websites, and advice on starting new grass-roots groups. Many organizations are beginning to assemble comprehensive educational materials to make teaching and learning about TNR easier. For example, the Neighborhood Cats TNR kit provides all necessary educational materials needed to launch a TNR program in one easily accessible package (www.NeighborhoodCats.org). TNR organizations are learning to be cohesive and focused and to define their mission and scope of work clearly. This aids them in being as effective as possible and improves their visibility and respectability.

While the level of technical knowledge about conducting TNR programs has certainly increased over time, the philosophical implications of TNR programs have even wider-ranging effects. Feral cat management is clearly interrelated with all other animal-related efforts in a community. This means that, to be effective, TNR groups have to develop a working relationship with municipal animal-control agencies and other animal-related programs. Feral caregivers also need each other and can accomplish more as part of a whole group or network than they can individually. Citywide efforts can work if they are truly comprehensive and wide reaching, as they are in San Francisco, California, and Newburyport, Massachusetts.

Feral cat problems have a direct impact on the intake and disposition of cats in shelters around the country. Feral cats themselves may be brought into shelters, where they are often euthanized, sometimes after being held for several days. The offspring of feral cats may be brought to shelters as well. Some of these offspring may be adoptable, adding to the numbers of cats needing homes. However, some will be euthanized due to disease or lack of socialization or because they are too young to be adopted and no foster home is available. Adoptions of colony kittens can contribute to problems in the community if the new owners do not sterilize their pets. It is also clear that discussions surrounding TNR and its implementation help shape society's views of and reactions to unowned cats. The discussion opens the door to new ideas beyond euthanasia of cats or other animals to control their population or deal with homeless animals. We are beginning to ask not why we should care about feral cats but rather how we can make a difference.

The Future

There is an ever-increasing body of knowledge being produced and published about feral cats. Researchers' long-term, detailed, follow-up study of feral cat colonies using several different control methods conducted in North Carolina was published in the *Journal of the American Veterinary Medical Association* in 2004. Three articles report on disease frequency in pet and feral cats (Nutter et al. 2004); reproduction and survival of kittens in feral colonies (Nutter, Levine, and Stoskopf 2004a); and live trapping efficiency of feral cats (Nutter, Levine, and Stoskopf 2004b). A scientific chapter on feral cats, with emphasis on the international perspective, is included in *The Welfare of Cats* (Rochlitz 2005). An in-depth and carefully crafted research project in Auburn, Alabama, comparing feline activities and territories before and after TNR will be completed and published in the near future. And a project to study the population dynamics of free-roaming owned and feral cats as of 2004 had just begun in a community in Texas.

Impressive strides have been made in bringing the plight of feral cats to public view and into the scientific and animal protection arenas. TNR can now be considered as an alternative to doing nothing or to euthanasia for feral cats currently in communities. Yet communities must grapple with the chain of events that results in establishment of feral cat colonies, particularly the initiating event, the deliberate abandonment or accidental loss of companion cats. They must find ways to increase the value of

cats in the minds of the public, to change people's behaviors so that it is no longer acceptable to leave cats behind or allow them outside without identification or sterilization, and to provide the public with the knowledge and impetus to help cats who appear to be homeless. Finally, those in the animal-care field must provide communities with the knowledge and resources to help cat owners trying to do right by their own cats and by homeless or feral cats in their neighborhoods.

Note
[1]Kittens younger than about eight weeks are generally the easiest to socialize. Kittens older than this may or may not socialize well within a few days to weeks. Adult cats may need a few days' "cooling off" before they can be definitively assessed as feral. Many previously owned cats when trapped and transported may seem unsocialized, but with time they return to their former socialized status. Adult feral cats can be socialized on occasion, but the process requires great care and commitment since these cats are often terrified and/or aggressive and generally require months to years of effort before they become socialized, if ever. They may also only be friendly with one or two people they know well. Adult feral cats in managed colonies may become more social with time, sometimes to the point where they are adoptable. This is another means by which colony size may be decreased over time.

Literature Cited

Anonymous. 2002. *Alley Cat Action*, Spring, 1.

Beran, G.W., and M. Frith. 1988. Domestic animal rabies control: An overview. *Reviews of Infectious Diseases* 10: S672–S677.

Berkeley, E.P. 1990. Feral cats. *Cat Fancy*, July, 20–27.

———. 2004. *TNR past, present, and future.* Washington D.C.: Alley Cat Allies.

Bester, M.N., J.P. Bloomer, R.J. van Aarde, B.H. Erasmus, P.J.J. van Rensburg, J.D. Skinner, P.G. Howell, and T.W. Naude. 2002. A review of the successful eradication of feral cats from sub-Antarctic Marion Island, Southern Indian Ocean. *South African Journal of Wildlife Research* 32: 65–73.

Cohen, A. 1992. Weeding the garden. *The Atlantic Monthly,* November, 76–86.

Courchamp, F., M. Langlais, and G. Sugihara. 1999. Control of rabbits to protect island birds from cat predation. *Biological Conservation* 89:(2) 219–225.

Fitzgerald, B.M., and D.C. Turner. 2000. Hunting behaviour of domestic cats and their impact on prey populations. In *The Domestic cat: The biology of its behaviour,* ed. D.C. Turner and P. Bateson, 151–175. New York: Cambridge University Press.

Fitzgerald, B.M., and J.A. Gibb. 2001. Introduced mammals in a New Zealand forest: Long-term research in the Orongorongo Valley. *Biological Conservation* 99: 97–108.

Hughes, K.L., and M.R. Slater. 2002. Implementation of a feral cat management program on a university campus. *Journal of Applied Animal Welfare Science* 5: 15–27.

Hughes, K.L., M.R. Slater, and L. Haller. 2002. The effects of implementing a feral cat spay/neuter program in a Florida county animal control service. *Journal of Applied Animal Welfare Science* 5: 285–298.

Johnson, K., and L. Lewellen. 1995. *San Diego County: Survey and analysis of the pet population.* San Diego: San Diego Cat Fanciers, Inc.

Johnson, K., L. Lewellen, and J. Lewellen. 1993. *Santa Clara county's pet population.* San Jose, Calif.: National Pet Alliance.

Levy, J.K., and P.C. Crawford. 2004. Humane strategies for controlling feral cat populations. *Journal of the American Veterinary Medical Association* 225(9): 1354–60.

Levy, J.K., D.W. Gale, and L.A. Gale. 2003. Evaluation of the effect of a long-term trap-neuter-return and adoption program on a free-roaming cat population.

Journal of the American Veterinary Medical Association 222: 42–46.

Meslin, F.X., D.B. Fishbein, and H.C. Matter. 1994. Rationale and prospects for rabies elimination in developing countries. *Current Topics in Microbiology and Immunology* 187: 1–26.

Neville, P.F., and J. Remfry. 1984. Effect of neutering on two groups of feral cats. *The Veterinary Record* 114: 447–450.

New, J.C., Jr., M.D. Salman, M. King, J.M. Scarlett, P.H. Kass, and J.M. Hutchinson. 2000. Characteristics of shelter-relinquished animals and their owners compared with animals and their owners in the U.S. pet-owning households. *Journal of Applied Animal Welfare Science* 3: 179–201.

Nutter, F.B., J.P. Dubey, J.F. Levine, E.B. Breitschwredt, R.B. Ford, and M.K. Stoskopf. 2004. Seroprevalence of antibodies against *Bartonella henselae* and *Toxoplasma gondii* and fecal shedding of *Cryptosporidium* spp., *Giardia* spp., and *Toxocara* cati in feral and pet domestic cats. *Journal of the American Veterinary Medical Association* 225: 1394–1398.

Nutter, J.P., J.F. Levine, and M.K. Stoskopf. 2004a. Reproductive capacity of free-roaming domestic cats and kitten survival rate. *Journal of the American Veterinary Medical Association.* 225: 1399–1402.

————. 2004b. Time and financial costs of programs for live trapping feral cats. *Journal of the American Veterinary Medical Association* 225: 1403–1405.

Patronek, G.J. 1998. Free-roaming and feral cats—Their impact on wildlife and human beings. *Journal of the American Veterinary Medical Association* 212: 218–226.

Patronek, G.J., A.M. Beck, and L.T. Glickman. 1997. Dynamics of dog and cat populations in a community. *Journal of the American Veterinary Medical Association* 201: 637–642.

Rosenblatt, B. 1992. Cats on campus. *The Animal's Agenda*, April, 20–21.

Sayres, E. 2000. Expanding the safety net: Creating a humane feral cat program in your community. Handout. No-Kill Conference. Tucson, Ariz. September 14–17.

Slater, M.R. 2002. *Community approaches to feral cats: Problems, alternatives and recommendations.* Washington, D.C.: Humane Society Press.

————. 2004. Understanding issues and solutions for unowned, free-roaming cat populations. *Journal of the American Veterinary Medical Association* 225: 1350–1354.

————. 2005. The welfare of feral cats. In *The welfare of cats,* ed. I. Rochlitz, 141–176. Dordrecht, The Netherlands: Springer.

Soulebot, J.P., A. Brun, G. Chapuis, F. Guillemin, H.G. Petermann, P. Precausta, and J. Terre. 1981. Experimental rabies in cats: Immune response and persistence of immunity. *Cornell Veterinarian* 71: 311–325.

Tabor, R. 1983. *The wild life of the domestic cat.* London: Arrow Books Limited.

————. 1997. *Understanding cats: Their history, nature and behavior.* Pleasantville, N.Y.: Reader's Digest.

Terborgh, J. 1992. Why American songbirds are vanishing. *Scientific American* May: 98–104.

Universities Federation for Animal Welfare. 1981. Feral cats: Notes for veterinary surgeons. *Veterinary Record* 108: 301–303.

WHO Expert Committee. 1988. Report of WHO consultation on dog ecology studies related to rabies control. *World Health Organization* 88.25: 1–35.

————. 1994. *Report of the fifth consultation on oral immunization of dogs against rabies.* World Health Organization 94.45, 1–24.

Dogs and Dog Control in Developing Countries

5

CHAPTER

J.F. Reece

Introduction

Of all the mammals with which humans have a close relationship, the domestic dog *(Canis familiaris)* has the longest association with man. The bond is believed to have begun some ten to twelve thousand years B.C. in Eurasia (World Health Organization [WHO] 1990) as wolves learned to follow the encampments of man to secure easy food. A degree of mutual acceptance developed between the two species, with each gaining something from the association. Mankind gained protection from having the animals around its camps and, probably, some assistance in hunting activities. Dogs gained a degree of protection from the human groups and from a ready and constant source of food arising from human hunting and other human waste, including excrement. Individual animals were then selected by man for their biddable character, and the ancestors of the current dogs were born.

Few human societies today do not have a relationship with dogs. Man-dog relationships are almost as numerous as the varieties of human society (World Health Organization 1990). In many cultures in Africa, in Zimbabwe and Kenya, for example, dogs are val-ued for the protection they afford to both men and livestock from human intruders and wild animals (Butler and Bingham 2000). In some cultures in western Africa and in southeast Asia, dogs are valued as a source of protein in the human diet. In Polynesia the two enjoy a complex relationship, as dogs can be seen as food, gifts, and offerings. In many cultures dogs are associated with the forces of the supernatural, either divine or demonic. Some religions consider dogs to be unclean in a spiritual sense, for example, Islam (Beck 2000). However, in some predominantly Muslim countries, such as Tunisia in North Africa, dogs are seen in a positive light. In contrast, Hindu, Jain, and Buddhist cultures, such as in India and Nepal, teach a "no kill" philosophy (yet are among the societies where the greatest levels of destruction of unwanted dogs are prevalent) (WHO 1990). In some developing countries, pet dogs are kept far more for social status than for companionship. Throughout much of the developing world, dogs are essential to the management of domestic waste, especially in areas of higher human population density, such as big towns and cities.

Dogs' activities in these areas are widely thought to keep the populations of other less desirable creatures, such as rats, mice, and cockroaches, under control.

Even among very similar societies the relationship with dogs may vary. In a number of European cultures, there is no word that readily corresponds to the English word "pet." The relationship between urban Americans and their pet dogs is different—if not in type, then in magnitude—from that seen among most of the dog-owning public in the United Kingdom. Within the United Kingdom, the relationship between many country folk and their dogs is very different from that of urban-dwelling people and their dogs.

The relationship between a community and its dogs is not always entirely positive, and many cultures identify similar problems associated with having dogs in their midst. For example, in South Africa, the Soweto community identified the problems caused by dogs as road accidents, barking and fighting, biting children and killing livestock, and uncontrolled fecal contamination (Beck 2000). Such problems exist in many cultures, throughout the developed and developing worlds.

It is against this background of a wide range of man-dog relationships that dogs in the developing world must be seen and understood. Knowledge about and understanding of the complexity of the relationships between dogs and local people is essential to any attempts to regulate the human-dog relationship officially and to control any problems caused by dogs.

Given the wide range of relationships between societies and the dogs associated with them, it is not surprising that the structures of canine population vary considerably too. Various attempts to classify the canine population have been made. These classifications all use the degree of dependence on and supervision by man. Beck, based in the United States, has identified three types of dogs seen: pets who never roam without supervision; pets who stray or roam; and ownerless animals who are free to roam (Matter and Daniels 2000). WHO recommends a four-point classification system (1990):

Restricted dogs, who are fully restricted or supervised and fully dependent on man for food and other resources;

Family dogs, who are semirestricted (and thus roam for part of the time) and fully dependent on one or more families for food and shelter;

Neighborhood dogs, who are either semirestricted or entirely free to roam and who are only semidependent on one or more families for food and shelter;

Feral dogs, who live wholly unrestricted lives and do not depend at all for food deliberately given by any person or group.

As a survival strategy in developing countries, neighborhood dogs in urban areas often behave the same as well-socialized pet dogs and are thus often indistinguishable from owned-but-straying dogs (Matter and Daniels 2000). In many Western societies, the stray dog population comes almost entirely from abandoned pets and often bears a striking resemblance to identifiable breeds. However, in developing countries, most of the stray dog population, whether neighborhood dogs or feral dogs, is much more uniform in conformation and appearance (Matter and Daniels 2000).

The proportion of the dog population that is owned varies considerably throughout the world. In Chad a maximum of 10.6 percent of the total dog population is considered "ownerless," while in Sri Lanka the figure is over 19 percent (Kayali et al. 2003). In Hong Kong 75 percent of the stray dog population is considered to arise from abandoned pet dogs (Dahmer, Coman, and Robinson 2000). Between 5 and 15 percent of the dog population in Tunisia was considered "stray." In much of Africa, many owned dogs are never restricted and stray freely: 78 percent of owned dogs in Nigeria and 54 percent in Zambia (Beck 2000). In Nepal and Indonesia, up to 70 percent of the dog population is associated with more than one household (WHO 1988).

The population density of dogs varies considerably throughout the world, too, although the figures arrived at are often little more than guesses. The figures given for the dog-to-man ratio vary from 1:3.5 in rural Tunisia, to 1:4.5 in the communal lands of Zimbabwe, to 1:8 in Sri Lanka and 1:16 in urban Zimbabwe (WHO 1988; Butler and Bingham 2000). Among the factors that contribute to this large variation are the socioeconomic class of the community, land type and use, and the degree of urbanization. Generally, dog population density rises as the human population rises (Butler and Bingham 2000).

These few figures show that throughout much of the developing world, a large population of dogs roams freely throughout the human community and is able to breed in an uncontrolled manner. It is these animals who are largely responsible for the various nuisances identified with human-dog association mentioned earlier. In addition to problems associated with noise, ordure, and aggression, much of the developing world is afflicted by zoonotic diseases that these free-roaming dogs are, in part, responsible for spreading. Estimates vary between sixty and one hundred for the number of diseases that may be transferred from dogs to man; however, many of these are somewhat esoteric and rare or theoretical in nature.

Zoonotic Diseases Spread by Dogs

A few diseases stand out as the main zoonoses associated with dogs: rabies, echinococcosis, and toxocariasis.

Rabies

Rabies is a viral disease of all mammals, including man. It is often said that rabies is 100 percent fatal but 100 percent preventable by vaccination. This is slightly misleading, since the disease is only 100 percent fatal once patients become symptomatic (Briggs 2002). Rabies has been recognized as a disease for perhaps five thousand years, and the relationship between a rabid animal's bite and a new case has also been known for a very long time. The disease is untreatable but preventable by either pre-exposure prophylactic vaccination or, because of the long incubation period, by post-exposure vaccination with concomitant administration of passive immunity through rabies immunoglobulins. In developing countries dog bites are the cause of the vast majority of human rabies cases. In India over 90 percent of human cases were caused by exposure to a rabid dog (WHO 1988). Although only twelfth on WHO's list of causes of mortality, rabies has a special place in societies where it is endemic because of the well-known and ghastly symptoms that accompany the disease. Official estimates put the total number of rabies cases worldwide as twenty-five to thirty thousand human deaths *per annum* (Kayali et al. 2003). There is considerable evidence that these figures may be underestimates, with work from Tanzania suggesting that the underestimation may be by a factor of between ten and one hundred (Cleaveland et al. 2002). Of these human rabies deaths, the largest number occurs in south Asia, most notably in India, though, curiously, recent work in India suggests that the number of human cases in that country may have been overestimated. Because of the close affinity between children and young dogs, most of the human cases are in young people (Wright 1991; Sharma, Kumar, and Chawla 2002). WHO states that 45 percent of rabies cases occur in children under fifteen years of age. Most of these cases are males, probably due to the bolder, more adventurous play of boys and youths, and most of the cases from the developing world occur among the socially disadvantaged. This partly explains the underreporting of cases and the low priority attached to rabies in most developing countries.

Echinococcosis

This is a disease caused by intermediate forms of the canine cestode worms *Echinococcus granulosus* and *E. multilocularis*. Dogs are infected with these parasites by eating hydatid cysts found in the offal of many mammals, including common ruminants. The ingested forms attach to villi and develop in the dog's small intestine. On maturity the worms produce eggs, typically thirty-four to fifty-eight days following ingestion by the dog. Eggs are produced for at least eighty days and in enormous numbers. *Echinococcus* eggs are passed in the dog's feces and then dispersed over considerable distances in the environment, where they are ingested by intermediate hosts such as sheep, goats, and other animals. When people ingest *echinococcus* eggs they become at risk of developing echinococcosis, which is the development of hydatid cysts in humans, commonly in the liver or lungs but also, and more seriously, in the brain (Macpherson and Craig 2000). The free-roaming dog population is at greatest risk of becoming infected, and this is especially true in areas where poor slaughterhouse hygiene is normal. In many cultures in the developing world, across much of North Africa, the Levant (the region of the eastern end of the Mediterraneqn Sea), and into south Asia, dogs are the principle method of disposing of unwanted offal from many small-scale, often unofficial, slaughterhouses. Education of slaughterhouse workers is often very poor, since they typically come from the most downtrodden and oppressed sections of society, and thus the risks associated with poor work practices are not appreciated (Hammond and Sewell 1990). Home slaughter of stock for consumption is also a common factor, since community dogs are likely to be given the unwanted offal. Some tribal peoples, especially in Kenya and Sudan, are particularly at risk of echinococcosis because of cultural practices that encourage very close associations between dogs and food preparation practices. There is also no veterinary care available to these people or their animals, so worm burdens in dogs remain high. Women of these tribes are at increased risk, because they are mainly involved in food preparation and disposal. Infection rates in dogs can be very high, ranging from less than 1 percent of dogs infected in Pretoria, South Africa, to 50 percent and 60 percent in Kenya, Sudan, and Tanzania. Similar high infestation rates among dogs are seen in China. In Kathmandu, Nepal, 5.7 percent of free-roaming dogs near slaughterhouses were infected, as were a smaller percentage in the rest of the city. In Uruguay 13.2 percent of the dog population was infected, and the infection was attributed to poor slaughterhouse practice (Macpherson and Craig 2000).

Toxocariasis

This is a disease caused by exposure to an environment contaminated by canine feces. *Toxocara canis* is a common roundworm (nematode) of dogs (Overgraauw and van Knapen 2000). Adult worms live freely in the lumen of the guts of dogs, where they feed off intestinal contents. They produce large numbers of eggs, which are shed in the feces. The eggs are not immediately infectious and must undergo development over several weeks or months in the environment before becoming infectious. (The time taken for development depends on environmental conditions.) Upon ingestion of contaminated soil or oral contact with soil-exposed hands, the larvae hatch and migrate via the bloodstream throughout the body as visceral larval migrans. In young dogs they migrate from the lungs up the trachea and into the gut, where they develop to maturity. In nontarget species, such as humans, however, the larvae remain as larvae in the various body tissues, where they survive for long periods but do not develop further. Dogs with a *Toxocara* infestation are not themselves infectious because of the period of larval development in the environment that is needed. Nursing bitches and young pups pose a risk, however, as pups can acquire infection from their dam's milk. Migrating *Toxocara* larvae pose a health risk to young children. Although a number of disease entities are recognized as a result of infection with *Toxocara* larvae, the most serious and best known is the ocular larva migrans form of the disease, where larvae, often many years after their ingestion, cause damage to the retina of the eye. This can result in loss of visual acuity and even blindness. Although the disease is generally considered in developed countries as a risk to children who play in playgrounds contaminated with dog feces, it clearly poses a risk to children in developing countries where high numbers of free-roaming dogs defecate freely throughout the environment and where infant and child hygiene has not reached the obsessive levels seen in some developed countries.

Control Issues in the Developing World

While figures for the incidence of echinococcosis and toxocariasis are not readily available, and those for rabies fatalities are subject to considerable error from poor reporting procedures in developing countries, it is obvious that large populations of poorly regulated dogs pose a risk to the health of the human population. Coupled with the types of problems associated with free-roaming dogs reported in Soweto, South Africa, there is a strong case for introducing some means of dog control in most developing countries. The success of such control measures depends heavily on an understanding of the dog ecology and the nature of the dog-human bond in the locale under consideration. Lack of appreciation of these issues is, I believe, one of the main reasons why efforts to control free-roaming dogs in developing countries so often fail.

In many developing countries, efforts to control the often large populations of free-roaming dogs typically focus on mass removal of dogs. In most cases, in south Asian countries, this is done by killing the dogs found on the streets. In many cases these campaigns do not discriminate between the owned-but-roaming-unsupervised animals and neighborhood dogs in an area. Consequently, there is often considerable antagonism between the government functionaries charged with collecting dogs and the population at large, particularly where, as in much of south Asia, there is a general religious (Hindu, Buddhist, and Jain) sentiment against killing animals. Societies often become very polarized, with some sections strongly advocating the removal of all dogs from the streets and other groups arguing equally forcefully to abandon the culling policies.

Many of the methods civic authorities use to remove dogs are less than satisfactory when viewed from an animal welfare perspective. The government employees charged with the task are often from the least-educated, socially deprived, and oppressed sections of society. In northern India, for example, only Dalits of the lowest caste, Harijan, will catch dogs. These poorly educated people are poorly trained and poorly supervised, since few higher officials in the government service want to be associated either with the Harijan dogcatchers or with the act of dog catching itself. The methods used to remove dogs vary. In some places, such as Kathmandu and, formerly, in Jaipur, it is done by indiscriminate use of poison, the most commonly used of which is strychnine. Not only does such poisoning risk poisoning other creatures, including children, but also few poisons are humane in action. (Strychnine, which causes respiratory arrest through paralysis of the respiratory muscles, for example, is clearly distressing to the poisoned animal.) Indiscriminate distribution of poison also has the environmental disadvantage of dead and dying animals left throughout the environment who must be removed.

In many places where poisoning is not used, dogs are caught and removed to some central facility to be killed. The techniques used for catching are often far from humane themselves. In India, where there is some of the most thorough animal welfare legislation in the world, the method laid down by law involves catching the free-roaming dog in a large sack (Prevention of Cruelty [Capture of Animals] Rules 1979). This method, which is used in the Jaipur animal birth control (ABC) program, has been examined by many veterinary surgeons and welfare activists and adjudged humane by all except one animal welfare group, which could provide no justification for its opinion. However, in much of the developing world, even where laws do exist, they are poorly enforced, and such is the case with dogcatching in India. Most municipal dogcatchers use other methods that are contrary to the provisions of the animal welfare legislation. This can include using long iron tongs, similar to very large fire tongs, with which the animals are grabbed by whichever part of their anatomy presents itself. This can often lead to penetrating injuries of soft tissues. In other cases the animals are lassoed variously with chains or ropes often held on poles. This method is favored in Hong Kong and throughout much of India. It is also the method advocated by the group referred to earlier that objected to the sack method. Catching dogs by nooses often results in partial or complete loss of consciousness due to cerebral anoxia through occlusion of the carotid and other arteries to the brain.

Having restrained the dog, no matter how poorly, the dogcatcher must then move the animal into a suitable vehicle for transport to central depots. With the sack method of catching, this is done by carrying the dog to the vehicle in the sack and then emptying the sack into the vehicle. With the tongs method, the dog is lifted up by the tongs and put in the vehicle. To make this process easier, the tail or a hind leg is often held by an assistant, and the animal is stretched to reduce struggling. With nooses and chains, the catcher will whirl the animal around his head on the end of the noose before releasing it, airborne, into the catching vehicle. Some catching teams carry truncheons with which to beat the animal if the dog attempts to bite during the catching process.

Once in the vehicle, animals may be held for many hours, even days, usually without food or water. In some cities in India, it is the practice to fill a caged vehicle until no more dogs can be stuffed in. In such cases some animals have to stand on dogs beneath them. Once returned to the central depot, these dogs may be electrocuted, gassed, or drowned. In a method documented in the city of Vishakhapatnam, the caged dogs were doused with water and the metal cage connected to the electrical supply to electrocute the animals en masse. In India, the electrical current is often variable in supply, and due to overcrowding, many animals are not in contact with the metal fabric of the cage. Thus, this method of electrocution was far from efficient, with some animals taking many minutes before expiring. Those who were not killed in the ordeal were clubbed to death.

It is unfortunate, given the considerable effort and the very serious welfare implications for the dogs concerned, that it is now well recognized that mass removal of dogs will not work as a means of controlling the population or the spread of diseases such as rabies. As long ago as 1988, WHO "strongly insisted that administrators obtain proof that elimination has a significant positive impact on rabies' endemnicity and/or epidemiology before deciding to continue dog removal" (WHO 1988). The evidence for this statement is fairly clear throughout the devel-

oping world. In Delhi a concerted effort at dog removal killed a third of straying dogs with no reduction in the dog population (Blue Cross of Hyderabad/Animal Welfare Board of India 2000). In Hong Kong approximately twenty thousand dogs were killed by the government and another thirteen thousand by welfare organizations every year, in an operation that has been described as "annual harvesting," similar to that practiced in wild animal control in Africa, with little impact on the free-roaming dog population (Dahmer, Coman, and Robinson 2000). In Ecuador the elimination of 12–25 percent of the dog population each year for five years did not reduce the population (WHO 1988). In rural Australia a 76 percent reduction in the free-roaming dog population failed to achieve a lasting reduction in the population, and the number of free-roaming dogs returned to pre-cull levels within one year (Beck 2000). In Kathmandu street dogs have been poisoned for at least 50 years with little long-term effect on the population. In Chennai (formerly Madras), India, the municipal authorities' dog-culling program had been in operation for 120 years yet is still required because of the dog problem (Blue Cross of Hyderabad/Animal Welfare Board of India 2000). Dog-removal programs do not control the dog population, or the various diseases and nuisances associated with dogs, because of their high reproductive potential and the continuing presence of an empty biological niche with unexploited resources. More puppies are born to the surviving animals, and more of them survive, and more dogs migrate into the area recently rendered dog-free. Dog removal may indeed be counterproductive when considered from a rabies-control perspective. The spread of rabies among the dog population is encouraged by high population turnover (Blancou 1988; Beran 1991). Rabies is also

overrepresented in young animals. Thus, by removing dogs, the rate of population turnover and the proportion of young animals are increased. Both lead to conditions that encourage rabies transmission. Many areas endemic for rabies already have high rates of dog population turnover and high proportions of young dogs in the population (Daniels and Bekoff 1989). In Tunisia 30–35 percent of the population is replaced each year. In Mexico 38 percent of the dog population is between three and twelve months of age (Beck 2000). In West Bengal, India, only a third of pups survive one year (Beck 2000). In Zimbabwe's communal lands, 71.8 percent of dogs die in their first year, and pup mortality is estimated at 52.6 percent in the first month of life (Butler and Bingham 2000). The causes of young dogs' deaths is not fully known and will vary from culture to culture but will include distemper and parvovirus infection; road and other accidents; active culling by man in some countries, particularly of female pups; fights; and starvation. Although the reproductive potential of dogs is high generally, it may not be as high in all environments as some workers have assumed. Figures from Jaipur show that breeding of street dogs in that city follows a unipolar seasonal pattern as is seen in many wild canids, but which is not considered normal for *Canis familiaris*. In Jaipur there is a very marked breeding season in autumn (Chawla and Reece 2002). Clearly, being receptive to breeding only once a year reduces the reproductive potential of the species. Anecdotal evidence, however, suggests these findings may not apply throughout the subcontinent, emphasizing the need for knowledge of the local ecology of the free-roaming dog population in any control program.

Despite the considerable mass of evidence and the advice of WHO, many municipal authorities in India and elsewhere in the developing world continue to chose the removal option over other alternatives of dog or rabies control. In part this is because of the lack of understanding and awareness of the issues involved. In part it is also because transient politicians and officials feel under pressure to act—and to be seen to act—when dog problems are drawn to their attention, as they frequently are, particularly by the better-educated and more influential members of society.

Not every attempt to remove dogs ends in their killing. Recently in Jodhpur in Rajasthan a removal program was begun which included keeping the dogs in pounds. This has also been attempted in Turkey. As a means of controlling the free-roaming dog population, this has not worked for the same reasons that killing the removed dogs does not work. Furthermore, keeping large numbers of dogs in pounds is expensive and difficult to do if the animals' welfare is taken into account. Diseases tend to spread more rapidly among large groups of dogs and establishing a social order within such groups results in fighting and injuries. The number of dogs found in the typical city in a developing country also precludes this approach. One Indian city, Hyderabad, is believed to have a dog-to-man ratio of 1:40 (Blue Cross of Hyderabad/Animal Welfare Board of India 2000), which implies a total dog population of between fifty and one hundred thousand. Jaipur, a city of roughly two million people, has an estimated fifty to sixty thousand dogs. Figures of this magnitude, typical for many cities, make establishing pounds impractical. In some Indian cities, the removed dogs are relocated to the nearest jungle area. This, too, does not control the population and has the added disadvantage of spreading problems associated with free-roaming dogs to other areas, usually with lower human and dog populations.

The relocated dogs can cause severe disruption to livestock in their efforts to find food, which are often unsuccessful and lead to dogs dying of starvation.

In some developing countries, some of the problems caused by street dogs are addressed through mass parental vaccination campaigns in an attempt to eradicate rabies from the cities involved. This method has been used on a truly heroic scale in parts of South America (Largi et al. 1988). A similar scheme was recently piloted successfully in Chad (Kayali et al. 2003). Millions of doses of rabies vaccine have been given annually to free-roaming dogs. This method has worked to control rabies in the areas where it is applied but, of course, does nothing to address the other problems of disease and nuisance caused by a burgeoning street dog population. Recently a modified rabies virus has been incorporated into an oral vaccine preparation for dogs. This should make mass vaccination of large proportions of the free-roaming dog population much easier, which will enable the threshold level required for rabies control to be reached. It is hoped that trials of this vaccine will be allowed by the Indian government shortly to control rabies in this country.

The control efforts, which are advocated by WHO and others, involve a three-part program featuring responsible pet ownership with licensing of pet dogs, sterilization and vaccination of free-roaming dogs, and habitat control (WHO 1990).

Responsible pet ownership requires educating the public in the correct ways to own a pet dog and care for it. It would include such matters as sterilization of animals; appropriate and timely veterinary treatment, including vaccination and anthelmintic administration; and the need to exercise control over pet dogs' activities by, for example, exercising the animal only on a lead and in an appropriate place. Governments play a role in this with a sensible licensing regime to regulate dog ownership. Licenses can be made less costly for sterilized and vaccinated dogs, thus encouraging these desirable actions. Such a regime of responsible pet ownership would be particularly valuable in many developing countries where the increasingly affluent middle classes have taken to keeping dogs as status or fashion symbols. This trend tends to mean that many people have no knowledge of correct dog care and appropriate social etiquette. In the Western world it is now commonplace for dog owners to be expected to clean up the ordure their charges leave in public places. Municipal laws demand such activity. However, in much of south Asia, especially, such a law would have little chance of success because of deeply ingrained attitudes based on caste and the quasi-religious concept of impurity and pollution that would prohibit much of society from even contemplating handling, even indirectly, their dog's feces. For licensing systems for dogs to be effective, they would need to be enforced and possibly accompanied by the removal, after suitable warnings, of unlicensed animals. This requires considerable municipal investment in identifying licensed dogs and humane removal and kenneling of apparently unlicensed dogs while awaiting confirmation of the animal's status. In much of the developing world, any licensing regime is, in effect, a means of boosting the income of the responsible government enforcers through bribery.

It is generally believed that dogs exist in very few places where they have no referral household or community (WHO 1990). The exception to this is around food markets, slaughterhouses, temples, and roadside restaurants, where sufficient food is available without the active involvement of humans in feeding the dogs. In north India, however, these conditions are common, and unofficial food sources are freely available to dogs. The availability of resources may be a limiting factor in the size of the free-roaming dog population (Butler and Bingham 2000). It thus follows that, if these resources can be controlled, the free-roaming dog population should also be controlled. In many developing countries, civic infrastructure does not include even basic sanitation and access to indoor, drained lavatories, much less the efficient disposal of household waste. Waste in developing countries has a much higher organic content than that in developed countries because the consumer culture has yet to develop, and very securely wrapped convenience foods do not feature in the typical diet. Many workers concerned with dog ecology in developing countries believe that the success of the dog population depends on the free availability of human waste food and feces, which enables females to maintain the high levels of fecundity required to offset the high mortality rate among pups and young dogs (Butler and Bingham 2000; Dahmer, Coman, and Robinson 2000). In contrast, workers studying in developed countries believe the availability of shelter may be the limiting factor determining dog population size (A.M. Beck, personal communication, June 23, 2004). Experience in India supports the food-availability hypothesis where areas, which are kept clean because they house senior government officials, for example, have very low dog populations. In contrast, areas with no civic amenities—where the population is obliged to put its rubbish out on the streets and where many are obliged to defecate in open spaces—have large dog populations. The amount of shelter available to dogs will be similar in each area or may, indeed, be lower in the dense, unplanned housing typical of poor areas. What does seem without doubt is that, were governments to make concerted and constant efforts to reduce the availability of food and shelter in the towns and cities of the developing world, the population of free-roaming dogs would be reduced. It has been suggested that, were a civic government to implement suddenly and rigorously such a plan for civic cleanliness and order, there might be a concomitant need to instigate some form of "humane culling" of the dog population. Failure to do so may otherwise result in large numbers of dogs with insufficient food fighting over the remaining resources, migrating to other areas with serious consequences to population stability in the new areas, and ultimately starving to death. A rigorous civic hygiene plan undoubtedly would result in a reduction in the nuisances caused by free-roaming dogs, including those diseases associated with the animals. This would be welcome in the fight against rabies, for example, but would confront animal welfare organizations in these cities with a difficult and unpleasant problem.

The third part of a plan to control free-roaming dog populations as envisaged by WHO is the introduction of sterilization and vaccination of dogs from this population. These plans, as previously mentioned, are known in much of the developing world as animal birth control (ABC) programs and in the Americas as trap-neuter-release (TNR) programs, have been part of WHO policy to control the health problems associated with large dog populations since 1990. There have been ABC programs in India since before this; however, the program in Madras (now Chennai) began in 1964 (Blue Cross of Hyderabad/Animal Welfare Board of India 2000). The concept is now widespread across many developing countries. Unfortunately most programs are conducted with little financial help from the civic authorities, with animal welfare organizations bearing most of the costs associated with them. Indeed, the motivation behind many ABC programs is driven by animal welfare rather than public health, which does cause some conflict, particularly with those medical doctors whose professional lives involve dog bite clinics that see dozens of bitten people each day. The basic premise behind ABC programs is that captured dogs would be sterilized, vaccinated against rabies, and returned to the exact location whence they came. They would thus maintain their position in the hierarchy of free-roaming dogs, preventing migration and population instability while not contributing to the number of puppies produced. In this way it was hoped that many of the problems with large, unsupervised dog populations would be controlled.

The Jaipur ABC Program

One of the problems with WHO's approach to dog population control was that it seemed counterintuitive. There was little positive evidence to prove that the methods advocated would work, even if it was reasonably well established scientifically that mass removal of dogs would *not* work. In an attempt to correct this situation, an ABC program was established in Jaipur in late 1994 with a view to collecting data on the efficacy of such programs. Initially the Jaipur program was a pilot program. Once the pilot had been completed with results that looked positive, the ABC program was expanded to cover most of the city. Jaipur, the rapidly expanding capital of the desert state of Rajasthan, has a population of about two million people. The methods and results of the Jaipur ABC program are detailed in Anderson et al. (1981).

The Jaipur ABC program has divided the city into areas and further subdivided these using major geographical features as the boundaries. Dogs are caught from one of these areas using the sack method referred to earlier. The location of each dog is recorded as accurately as possible, and the dogs are transported back to the ABC kennels and veterinary operating suite located in an animal welfare nongovernmental organization (NGO)'s premises. The dogs are kenneled individually, given a quick veterinary examination, and registered before being allowed to settle in. In the Jaipur program, approximately 10.3 percent of dogs captured are killed humanely since they are found to be suffering from serious disease or illness or to be temperamentally unsuited to life on the streets among a high-density human population. (The concept of a strict "no kill" policy in the context of a major ABC program is nonviable if only because of the number of animals involved.)

The next day the dogs are fasted and given pre-medication. They are prepared individually for surgery and given anesthetic, antibiotics, and analgesics. All animals are vaccinated against rabies using a modern vaccine that gives three years' immunity. The dogs are marked permanently by removing a notch from the cranial border of the left pinna and a five-digit, alphanumeric, unique tattooed number in the right pinna. The dogs are then sterilized by complete ovariohysterectomy through a right flank incision; males are sterilized by castration through a single pre-scrotal incision. The Jaipur program concentrates on sterilizing female animals since they produce the puppies. Prepubescent male puppies are also castrated. Some programs sterilize all dogs, including adult males. With limited resources available, however, it is hard to see why castration of even

large numbers of male dogs is attempted since the remaining unaltered males will continue to sire pups by every unaltered female available. The limited surgical skill of some veterinary surgeons in some developing countries may account for this policy difference, however, since castration is the easier procedure.

Once the surgical procedure is completed, the animals are returned to their individual kennels to recover. They are examined by veterinary surgeons daily until they are considered to have recovered sufficiently to endure the rigors of life on the streets. At all stages of the ABC program, the dog is accompanied by a registration card to avoid any confusion as to his or her identity and location. Records are maintained of all information deemed relevant so the program can be monitored carefully. The Jaipur program aims to catch unaltered adult male dogs, in addition to the sterilized individuals, so that they may be vaccinated against rabies and so identified by an ear notch and tattoo. The adult males are also returned to their exact location in the city. By vaccinating only these adult dogs, the hierarchy is less disturbed (since the males maintain their own territories), but the percentage of the total dog population that is vaccinated against rabies is increased. Research from rabies-control programs in Europe and elsewhere and epidemiological theory indicate that a certain threshold percentage of vaccinated dogs must be achieved to prevent continuance of the urban rabies cycle (Margawani and Robertson 1995). According to WHO this threshold percentage for rabies is about 70 percent, though exactly how this figure has been derived seems unclear from the literature.

The Jaipur program has attempted to record all manner of data on its effects and on the ecology and behavior of the dog popu-

lation it is trying to control. As of 2004 more than thirty thousand animals had entered the program and more than twenty-four thousand sterilization and vaccination operations had been performed. An additional three thousand animals had been vaccinated against rabies. Population censuses indicate that about 70 percent of the female population had been sterilized and vaccinated. The total population in a smaller representative area of the total area covered by the ABC had declined by 28 percent from its peak. It has been established that dogs in Jaipur breed seasonally (in late autumn) and have an average litter size of 5.62 pups.

The program does not have an active re-vaccination component because the available scientific evidence suggests that street dogs do not usually live long lives (Butler and Bingham 2000; Coyne et al. 2001). The vaccine given confers protection for three years, according to the manufacturer's information, and possibly longer if given, as it is in the program, intramuscularly (Daniels and Bekoff 1989). However, some dogs are recaught for other reasons or by mistake. From these the Jaipur program has some migration and longevity data. Of recaught dogs 21.5 percent had traveled less than five hundred meters from the place of original capture and release. Only 15.2 percent of recaptured dogs had survived longer than a thousand days from the date of their original release.

Arguments about animal welfare in developing countries carry little weight with governments and decision makers. However, if the concept of ABC programs, together with the other dog-control measures mentioned, can be shown to have a positive effect on human health, then governments may show greater interest in implementing these control programs, which would improve the animal welfare situation. To this end the Jaipur ABC program has attempted to collate data on human rabies cases occurring in the city. As with much of the developing world, disease-reporting procedures leave much to be desired. However, figures for human rabies cases from the main state hospital in the city suggest that the number of cases has fallen in the area covered by the ABC program from a pre-ABC peak of ten cases a year to no reported cases in 2001 and 2002. In areas of the city not served by the ABC, the number of cases has risen as the outlying areas develop. The total number of cases seen in the hospital, regardless of the place of origin, has remained approximately static. This would seem to suggest that the program is having an affect on the levels of rabies infection within Jaipur city.

In an attempt to prove that the ABC program benefits the dogs of Jaipur, a study of the incidence rates of the two commonest disease processes of street dogs (e.g., transmissible venereal tumor and parasitic mange) was undertaken from the records maintained by the ABC program. Although subjective assessment of the city's dogs' condition indicates that ABC dogs are in better condition than those who have not been through the ABC program and that dogs in Jaipur are in better condition than those elsewhere, this study failed to indicate any difference in the diseases' incidence rates.

The various results of the Jaipur ABC program indicate that a concerted effort to sterilize and vaccinate free-roaming dogs from the city's streets may indeed stabilize or reduce the dog population and control rabies, the most serious disease associated with dogs.

Armed with data such as these, one would think that the program would be applied throughout the developing world. Unfortunately this has not been the case to date, for a number of reasons. In south

Asia government is extremely bureaucratic and cautious. Dog control does not readily fall within any particular department's sphere of influence: health departments claim that dog control is not their problem, and veterinary departments claim rabies is a human disease. Improvements in civic infrastructure are the responsibility of other departments that have little incentive to be involved in the "degrading" area of waste management when larger development projects such as road and bridge construction are available. In India, Nepal, and Sri Lanka, most of the effort promoting ABC programs as a part of the total control of free-roaming dogs has come from animal welfare organizations. In the case of India this has, until lately, been greatly helped by support from government due to former minister Maneka Gandhi's passionate interest in animal welfare. (India has one of the most advanced government structures in the world for improving animal welfare.) The human health issues have not been emphasized, so ABC programs and their proponents are seen as being "for" dog welfare protection and advancement rather than attempting to help the human population at large. Unfortunately, many organizations undertaking ABC programs in developing countries are somewhat economical with the truth and creative in their accounting procedures, often encouraged in this approach by per capita payments for each dog entering the program. Thus achievements may be on paper only. Opponents of humane dog-control measures or those who remain to be convinced are thus handed plenty of ammunition by examples of where such measures have not achieved what was claimed for them.

It is interesting to note that free-roaming dogs and their associated problems, particularly rabies, were controlled in the United Kingdom

and some European countries in the early part of the twentieth century by a strictly enforced licensing regime, along with stray elimination programs and rigid quarantine procedures and concomitant improvements in civic hygiene. In England, for example, for much of the twentieth century, it cost as much to license ownership of a dog for a year as it did for a man to obtain government permission to take a wife for life! The fact that these measures were successful at controlling free-roaming dogs and rabies emphasizes that control is possible and that control measures must be suitable to the society and situation in which they are applied.

Conclusion

The roles of dogs in developing countries are varied and range from the venerated to the impure, from the tolerated to the loved. In many situations dogs undoubtedly do sterling work for their community as guard dogs, affording protection against a dangerous, uncontrolled world and providing a means by which much human waste is removed from the environment of man (thus suppressing populations of other more pestilential creatures such as rats and cockroaches). Unfortunately dogs' very success at living with and relying on man can create problems for both the dogs and their associated human populations. The dogs suffer from very short life expectancies and high rates of mortality, among the young especially, and these deaths are often unpleasant. The human population is subjected to minor problems by a large free-roaming dog population, including noise and environmental soiling by ordure, and to some major public health issues, such as rabies, from which about thirty thousand people die each year, mainly in developing countries. Some measure of control of the dog population would seem desirable in many of these countries. The control measures applied and the future development and refinement of the human-dog bond must be in accordance with the local customs, beliefs, and wishes of the human population as well as the ecology of the dog population locally.

Literature Cited

Anderson, R.M., H.C. Jackson, R.C. May, and A.H. Smith. 1981. Population dynamics of fox rabies in Europe. *Nature* 289: 765–771.

Beck, A.M. 2000. The human-dog relationship: A tale of two species. In *Dogs, zoonoses, and public health,* ed. C.N.L. Macpherson, F.X. Meslin, and A.I. Wandeler, 1–16. Oxford: CABI.

Beran, G.W. 1991. Urban rabies. In *The natural history of rabies,* ed. G.M. Baer, 427–433. Boca Raton, Fla.: CRC Press.

Blancou, J. 1988. Epizootology of rabies: Eurasia and Africa. In *Rabies,* ed. J.B. Campbell and K.M. Charlton, 242–265. Boston: Kluwer Academic Publications.

Blue Cross of Hyderabad/Animal Welfare Board of India. 2000. *Summary of a seminar on management of stray dog population and rabies control.* June.

Briggs, D.J. 2002. Purified chick embryo cell vaccine: Rabies vaccine for a new millennium. *Indian Journal of Internal Medicine* 11(6) Supplement 2: 1–4.

Butler, J.R.A., and J. Bingham. 2000. Demography and dog-human relationships of the dog population in Zimbabwean communal lands. *Veterinary Record* 147: 442–446.

Chawla, S.K., and J.F. Reece. 2002. Timing of oestrus and reproductive behaviour in Indian street dogs. *Veterinary Record* 150: 450–451.

Cleaveland, S., E.M. Fevre, M. Kaare, and P.G. Coleman. 2002. Estimating human rabies mortality in the United Republic of Tanzania from dog bite injuries. *Bulletin of the World Health Organisation* 80: 304–310.

Coyne, M.C., J.H.H. Barr, T.D. Yale, M.J. Harding, D.B. Tresman, and D. McGavin. 2001. Duration of immunity in dogs after vaccination or naturally acquired infection. *Veterinary Record* 149: 509–515.

Dahmer, T., B. Coman, J. Robinson. 2000. *Ecology, behaviour, and persistence of packs of stray/feral dogs with implications and practical recommendations for control.* Final report to Department of Agriculture, Fisheries, and Conservation, Government of Hong Kong. March.

Daniels, T.J., and M. Bekoff. 1989. Population and social biology of free ranging dogs. *Journal of Mammology* 70(4): 754–762.

Hammond, A., and M.H.H. Sewell. 1990. Echinococcosis. In *Handbook on animal diseases in the tropics,* 4h ed., ed. M.H.H. Sewell and D.W. Brocklesby, 117–119. London: Bailliere Tindall.

Kayali, U., R. Mindekem, N. Yemadji, P. Vounatsai, Y. Keninga, A.G. Ndoutamia, and J. Zinsstag. 2003. Coverage of a pilot parental vaccination campaign against canine rabies in N'Djamena, Chad. *Bulletin of the World Health Organisation* 81(10): 739–744.

Largi, O.P., J.C. Arossi, J. Nakajataa, and A. Villa-Nova. 1988. Control of urban rabies. In *Rabies,* ed. J.B. Campbell and K.M. Charlton, 407–422. Boston: K.M. Kluwer Academic Publications.

Macpherson, C.N.L., and P.S. Craig. 2000. Dogs and cestode zoonoses. In *Dogs, zoonoses and public health,* ed. C.N.L. Macpherson, F.X. Meslin, and A.I. Wandeler, 177–255. Oxford: CABI.

Margawani, K.R., and I.D. Robertson. 1995. A survey of urban pet ownership in Bali. *Veterinary Record* 137: 486–488.

Matter, H.C., and T.J. Daniels. 2000. Dog ecology and population biology. In *Dogs, zoonoses, and public health,* ed. C.N.L. Macpherson, F.X. Meslin, and A.I. Wandeler, 17–62. Oxford: CABI.

Overgraauw, P.A.M., and F. van Knapen. 2000. Dogs and nematode zoonoses. In *Dogs, zoonoses, and public health,* ed. C.N.L. Macpherson, F.X. Meslin, and A.I. Wandeler, 213–256. Oxford: CABI.

Prevention of Cruelty (Capture of Animals) Rules 1979 made under ss38(2)(i) Prevention of Cruelty to Animals Act 1960. Government of India, New Delhi.

Sharma, N., V. Kumar, and M. Chawla. 2002. *Profile of animal bite cases in ARC, SMS Hospital, Jaipur.* APCRICON Souvenir.

World Health Organization (WHO). 1988. *Report of WHO consultation on dog ecology studies related to rabies control.* WHO/Rab.Res./88.25.

———. 1990. WHO/WSPA guidelines for dog population management. WHO/ZOON/90/166.

Wright, J.C. 1991. Canine aggression towards people. *Veterinary Clinics of North America: Small Animal Practice* 21(2): 299–314.

International Animal Law, with a Concentration on Latin America, Asia, and Africa

CHAPTER

Neil Trent, Stephanie Edwards, Jennifer Felt, and Kelly O'Meara

It is, of course, a challenge to undertake an overview of international animal protection law within the confines of a single chapter. The countries reviewed here are exemplars chosen to represent various animal welfare issues in each region.

The status of domestic animal protection laws in Asia, Africa, and Latin America varies, as one might imagine, from country to country. Countries with high per capita incomes are more likely to have a large number of animal protection organizations, whose existence normally leads to the passage of protective legislation.[1] The sociopolitical, cultural, and religious backgrounds of each country, as well as previous colonization, also influence whether it has animal protection legislation and whether these laws are enforced. Previous colonization is the case in many former British colonies, which often have very good laws but neither the means nor the interest to enforce them. With some exception, countries within each region of the world follow similar patterns of law and enforcement. (Logically, it would follow that countries with the highest number of animal protection groups per land area or per population would be the most

likely to have an animal protection law, yet these concepts do not necessarily correlate, though it may reflect increased interest in animal protection as a concept [Table 1]). International animal protection can be best understood by placing countries in one of four descending levels of animal protection. Countries of Asia, Africa, and Latin America can be found in the bottom three categories (Irwin 2003).

Model Animal Protection

The greatest degree of animal protection is found in North America, Northern Europe, and Australia/ New Zealand. These regions exhibit the highest levels of such protection and have comprehensive animal welfare legislation.

Animal legislation in these countries includes laws protecting companion animals, livestock, and wildlife. Their statutes describe what behavior is considered humane treatment of animals and what is considered animal abuse, and they are regularly enforced. There is also a high level of enforcement, yet conditions for animals are still not ideal and laws are not uniform from one country to another. For example,

while the United Kingdom is steeped in animal protection legislation, as of 2005 it had not yet banned dog and cat fur products, which due to their inhumane production, have cause a worldwide furor—and legislative prohibition in the United States and elsewhere. Australia, which *has* officially banned the sale of dog and cat fur, had as of 2005 no blanket federal legislation concerning domestic animal welfare, though it did have strong animal welfare laws within each of its territories.

A number of European countries have made great advancements in animal welfare protection in the last few years. As of 2005 the European Union (EU) was considering a ban on the import, export, sale, and production of cat and dog furs and skins. Though some countries strongly supported this ban, others, like the United Kingdom, felt that it is not the EU's place to intervene in individual countries' affairs. Austria, on the other hand, had taken huge steps in advancing animal protection by passing in May 2004 one of Europe's toughest animal rights laws, the Animal Protection Act of 2004. It prohibits caging of chickens, cropping of dog's tails and ears, chaining of dogs, and use of wildlife

Table 1
Animal Protection Activity in Selected Countries

Country	Law	No Law	No Law but Draft of Law in Progress or Under Review	Total Population in Millions*	Land Area-Hundreds of Square km*	Number of Animal Protection Organizations (2004)**	Number of APOs per million people	Number of APOs per Hundred Square km
Australia		•		19.91	7,617.93	355	17.83	0.05
Austria	•			8.17	82.44	122	14.93	1.48
Spain		•		40.28	499.54	108	2.68	0.22
UK	•			60.27	241.59	752	12.48	3.12
Antigua	•			0.07	0.44	4	57.14	9.09
Anguilla	•			0.01	0.10	1	100.00	10.00
Bahamas	•			0.30		8	26.60	
Costa Rica	•			3.96	50.66	15	3.79	0.29
Honduras		•	•	6.82	111.89	2	0.29	0.02
Mexico		•	•	104.96	1,923.04	83	0.79	0.04
Panama	•			3.00	75.99	7	2.33	0.09
Bolivia		•		8.72	1,084.39	21	2.41	0.02
Brazil	•			184.10	8,456.51	93	0.50	0.01
Chile		•	•	15.82	748.80	67	4.24	0.09
Colombia	•			42.31	1,038.70	26	0.62	0.03
Peru	•			27.54	1,280.00	12	0.44	0.01
China		•		1,298.85	9,326.19	38	0.03	0.004
India	•			1,065.07	2,973.19	326	0.31	0.11
Japan	•			127.33	374.74	54	0.42	0.15
Korea	•			48.60	98.19	20	0.41	0.2
Philippines		•		86.24	298.17	16	0.19	0.05
Russia		•	•	143.78	1,699.80	38	0.26	0.02
Botswana	•			1.56	585.37	4	2.56	0.01
Kenya	•			32.02	569.25	21	0.65	0.04
South Africa	•			42.72	1,219.91	90	2.11	0.16
Uganda	•			26.40	199.71	9	0.34	0.05
Zimbabwe		•		12.67	386.67	24	1.89	0.06

*Source: *CIA World Factbook*. www.cia.gov/cia/publications.factbook.

**Source: *World Animal Net Directory*.

in circus acts (Associated Press 2004). Spain, with a mid-to-high level of animal protection, has been experimenting in the last two years with strengthening animal-cruelty laws. Several cities, including Barcelona, had condemned bullfighting. While there is no official ban at the provincial level, people's protests against bullfighting show that they are ready for tougher animal protection laws (Trent 2004b). The first European regulation at the municipal level to ban euthanasia as a means of animal control passed in Catalonia in January 2003; the Law for Animal Protection takes effect in all of Catalonia in 2007. Yet some cities, like Barcelona, have passed similar legislation independently (Abend and Fingree 2004).

Australia

Although Australia does not have a federal law protecting domestic animals, each individual state and territory has its own animal welfare legislation. Queensland in particular introduced a thorough and comprehensive animal protection act in 2000 (Queensland Animal Care and Protection Act 2001). Animal protection organizations in Australia have been lobbying for some time and hope to pass a federal animal protection law.

South Africa and the Caribbean Islands

South Africa and the Caribbean Islands, along with Southern and Eastern Europe, comprise the second level of animal protection. Animal welfare laws are the norm, but enforcing them is the biggest challenge. The laws in South Africa and the Caribbean, passed during former British rule, do not necessarily represent the concerns of current governments. Animal protection presence is high in most of the areas' regions, yet there is room for improvement in their programs.

South Africa has two animal protection laws, the Animal Protection Act 24 of 1962, which covers all animals, and the Performing Animals Act, which includes working and performing animals. Enforcement of these laws is largely left up to the National Society for the Prevention of Cruelty to Animals (NSPCA). If animal abuse is suspected, the law allows NSPCA member organizations to enter the suspect premises and seize the animal involved. It also has the right to arrest a person who tries to prevent its personnel from entering a premises and/or removing an animal. The problems arise in actually punishing offenders under these laws. Because there is no separate court to hear animal-related cases, these cases are regularly pushed aside to address other criminal cases. Since crime is high in South Africa, animal abuse cases can take up to three years to get through the court system. Such enforcement problems are evidence of the need for improvement (M. Meredith, executive director, National Council of SPCAs, personal communication with S.E., June 24, 2004).

The Caribbean enjoys a moderate presence of animal protection groups, and most islands have animal protection laws in place (Table 1). Yet, as stated earlier, where these laws do exist, largely due to current or prior British influence, they do not necessarily reflect the priorities of the current governments. For example, the Bahamas, a former British colony, has an animal welfare act of British origin. Antigua and Barbuda, independent states within the British Commonwealth, have animal-cruelty laws, but the penalty for noncompliance is no more than a fine. Anguilla, which is still a British colony, has laws that prohibit animal cruelty and name the local police as enforcers, yet there are no local government funds to support animal control or animal welfare. Several Caribbean countries have laws against cruelty, dogfighting, and cockfighting, but most of the penalties for animal abuse in these countries generally involve a fine and are not usually implemented (Trent 2004a).

Central and South America and Asia-Japan

Central and South America and part of Asia (Japan), along with the Middle East, have relatively weak animal protection programs, and enforcement of such laws in many of these countries is minimal. The high economic status and high standards of living in many of the countries in these regions normally would indicate advanced protection laws and programs, but that is not the case. Instead, cultural challenges and traditions are obstacles for animal protection. However, most of these areas have exhibited a growing interest in increasing animal protection programs and law enforcement. If this trend continues, countries within this region, with the cooperation of their governments, should be able to improve and/or enforce their existing animal protection legislation.

Central and South America

In recent years concern for animal protection in Latin America has been growing. Peru, Costa Rica, Colombia, and Brazil have federal animal welfare laws that specifically protect companion animals and define animal cruelty. Costa Rica and Peru have made humane education mandatory in the curriculum for schoolchildren. Costa Rica and La Paz, Bolivia, have outlawed circuses that use animals; Tegucigalpa, Honduras, and La Paz have passed ordinances to ban dogfighting; and Mexico City has identified an enforcement squad that will work strictly on animal issues and enforcing the federal district's animal welfare law, and government organizations are looking at standards for the transport and sacrifice of livestock. Yet, several countries in the region have no animal welfare legislation and no current plans to develop any.

Creating and passing animal protection legislation in Latin America is dependent upon a series of variables, including economics, culture, and religion. In each country the state of the government can determine the success of any type of law or regulation. Even countries that put forth the best effort will not succeed if corruption rules in the place of communication. The culture of animal ownership and what individuals see as being animals' role in society are additional variables that affect legislation.

Human health issues have affected animal welfare incidentally in a positive manner around the world. Species from dogs to cows have benefited from increased attention and advances in veterinary care as a consequence of efforts made to fight diseases that can be transmitted from animals to humans. With education campaigns that document the effects of such zoonotic diseases, health departments in the majority of Latin American countries, and international organizations working in those countries, are persuaded to support the animal welfare movement. A classic example of this dynamic can be seen in the approach to rabies control around the world. In many countries you can travel to the most remote areas and witness a rabies vaccination campaign that benefits human and animal populations alike.

Similarly, the emergence of bovine spongiform encephalopathy (so-called mad cow disease) has acted as an economic driver for improved animal welfare standards in Latin America. The possibility that mad cow disease could decimate a livestock industry has forced the ministries of agriculture in several countries (e.g., Argentina, Brazil, and Chile) to evaluate their livestock transport and handling practices, though they are not the first to do so (Appleby 2003).

Tourism, the predominant economic driver of many Central and South America countries, and a potential economic engine for the others, has caused some countries to work on specific animal welfare problems. Tourists from countries without large numbers of visible stray and street dogs, for example, can be strongly affected by the sights of malnourished, sick, or uncared-for animals congregating around their hotels and restaurants when they travel. They complain to hotel and restaurant personnel and carry the word back to others once they return home. Such bad publicity can generate a response from countries looking for tourist business.

Central America

Mexico

Mexico has no national animal welfare law, but "official norms" exist that address issues of animals in research and animal transport and sacrifice. (Another, as of 2004, was soon to be released on maintenance and care.) In February of 2002, Mexico City passed an animal protection law that put in place regulations and criteria to protect the lives of animals, ensure their respectful and dignified treatment, and foster the participation of the social and private sector in complying with these regulations within the city's federal district.

In 2001 the International Fund for Animal Welfare (IFAW) opened a regional office in Mexico City, where it has begun working fervently on issues particular to Mexico. IFAW staff has been working with the National Animal Health Council, a consulting firm for the Ministry of Agriculture, since 2002, helping to draft a federal animal welfare law. The veterinary school at the National University of Mexico has begun a program to train inspectors on implementing the animal welfare law in the federal district. Although it seems much has been done, animals in Mexico do not live in health and comfort. In Mexico City, in particular, which has a population of around twenty million, the federal district has a lot of work to do, and one can only hope that the rest of the country will follow (F. Galindo, D.V.M., campaign officer, IFAW, personal communication with J.F., July 29, 2004).

Costa Rica

Costa Rica has adopted an animal welfare law that looks at issues ranging from companion animals to work animals and from animals involved in sports and experimentation to wildlife. The law appears to be fairly general, but its introduction explains that cruel acts against animals damage human dignity, and it specifically states that its aim is to foster respect for all living things. It suggests animals should have adequate food and water, should have the ability to exhibit behaviors normal to the species, and should be free from pain and distress.

Local and international animal welfare organizations have done much to add more detail to the law and expand its scope. The World Society for the Protection of Animals (WSPA), through its regional office in Costa Rica, has been behind a series of efforts to improve animal welfare in the country. A handful of very successful local organizations promotes this effort, dedicating its time and lending its expertise. These organizations enjoy good working relationships with the government and are interacting successfully with the ministries of environment, health, and education toward improved animal welfare standards (G. Huertas, regional director, WSPA Latin America, personal communication with J.F., June 15, 2004). The ministry of education, for example, has included humane education in the national curriculum, and the ministry of agriculture is currently working on a transportation decree for livestock that is heavily focused on animal welfare. (On a separate note, circuses using wild animals have recently been outlawed in the country.)

Costa Rica is greatly affected by tourism and the tourist dollar. In one area in particular, the street/ stray dogs are called "tourist dogs" because they survive on food dispensed by whatever tourist decides to "adopt" them that week. Despite Costa Rica's high profile as a tourist destination, it is a struggle to bring the welfare of companion animals, as well as livestock, to the attention of the majority of the population. Even though the country's animal welfare law, Ley De Bienestar De Los Animales, provides a necessary foundation, its enforcement is practically nonexistent.

There are signs of hope, however. Travelers have expressed great concern for Costa Rica's tourist dogs, and, as a result, there is additional pressure on the government to strengthen the language of the animal welfare law and its enforcement strategy. Local organizations show a constant willingness to be involved and to push for stronger legislation and improved enforcement (L. Schnog, president, Asociacion Humanitaria Para la Proteccion Animal de Costa Rica, personal communication with J.F., June 17, 2004), and humane education provides an essential component for future improvements. Such positive steps demonstrate a commitment to animal welfare and the desire to make the necessary changes to prevent the unnecessary suffering of animals in the region.

Panama City, Panama

The city of Panama has drafted a municipal ordinance that looks at the welfare of companion animals (Municipal Resolution No. 20, 1990). Panama has its own national animal protection law, the Codigo Administativo–Tratamiento de Animales Domesticos, 1941, but this law is not thorough, nor is it often enforced.

Drafters of the ordinance used an administrative code and a sanitary code to create this legislation. Working animals dominate the ordinance, and strict guidelines are presented. The ordinance prohibits excessive beating of work animals and prohibits such animals from carrying excessive weight. Mistreatment of animals for not working as quickly as their owners would like and abandonment of an animal no longer able to work are prohibited as well. Animals should not be made to work if they have a broken or dislocated bone. Each of these infractions is punishable by a modest fine. The ordinance also addresses bullfighting, only allowing it on festival days. Any police officer who fails to enforce this is subject to a fine. When discussing domestic animals, the ordinance pairs maintenance of dogs with health issues and concerns. It does make clear, however, that anyone who mistreats a domestic animal, fails to provide sufficient food, or allows an animal to suffer is subject to a fine or ten to twenty days in jail and that those who witness cruelty toward domestic animals are obligated to report it to the Panama City Humanitarian Office.

Although it may seem that animal welfare issues are largely covered, enforcement of the ordinance is not widespread, and the majority of the activities specifically prohibited in the document are still allowed to occur daily.

Panama City's mayor in 2004 was very sympathetic to animal welfare issues, and the local animal welfare organization was working on a draft proposal for a national law that would outline animal welfare concerns in more detail. It was to be presented in September 2004 after governments had changed (A. de Llorach, Fundacion Humanites, personal communication with S.E., October 22, 2004).

Honduras

A demonstrated knowledge of the importance of protecting species is crucial to any forward movement on animal protection issues. Honduras has legislation protecting animals of national significance, such as the white-tailed deer and the scarlet macaw. Local Honduran animal welfare organizations are in the process of drafting a proposal for a law that would cover domestic animals. A struggle to get the proposal passed into law was anticipated as of 2004 as domestic animals are not considered by many to be a priority species (K.J. Duarte, Asociacion Hondurena Protectora de los Animales y su Ambiente, personal communication with J.F., June 12, 2004). As a result of several dog attacks on children, the capital city of Tegucigalpa outlawed dogfighting in 2004. Although this action can be seen as advancement, when it is difficult to determine the capacity of the government to work on such issues, any improvement is compromised by the lack of communication and transparency surrounding it.

South America

Peru

Peru benefits from the existence of a well-known animal welfare organization that has worked well with the government for several years. After a series of successful animal programs in the capital, Lima, this organization was able to demonstrate to the government the benefits of animal welfare and the importance of having a law that outlined animal welfare standards (R. Quintanilla, Amigos De Los Animales, personal communication with J.F., June 12, 2004; with S.E., November

22, 2004). The Law for Protection of Domestic and Captive Wild Animals (Law No. 27265, 2000) is comprehensive, includes companion animals and wildlife, and covers topics from pet ownership to the role of the authorities in animal protection. Its goal is to prevent all mistreatment of and acts of cruelty toward animals caused directly or indirectly by humans. It also aims to foster respect for the lives of animals through education, to disseminate these ideals throughout the Peruvian population, and to lay down rules for pet owners, starting with the basics of providing adequate food and water and proper living conditions. The role of the authorities is defined in the law, which stipulates that police should provide adequate support and that government organizations, such as the ministry of health, should take responsibility for a program that would address the issue of overpopulation. The document also addresses issues such as animal experimentation and transportation of circus animals.

The law puts a great deal of emphasis on education and health and the fact that those government organizations charged with addressing public health and education should take responsibility for animal welfare concerns within the scope of their focus. Since passage of this law, these government agencies have done just that. In partnership with the police force, the local animal protection organization has been able to investigate a number of cruelty cases and seek prosecution (R. Quintanilla, personal communication with J.F., June 12, 2004). Perhaps the law's most notable success is the fact that the ministry of education has included humane education in the curriculum of schoolchildren. It must be noted, however, that political instability over the years has slowed the progress of improved animal welfare standards.

Although there have been suc-cesses, many animal welfare issues in the country are still waiting to be addressed. The law may be enforced at times in Lima, but enforcement is virtually nonexistent outside the city borders. Communication among officials is weak, and the push for enforcement of law lies primarily with the animal welfare organization and not within the police department. There is little familiarity with the law throughout the rest of the country, and few individuals are willing or able to dedicate their time to these issues. The streets continue to be filled with stray dogs in poor condition; however, with the inclusion of humane education in the curriculum for all of Peru that will reach children from each corner of the country, there is hope that the general welfare of animals in Peru will continue to improve.

Brazil

Brazil has two laws that pertain directly to animal welfare issues. The first is a presidential decree that prohibits animal cruelty, requires adequate care of animals, and discusses punishment for non-compliance (Presidential Decree 24.645, July 10, 1934, President Getulio Vergas). The law provides an extensive list of what is to be considered as cruelty to animals and even includes a section on transport of animals and transport vehicle conditions. The second law (Federal Law 9.605/98—Art. 32. Environmental Crimes Law, 1998) states that anyone who abuses or mistreats, wounds or mutilates a wild, domesticated, or domestic animal, whether native or exotic, will incur a punishment of three months to one year in jail and a fine.

It is fair to say that the early passage of an animal welfare decree was due in large part to influence from citizens around the world who had settled in Brazil. Despite the fact that animal welfare has been on the books in that country for a number of years, many obsta-cles still must be dealt with. Although Brazil is similar in size to the United States, its road structure is quite different, and dissemination of information and communication is difficult. The diversity of the population also presents obstacles, and belief systems with regard to animals vary from village to village. Although the laws may have been present for a long time, their enforcement has not.

Brazil, like Costa Rica and Colombia, benefits from a regional WSPA office that has worked successfully in collaboration with local organizations on a variety of issues. The presence of well-organized local animal welfare organizations has enabled many of the issues to be brought to the forefront of the news, and many of these groups are working on municipal ordinances that will complement and strengthen the country's laws (E. Mac Gregor, WSPA Brazil, personal communication with J.F., June 2, July 2, August 3, 2004).

Chile

Chile has more than two dozen animal protection organizations working on issues ranging from marine mammals to stray dogs. Some groups are working toward banning animal experimentation; others are concerned with the plight of workhorses. Despite the overwhelming presence of animal welfare groups, the country has no national animal welfare law. A coalition has been working unsuccessfully for over ten years to get a particular piece of legislation passed (C. Sprohnle, Agrupacion Cultural Amor a los Animales, personal communication with J.F., May 10, May 11, July 20, 2004). The proposed law has gone through several changes to accommodate various concerns but, as of 2004, without success. It looks much like the animal protection laws in local regions of the country: it covers domestic animals and wildlife, includes animal experimentation, and aims to establish norms to understand, protect, and respect animals as living beings and as part of nature with the goal of providing them with adequate care and avoiding suffering.

The law also aims to include humane education in the national curriculum and provides general guidelines for the care of companion animals. It outlines punishment in terms of fines to be paid or public service. The great challenge has been to identify someone within the government to sponsor the legislation and work for its passage.

Concerns have been raised that once there is an animal welfare law, there will be problems with its enforcement. In most countries, police salaries are low, and the incentives to receive new information and incorporate new practices into the daily job are not there.

Bolivia
Once considered to have the lowest level of awareness of animal welfare issues, Bolivia in 2003–2004 alone prohibited dogfighting and circuses that use wild animals in the city of La Paz. Both efforts were led by the local animal welfare organization that has worked with the government on several programs over the past years (S. Carpio, Animales SOS, personal communication with J.F., July 2, 2004). As of 2004 Bolivia had no national animal welfare legislation, but with the passage of the two municipal ordinances mentioned above, it was clear that animal welfare was starting to capture the attention of government officials. The instability of Bolivia's government has made it difficult in the past to work on such issues, but, it is interesting to note, in 2004, when political instability was at a high, this was clearly not the case. The key to these huge gains in animal welfare was the work of the local animal welfare organization and of several government officials concerned with the issue. Although these are positive outcomes for animal welfare, there

is still the challenge of getting a law actually on the books and a commitment to enforcing that law.

Colombia
Despite the sometimes volatile political situation in Colombia, there is no evidence that politics has impaired efforts to increase the country's animal welfare standards. An animal welfare law was passed a little over a decade ago. The effort was led by a veterinarian and backed by several local animal protection organizations. As in Costa Rica, Colombia enjoys the presence of a regional WSPA office that is able to lend support and act as resource for information for local groups working to effect change. This does not discredit the efforts of and impact that many well-organized and well-run local animal welfare organizations have had on their own. Instead it complements their efforts.

When the Colombian law was passed, the government required that bullfighting and cockfighting be omitted from the text. Local organizations have been working to negotiate prohibitions against these activities. The effort is to include dogfighting, increase fines, and make cruelty toward animals a felony. There have been problems with enforcement of the law, and police officers are reluctant to charge people with animal cruelty (C. Ochoa, Vidanimal, personal communication with J.F., July 29, 2004.)

As it stands, the law states that animals in the national territory have protection against suffering and pain caused directly or indirectly by humans. The law, which covers companion animals, wildlife, and work animals, seeks to prevent pain and suffering, promote health and well-being, ensure good hygiene and appropriate conditions, eradicate animal cruelty, and develop an educational program, among others. The law also sets fines for cruelty and provides a

comprehensive list of acts against animals deemed to be cruel.

Colombia and the organizations working on animal welfare issues have made great strides and achieved some successes. There is still a long road ahead, but these groups have the benefit of having worked on these issues for several years and have seen what has worked and what has not, which will help them determine the next steps.

Asia: Japan
Unlike other countries in its region, Japan enjoys a mid- to high level of animal protection presence, with legislation to support the efforts. However, the legislation is not always enforced consistently.

There is extensive animal welfare legislation, amended in 1999, addressing the proper treatment and care of companion animals. The law requires owners to care for their animals "in a proper manner" and recommends spay/neuter as an answer to overpopulation.

The Law for the Humane Treatment of Animals mandates the establishment of an Animal Welfare Council and requires the government and local public bodies to make an effort to educate the people on the concept of animal welfare. To popularize animal welfare, the legislature designates a "Be Kind to Animals Week." The law also specifically states the punishment for several levels of abuse, all of which involve a fine but no imprisonment. It also provides suggestions for promoters of animal welfare; advising them of effective ways to spread their message (Law for the Humane Treatment and Management of Animals—Law No. 105, October 1973, revised December 2000). The law itself is quite thorough; the problem is that law without enforcement is ineffective.

Little consideration is given to the treatment of farm animals. A related livestock ordinance, The Guidelines for Rearing Industrial Animals, makes recommendations for hygiene and prevention of animal abuse, yet does not specify any penalty for abusers. Livestock animals could be considered as covered under the Law for Humane Treatment of Animals Article 8, which addresses businesses dealing with animals; defines an animal as a mammal, bird, or reptile; but says specifically that it does not include animals on livestock farms (Kishida and Macer 2003). In Article 27, which describes penalties for abuse, several livestock animals are included (Law for the Humane Treatment and Management of Animals—Law No. 105, October 1973, revised December 2000). So the law does protect livestock animals from clear abuse but does not address humane living conditions or humane slaughter (Kishida and Macer 2003).

Despite its advanced law, Japan could use stricter livestock laws and increased enforcement of the companion animal law, although it does show interest in this improvement.

Asia and Africa (excluding Japan and South Africa)

Asia

Asia and Africa, along with most of the member countries of the former Soviet Union, experience the lowest levels of animal protection. Most countries in these regions do not have any animal protection laws, and those that do have extreme problems with enforcement. In Asia, problems tend to stem from lack of provision for stray animals, lack of protection for wild and captive animals, and minimal awareness of animal welfare as a concept. The biggest obstacles in African countries are financial and cultural. In many of these countries there is little concern for the animals, because so many of the people are struggling for survival.

In many Asian countries, particularly Korea, China, Vietnam, and the Philippines, the inhumane slaughter of dogs and cats for the purpose of human consumption is a common practice despite laws against it.

Korea

Although Korea adopted the Korean Animal Protection Law, which should protect dogs and cats from cruelty, in 1991, this law is not often enforced. While it is not an everyday practice, many Koreans feel that eating dog/cat meat is a part of their culture and has many health benefits. Some feel that giving up this tradition would be conforming to Westernization. Others feel that this is a practice that began after the Korean War during a period of widespread starvation. Eating of dog meat grew in prevalence during reconstruction largely due to the claims, made by some, that dog meat had extensive health benefits (Korean Animal Protection Society 2001). Yet the problems lie not in the actual consumption of dog meat but in the cruel manner in which the dogs are kept and slaughtered. The Korean Animal Protection Law states that its purpose is to prevent the mistreatment of animals and to encourage respect for animals (Korean Animal Protection Law, May 7, 1991). This law states that no one may kill an animal in a cruel manner nor may he or she inflict unnecessary pain upon an animal. Despite these provisions, dogs and cats are often killed purposefully in an inhumane manner because some believe that the fear and suffering experienced by the animal enhances the quality of the meat.

A related Korean livestock ordinance makes a distinction between livestock animals and pets. It specifically names animals that are considered as livestock, and except for a three-year period (1975–1978), dogs have not been included in the list of livestock animals (Korean Animal Protection Law, May 7, 1991). Despite this exclusion, eating dog still occurs. Although keeping dogs as pets has become popular, many Koreans also see a distinction between dogs bred as pets and those who are traditionally bred for consumption.

An amendment to the 1991 law, which was to be submitted to the Korean Parliament in July 2004, would make a distinction between dogs bred as pets and all others. The government explained that, by amending the law, it hoped to further protect pets and change the negative perception of foreigners regarding animal abuse in Korea. The proposed amendment included rules regarding vaccination and identification of pets and the management of stray animals and sheltering facilities. The amendment also specified acts of animal abuse to improve the efficiency of the Animal Protection Law. While the amendment could provide further legal protection for pets, some are concerned that distinguishing between pets and other dogs would classify non-pet dogs, by default, as livestock and thereby legalize their consumption (Korean Animal Protection Society 2004).

Philippines

Animals in the Philippines have a similar problem: they are protected by legislation without enforcement. A general Philippine law relating to animals, Republic Act 8485, or Animal Welfare Act of 1998, lists the species considered as livestock. It does not include dogs, although it does mention dogs under "pet animals," which means that dogs cannot be eaten legally. The Metro Manila area has specific legislation banning the killing, serving, or eating of dogs (Republic Act No. 8485: The Animal Welfare Act of 1998).

The Philippine Animal Welfare Act prohibits the torture of animals and/or their killing in an unnecessarily inhumane manner. It also prohibits those who operate a pet store, zoo, or veterinary hospital from owning slaughterhouses. Facilities supporting a pet store, zoo, or veterinary hospital must display on the premises a sign stating that they have established clean and sanitary conditions for the animals and would not cause them pain and/or suffering.

It an attempt to regulate enforcement, the law mandates the creation of a Committee on Animal Welfare, which should be in charge of implementing and enforcing the Act.

China

While law enforcement can be a problem in many Asian countries, in mainland China there is no domestic animal protection law to enforce. Although a draft Animal Welfare Act was being considered in May 2004, Beijing inexplicably withdrew the proposal. This law would have banned organized animal fighting and mandated humane slaughter of livestock (ABC Radio Australia News 2004). The legislation would have been a timely protection for animals in China because the export of animals is increasing, as is the domestic demand for milk and dairy products. China already has laws protecting wildlife and exotic animals, but this would have been the first law to protect domestic and farm animals. The nonexistence of domestic animal welfare legislation makes China a paradox, because the people of China seem to want more advanced animal protection. Despite steep government license fees, keeping dogs and cats as pets in China is becoming more and more popular, especially in metropolitan areas such as Beijing. Yet the 2003 Severe Acute Respiratory System (SARS)] outbreak was a setback for pets in China (Lev 2003). Confusion over how the virus was spread led to rumors that dogs and cats could spread SARS. Out of fear many people abandoned or killed their pets. Some

local government officials responded by saying that any abandoned animals or animals exhibiting signs of illness would be put to death. Some people fearing that their animals would face a cruel death took their pets to be euthanized, instead. Fortunately, not all veterinarians would euthanize pets based on the public fear of SARS, and many disagreed with euthanasia as a way of ensuring pet safety (Epstein 2003).

Further evidence of interest in animal welfare comes from the Chinese public's rejection of bullfighting. When Beijing's Wildlife Park began building a bullfighting stadium in hopes of increasing tourism, the public outcry was so great that officials decided to drop the idea entirely. Protests came not just from animal rights groups but from the community as well. The outcry represents the Chinese people's increased interest in animal protection (Trent 2004b). As the Chinese are exposed to informational resources now more than ever before, often via the Internet, people are engaging in grass-roots actions on a number of issues, one of these being animal welfare. Unfortunately the increased interest in animal welfare has not been reflected through legislation in mainland China.

Taiwan

In contrast to mainland China, Taiwan has comprehensive animal protection legislation. The Taiwan Animal Protection Law, which prohibits the mistreatment of animals in detail, outlaws animal fights, human-animal fighting, or animal fighting as entertainment and prohibits gambling on any animal-related sport, including racing. Abandonment of animals is prohibited, and the law specifies that animals must be provided with a healthy living environment and situation. Provisions for transport of animals is also discussed in detail, mandating such transport take

into consideration the shelter, lighting, temperature, and ventilation involved in the transport (Animal Protection Law; Stray Dog Control in the Republic of China on Taiwan, November 4, 1998).

Under this law, animals are categorized as pets, economic, scientific, or feeder animals. Animals in the pet category may not be killed at will. There are also regulations concerning the treatment of experimental and scientific animals. The number of animals involved and the pain and distress incurred in animal experimentation must be kept to a minimum.

The Taiwan Animal Protection Law also calls for counties and/or municipalities to set up animal shelters to house stray and unwanted animals. As a result, several animal shelters have been built throughout the country; however, the lack of an overall animal control program means these shelters are less than efficient. Despite the law, stray dogs remain a huge problem in Taiwan.

Russia

While the lack of law enforcement has been a problem for some parts of Asia, in Russia the law itself is the problem. In 1998 Russia banned veterinarians from using ketamine to sedate animals, making it nearly impossible for them to perform surgeries without inflicting pain. For years, Russian veterinarians used ketamine legally, and without any interference. Yet in 1998 the Ministry of Agriculture undertook a sweeping review of drugs permitted for use in veterinary medicine. Ketamine didn't make the cut, due only to an oversight (Trent 2004c).

After much protest Russia lifted the ban in 2004. Though this seems to be a step in the right direction, the government still makes it impossible for veterinarians to gain access to ketamine by requiring them to obtain a license for the drug and then refusing to grant them one. Veterinarians who have attempted to access ketamine without a license have been arrested and fined (Trent 2004c).

India

India serves as a good example of a country with strong animal protection laws. As a former British colony, India has in place extensive legislation at the federal and state levels. The main federal law (The Prevention of Cruelty to Animals Act of 1960) includes an array of provisions governing the treatment of nearly every category of animal—domestic, farm, wild, captive, or other. The law's provisions cover proper transport, breeding, and housing of these types of animals.

Each state has equally strict laws that range from governing particular species, such as the Assam Rhinoceros Preservation Act 1954, to covering large groupings of animals, such as the Rajasthan Animals and Birds Sacrifice (Prohibition) Act 1975.

Still in existence today is an Animal Welfare Board of India, a legally constituted body created under the 1960 act that oversees the federal law. In addition, the Indian constitution states,

> It shall be the duty of every citizen of India to protect and improve the natural environment including forest, lakes, rivers, and wildlife, and to have compassion for living creatures. (Constitution of India, Article 51-A 1950, last amended 2002)

However impressive this body of legislation is, it is largely ignored. As India has an immense human population, many of whose members live in extreme poverty, animal protection goes unnoticed, and the laws are rarely enforced.

Africa

The situation for animals in Africa is similar to that in Asia, except that African countries have passed even less animal protection legislation. There is little animal protection activity in any African country, except South Africa. Though most countries have wildlife protection acts, the majority of them have no federal protection laws for companion or domestic animals; if they do have legislation, enforcement is a problem. There are few animal protection groups, and even in areas where they work, their visibility and influence is limited.

Uganda and Botswana

Uganda has been working over the last few years on revising its 1958 Animals Act. The government is gathering information regarding

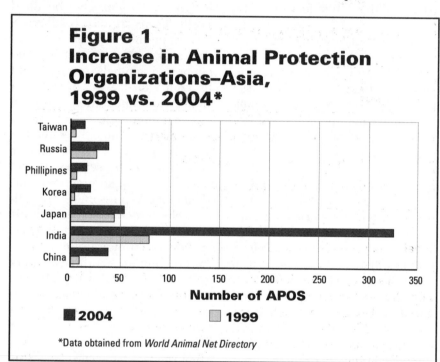

Figure 1
Increase in Animal Protection Organizations–Asia, 1999 vs. 2004*

Number of APOS

■ 2004   ▢ 1999

*Data obtained from *World Animal Net Directory*

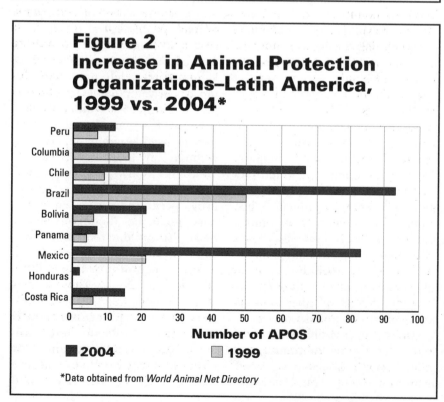

Figure 2
Increase in Animal Protection Organizations–Latin America, 1999 vs. 2004*

Number of APOS

■ 2004   ▢ 1999

*Data obtained from *World Animal Net Directory*

the improvements needed and has asked the Uganda SPCA for its input several times. Botswana, too, is looking to revise its animal laws. The Parliament of Botswana is considering a revised version of the 1977 Cruelty to Animals Law. A proposal written by a British Consul in 1999 would update the 1977 law. The proposal is much longer and more thorough than the original, but no decision has been made yet about whether this revised version will be passed (K. Menczer, Uganda SPCA, personal communication with S.E., June 14, 2004).

Kenya

Kenya also has a law protecting domestic animals, known as CAP 360 (Prevention of Cruelty to Animals, CAP 360, 1983) and based on the U.K. Animal Protection Act. This law is often difficult to enforce, despite the efforts of the many animal protection organizations in Kenya. Lack of enforcement is often due to police and prosecutors' ignorance of the law. Getting animal abuse cases through the court is often a very slow process, and penalties are minimal. Kenya has an Animal Transportation Act that is policed by the Kenya SPCA (KSPCA), with branches in Nairobi and Mombassa. This law tends to be difficult to enforce due to the size of the country (K. Menczer, personal communication with S.E., July 14, 2004). A common infraction of this law is the shipment of camels from Arab states to Kenya. Often the camels are not provided with adequate food and water for their long journey. Thirst and hunger lead camels to stampede, causing many injuries. More recently, the KSPCA has been able to work with the shippers to ensure proper care for the camels, and the camel shippers have shown greater willingness to abide by the Animal Transportation Act.

Kenya has a relatively effective humane slaughter act, which requires that all food chain animals be stunned before slaughter. The

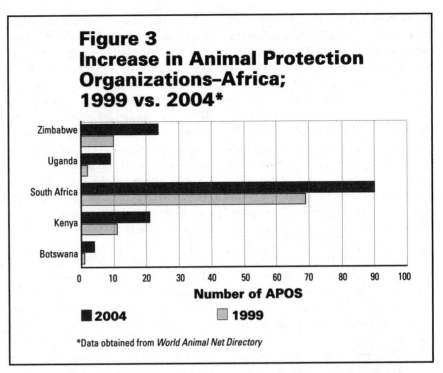

Figure 3
Increase in Animal Protection Organizations–Africa; 1999 vs. 2004*

Number of APOS

■ 2004   ▨ 1999

*Data obtained from *World Animal Net Directory*

KSPCA, which polices this act, repairs and supplies ammunition for the captive bolt stunners used in the slaughterhouses. It also does periodic spot-checking to ensure the law is being enforced (A. Kahn, executive officer, Kenya SPCA, personal communication with S.E., June 17, 2004).

(Other countries, such as Uganda and Egypt are addressing the livestock issue. Several humane organizations have emerged recently in Uganda and are working toward the development of a relationship with Islamic elders to introduce a pre-stun concept in the slaughtering process that could fall within Islamic religious parameters. Currently, the halal method of slaughter does not provide for desensitizing or pre-stunning of animals. One of the authors [N.W.T.] reports that these humane organizations hope that, by working together, they will be able to harmonize religious and cultural practices with humane considerations. There had been little animal protection structure in Egypt, but there has been an enormous growth in the past several years. In 2004 several organiza-

tions joined forces to establish an Egyptian Federation for Animal Welfare and are working on developing a draft of animal welfare legislation for Egypt. This group is striving to address many different animal protection issues, but its main focus is on combating the existing barbaric methods of livestock slaughter and of companion animal population control. It is also actively developing a website that would promote sharing of information and resources for newly emerging animal protection groups in the Middle East and North Africa.)

Zimbabwe

In Zimbabwe, enforcement of animal protection laws is nearly impossible due to civil and political unrest. Although Zimbabwe has extensive protection legislation, the concept of animal welfare no longer carries the weight it once did. It is a classic example of a regional paradox; because of the country's history as a former British colony, logic would lead to the conclusion that it would exhibit the first or second level of animal protection. It does indeed have animal legislation, underpinned by British law, that was heavily enforced until political strife shifted political priorities. Recent civil unrest clearly has had a negative impact on animal welfare in Zimbabwe. Many people have lost their land and their homes as part of a political decision to seize and redistribute lands. Because the lands are taken violently, people often have fled their homes and left behind their animals. The abandoned animals, which include pet and farm animals, face starvation, chaos, and, often, abuse. Because private reserves have been seized as well, wildlife has been left susceptible to poachers (Collier 2004).

The high rate of poverty and unemployment in Zimbabwe, added to the political instability, has caused deplorable living conditions for humans. When people are struggling for survival, they cannot feasibly care for the animals. Also, because of the depletion of natural resources, wildlife has become a viable source of food. The Zimbabwe

SPCA is doing what it can to protect the animals, but even with the support of the Zimbabwean police, it faces suspicion and obstinacy from the Zimbabwean militia. Animals have been abused and tortured to illustrate political philosophies. Though the fate of animals was once a high priority to Zimbabwe, and would most likely be again when the country regains stability, it will surely take many years to regain the high standard of animal protection the country once enjoyed.

There have been some improvements in conditions for animals in Africa, and several countries are looking into updating their laws. However, for the laws and protection for animals to increase, there needs to be a change in the public view of animals. At present, dogs usually are kept for guarding purposes rather than as pets and are seen as disposable. Many people have had no education on the proper care for an animal and think that dogs can find food and water on their own. It is also unusual for people to spay or

neuter their animals, which leads to an overpopulation problem.

Another obstacle to improvements for animals is the conflict between land conservation and the human need for land. Because of the high rate of poverty and depletion of natural resources, indigenous peoples feel they should be able to use the land and the wildlife for their own survival and sustenance. This is especially the case with tribes that have traditionally used animals as a food source. Most African countries have laws that prohibit hunting and sale of wildlife, but these often are disregarded to feed families and sometimes to gain income from illegal trade. The laws are difficult to enforce and are usually not a priority among other issues in Africa.

Conclusion

The state of animal protection in Latin America, Asia, and Africa depends on each country's economic status, combined with the

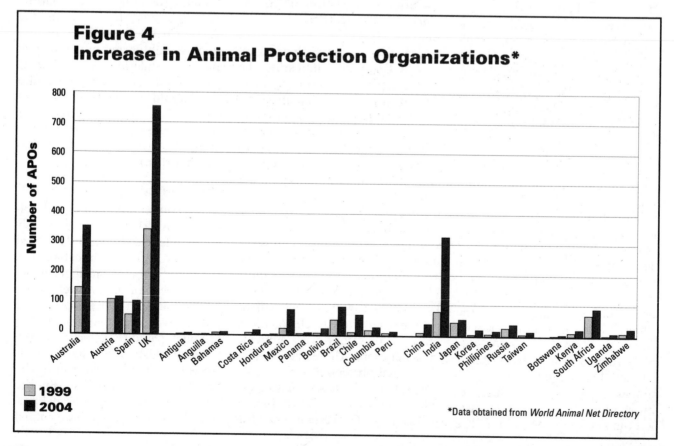

Figure 4
Increase in Animal Protection Organizations*

Data obtained from World Animal Net Directory

cultural and sociopolitical issues unique to each. In regions where animal protection traditionally has not been a concern, such as is typically the case in parts of Africa and Asia, there is a long way to go. For the most part, African legislation regarding domestic animals is rare, and when it does exist, it is rarely enforced. Asian animal protection legislation exists at about the same level as in Africa, though a few more countries do have laws in place. Challenges to enforcement tend to be cultural rather than economic. South Africa and the Caribbean, which have the highest presence of animal protection of regions under review, still have problems with enforcement. Central and South America and Japan fall at about the mid-level in regard to animal welfare presence, but they have demonstrated interest in improving and enforcing their laws.

The increased presence of animal welfare organizations in all of these regions is the first step in raising awareness (Figures 1–4). Human health issues and tourist reactions are key drivers in improvements in animal welfare, in passing animal welfare legislature, and in making animal welfare an important government issue. To achieve model animal protection, the countries of Latin America, Africa, and Asia must overcome the political and cultural obstacles unique to their regions that prevent animal protection from becoming a priority.

Note

[1] It should be noted that the mere existence of law does not translate into enforcement of the law: Japan, a relatively wealthy country, has legislation but lacks enforcement, thus its level of animal protection falls well below those of other countries with similar level of economic development, such as the United States, the United Kingdom, and Australia.

Literature Cited

ABC Radio Australia News. 2004. *Beijing rejects animal welfare laws* (19:14:15). May 17. *http://www.abc.net.au/ra/new stories/RANewsStories_110993 1.htm.*

Abend, L., and G. Fingree. 2004. Abandoned pets find haven. *Christian Science Monitor.* June 23: *http://www.csmonitor.com/2004/0623/p15s02-woeu.html.*

Appleby, M.C. 2003. Farm disease crises in the United Kingdom: Lessons to be learned. In *The State of the Animals II: 2003*, ed. D.J. Salem and A.N. Rowan, 149–157. Washington, D.C.: Humane Society Press.

Associated Press. 2004. Austria puts bite on cruelty. *The Dallas Morning News,* May 28: 28A.

Collier, P. 2004. Zimbabwe animals rescued after farmers flee. Animal News Center (ANC), January 31. *http://www.buzzle.com/editorials/text1-31-2004-50049.asp.*

Epstein, G. 2003. Amid SARS epidemic, China panics over pets. *The Baltimore Sun,* May 6. *http://www.animalschina.org/english/news/2_news_05.htm.*

Irwin, P.G. 2003. A strategic review of international animal protection. In *The state of the animals II: 2003*, ed. D.J. Salem and A.N. Rowan, 1–8. Washington, D.C.: Humane Society Press.

Kishida, S., and D. Macer. 2003. Peoples' views on farm animal welfare in Japan. In *Asian bioethics in the twenty-first century,* ed. S. Song, Y. Koo, and D.R.J. Macer. Eubios Ethics Institute. http://www.biol.tsukuba.ac.jp/~macer/ABC4.htm.

Korean Animal Protection Society. 2001. *Animal issues: The treatment of dogs in Korea.* *http://www.koreananimals.org/dogs.htm.*

———. 2004. Animal protection law: Korean animal protection law. *http://www.koreananimals.org/dogs.htm.*

Lev, M.A. 2003. SARS rumors doom dogs in China. *Chicago Tribune,* May 7. *http://www.homeagainid.com/news/article.cfm?storyid=9197.*

Trent, N. 2004a. Caribbean animal laws: Overview, what works and what doesn't. PowerPoint presentation, May 23.

———. 2004b. No bull: Barcelona condemns bullfighting as the blood sport loses favor. *http://www.hsus.org/ace/21160.*

———. 2004c. Russia's crackdown on ketamine smacks of a more repressive era. *http://www.hsus.org/ace/21425.*

Progress in Animal Legislation: Measurement and Assessment

7

CHAPTER

Andrew N. Rowan and Beth Rosen

Introduction

British philosopher John Stuart Mill once said: "All great movements experience three stages: Ridicule. Discussion. Adoption." (in Wiebers, Gillan, and Wiebers 2000, 169). As movements reach the level of adoption into mainstream society, they acquire a certain level of legitimacy, often reinforced through the passage of legislation that validates the fundamental principles they promote. Contemporary theorist Bill Moyer's (1987) conceptualization of a social movement's evolution adds greater complexity to Mill's assertion.

Moyer asserts that a social movement has eight stages, which operate cyclically (although the various goals within the movement may be at different stages at any one time). The first three stages cover the early organization and recruitment of adherents. The movement then typically gains momentum from a "trigger event"—one that brings public awareness to a social problem—that pushes the movement into stage four. In this stage, the media "discovers" the movement, and the wider public begins to attend to the movement's issues. This is a relatively short phase (for the modern phase of the animal protection movement, it lasted for

about fifteen years, until 1990) (Herzog 1995). In stages five and six, some movement followers enter the dead-end phase five. These followers perceive the lack of major legislative change emanating from the media attention as a failure and either burn out or develop much more aggressive techniques. Stage six is peopled by those followers and organizations that take advantage of the media attention to get at least some of the issues onto the public agenda, leading to some concrete achievements. Ultimately Moyer defines social movements as "collective actions in which the populace is alerted, educated, and mobilized, over the years and decades, to challenge the power holders and the whole society to redress social problems or grievances and restore critical social values" (Moyer 1987, 3).

The animal protection movement has historically relied on legislation as a key element to promote and enact its reform agenda. Moyer's model helps to place and analyze when, why, and how the movement (or parts of it) gets its issues onto the public agenda. Over the years, animal organizations have committed significant effort and resources to the passage of leg-

islation leading to greater legal protection for animals. However, some eras have led to the passage of more laws than have other eras. From 1900 to 1950, only one federal law addressing animals was passed, although individual states did pass or amend animal protection laws during this period. Table 1 lists the federal laws passed and amended that deal with animal protection, demonstrating the considerable success and increase in political influence that the animal movement has enjoyed in the second half of the twentieth century.

Federal law is only one dimension of the movement's legislative reform, however. Its political influence has reached not only Congress but also state legislatures, which are also much more active in addressing animal issues. One of the more significant accomplishments for the animal protection movement has been the passage over the last two decades of felony-level animal-cruelty statutes that permit certain abuses against animals to be prosecuted as felonies rather than as misdemeanors, as in the past. Nine states passed felony animal-cruelty laws between 1994 and 1997 (Table 2) and the pace accelerated between 1998 and

Table 1
Federal Legislative Summary, 1958–2003

Year	Federal Legislation Passed/*Amended*
1958	**Humane Slaughter Act**
1959	Wild Horses Act
1962	Bald and Golden Eagle Act
1966	Endangered Species Act **Laboratory Animal Welfare Act**
1970	Animal Welfare Act *(amendments to Laboratory Animal Welfare Act)*
1971	Wild Free-Roaming Horse and Burro Act
1972	**Marine Mammal Protection Act**
1973	*Endangered Species Act amendments* CITES
1976	*Animal Welfare Act amendments* Horse Protection Act Fur Seal Act
1978	*Humane Slaughter Act amendments*
1985	*Animal Welfare Act amendments (focus on alternatives and pain and distress)* PHS Policy on animals in research revised
1990	*Animal Welfare Act amendments*
1992	Wild Bird Conservation Act
1993	International Dolphin Conservation Act Driftnet Fishery Conservation Act NIH Revitalization [Reauthorization] Act mandates development of research methods using no animals
1995	USDA ends face branding
1999	Ban on the interstate shipment of "crush videos"
2000	Chimpanzee Health Improvement, Maintenance, and Protection Act
2002	Dog and Cat Protection Act Interagency Coordinating Committee on the Validation of Alternative Methods (ICCVAM) Authorization Act Safe Air Travel for Animals Act Ban on interstate transportation of birds and dogs for fighting purposes
2003	Captive Exotic Animal Protection Act

Source: Unti and Rowan 2001, 34–37; HSUS 2004.

Even with the greater momentum in the states to enact state felony anti-cruelty legislation, other legislative initiatives were not successful. The animal protection movement began to adopt a new tactic, the citizen-initiative ("direct democracy") process, in the twenty or so states that allowed such petitions. Between 1990 and 2002, twenty animal protection initiatives were passed, and six anti-animal measures were defeated. Overall, thirty-nine initiatives that affected animal protection were introduced during the period and, in twenty-six cases, the result was a win for animal protection.

However, passage of new legislation does not necessarily provide satisfactory protections for animals. The new legislation must be supported by adequate funding and effective enforcement. Little if any legislation is perfect, and usually continuing efforts to improve a statute will be needed.

As the animal movement has gained more political authority and public acceptance, it needs better ways to assess and follow its progress—or lack thereof—towards its goals. In this era, in which nonprofits and funding agencies are demanding better measures of effectiveness, the animal movement needs to examine how it looks at the progress it is (or is not) making in gaining better legal protection for animals.

Federal Legislation

Between 1958 and 1972 three major pieces of federal animal protection legislation were passed, the Humane Slaughter Act (1958), the Animal Welfare Act (1966), and the Marine Mammal Protection Act (1972). These serve as the basis for the following analysis. Given that before 1958, the last federal animal protection legislation that had passed was in

2001, as an additional sixteen states adopted felony legislation. As of 2003 forty-one states and the District of Columbia had felony level animal-cruelty statutes on their books, and Nebraska, Montana, Connecticut, Texas, Nevada, Virginia, and Colorado had upgraded their original felony animal-cruelty laws.

1906, these three legislative victories, plus the other legislation listed in Table 1, demonstrate the rise of the animal movement from political oblivion in the first half of the twentieth century to a position where lawmakers would listen if the context and the proposal were timely and supported by the societal and political mood. (The Endangered Species Act was also passed during this period and was supported by many animal protection organizations, but it is not strictly animal protection legislation, that is, it does not seek to prevent or prohibit animal distress or suffering caused by the human use of animals.)

The Humane Slaughter Act (HSA) established a very basic humane standard of care for farm animals during slaughter (namely, that they should be made insensible to pain). The Animal Welfare Act mandates humane standards for the handling, treatment, and transportation of "any warm blooded animal used for research, testing, experimentation, or exhibition purposes," although farm animals used in food production and birds, mice, and rats used in research are excluded from its coverage. The Marine Mammal Protection Act imposes a moratorium on "harassing, hunting, capturing, or killing all marine mammals" (Animal Welfare Institute 1990, 190).

Humane Methods of Slaughter Act: An Assessment

In the early days of The Humane Society of the United States (HSUS), after its split from the American Humane Association (AHA) in 1954, Fred Myers, HSUS president, was determined to instill a broader vision of the importance of nationally organized initiatives and to lead local organizations in setting their sights on achieving larger strategic objectives (HSUS 1956). One of the

points of tension in the internal AHA schism concerned the pre-slaughter handling and slaughter of animals used for food. Therefore, it is not surprising that the first national campaign that the newly formed HSUS launched focused on that issue. During 1955 and 1956, The HSUS diverted every available dollar from its budget into the drive for slaughterhouse reform and generated widespread publicity on the issue. Myers lined up significant sources of public support for the HSA and testified on its behalf in 1958, the year in which it passed (Unti 2004).

Myers took great encouragement from the fact that, between 1954 and 1958, the animal protection movement had united to achieve passage of a federal humane slaughter law that would spare approximately 100 million animals a year from pain and suffering. It was also a vindication of the vision that had driven the formation of The HSUS, namely, the idea "that hundreds of local societies could lift their eyes from local problems to a great national cruelty" (Unti 2004, 6). Passage of the HSA represented the first time since enactment of the 28-Hour Law (regulating how long livestock could be transported without being given a food and water rest) more than fifty years earlier that the federal government had agreed to address an animal welfare issue. By and large, animal protection in the 1950s was perceived to be the domain of the state legislatures (e.g., anti-cruelty and related legislation).

The HSA required slaughter plants selling meat to the U.S. government (roughly 80 percent of all U.S. meatpacking plants) to abide by humane methods of slaughter set by the federal government. The U.S. government was the largest purchaser of meat, buying $300 million worth annually (Unti 2004, 45). According to the law, cattle, sheep, swine, goats, horses, mules, and other equines must be slaugh-

tered humanely, usually by rendering these animals "insensible to pain by a single blow or gunshot or an electrical, chemical, or other means that is rapid and effective, before being shackled, hoisted, thrown, cast, or cut" (7 U.S.C.A. §1902). One loophole in the law permitted the armed forces to purchase meat that did not have to be certified as humanely slaughtered

Table 2 States with Felony-Level Anti-Cruelty Statutes

Year Enacted	State(s)
1986	Wisc.
1987	
1988	Calif.
1989	Fla.
1990	
1991	
1992	Neb.
1993	Mont.
1994	Del., Mo., N.H., Wash.
1995	La., Ore., Pa.
1996	Conn.
1997	Tex.
1998	Ind., N.C., Vt.
1999	Ariz., Ill., Nev., N.Y., Va.
2000	Ala., Ga., Iowa, S.C.
2001	D.C., Md., Minn., N.J., Tenn.
2002	Colo., Ohio, Me.
2003	Ky., W.V., Wy.

Source: *www.hsus.org*: Legislation and Laws—Citizen Lobbyist Center.

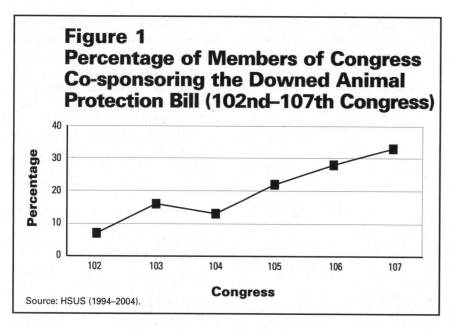

Figure 1
Percentage of Members of Congress Co-sponsoring the Downed Animal Protection Bill (102nd–107th Congress)

Source: HSUS (1994–2004).

as long as the purchased amount did not exceed $2,500. While it is unclear exactly how much meat fell into this category, "a considerable portion of that volume [was] understood to be acquired in lots of $2,500 or less"(Animal Welfare Institute 1990, 55).

Under the concerted efforts of Sen. Robert Dole (R-KS) and Rep. George E. Brown (D-CA), the HSA was amended and renamed the Humane Methods of Slaughter Act (HMSA) in 1978. With this strengthened law, not only plants that sold meat to the government but also all plants that wanted to be U.S. Department of Agriculture (USDA)-certified had to follow the humane methods of slaughter guidelines. Federal inspectors had the authority to shut down inhumane slaughter operations until they were modified to comply with humane standards (although such action was very rare). Any meat imported into the United States had to be from humanely slaughtered animals. In 2002 the HMSA was amended further to request that the Secretary of Agriculture report to Congress on the condition of nonambulatory livestock (downed animals) in slaughter houses.

"Downer" animals had become a focus of increased animal protec-

tion concern well before 2002. Since the 102nd Congress in 1994, animal protection groups had lobbied for passage of the Downed Animal Protection Act, which would end the slaughter of downed animals for human consumption. The bill requires that any downed animal be euthanized before it reaches the slaughterhouse. A decade after its first introduction in Congress, the Downed Animal Protection Act was added to the 2004 agriculture appropriations bill, only to be removed at the last minute. Shortly thereafter, when the first case of so-called mad cow disease was discovered in the United States, Agriculture Secretary Ann Veneman announced that downed animals would be banned from the human food chain. While this administrative reaction could be construed as something of a victory for animal advocates, as of 2005, the movement was still pushing for passage of the Downed Animal Protection Act to give greater permanency to the existing administrative ban.

In assessing progress on the downed animal issue, a more nuanced measure is needed than simple passage of the bill into law. One possibility is to follow the level of support via the number of cospon-

sors who sign on in each Congress. Figure 1 illustrates the steady increase in the proportion of members of Congress who have cosponsored the Downed Animal Protection Act, showing how support for the legislation has risen over time.

While this increase may be a measure of the effectiveness and impact of lobbying by animal activists, other forces are at work as well. In *The Washington Post* Warrick (2001) exposed the abusive violations of the HMSA in various slaughter facilities, describing in detail how cattle remained alive throughout the slaughter process. Relying on the accounts of slaughter facility workers, inspectors, and technicians, Warrick also described how such facilities were allowed to continue to operate despite being cited for numerous violations of the HMSA.

The *Washington Post* article prompted Sen. Robert Byrd (D-WV) to deliver a speech on July 9, 2001, in the U.S. Senate asking for stricter oversight of U.S. slaughter facilities. In this passionate speech, the first ever of its kind on farm animals, Byrd exclaimed: "The law clearly requires that these poor creatures be stunned and rendered insensitive to pain before this process begins. Federal law is being ignored. Animal cruelty abounds" (*Congressional Record 2001*, S7311). Between 2001 and 2004, $1 million was appropriated to the USDA to hire seventeen regional managers to oversee enforcement of the HMSA, as was an additional $5 million to hire at least fifty inspectors to work solely on ensuring compliance with the law (HSUS 2004).

Even taking into account the 1958 passage of the humane slaughter legislation, its subsequent amendments, and the increase in funding for it, the structural problems with enforcement of the Act remain in place. As the animal movement continues to investigate slaughter facilities and gain political ground, it presses to have the HMSA amended again to include poultry under its humane standards. In 2004 People for the Ethical Treatment of Animals (PETA) conducted an undercover investigation of a slaughter facility. The findings of the investigation, including chickens being kicked and thrown against a wall, reached major media outlets throughout the country. The video footage not only prompted public outrage, but it also created an opportunity for the movement to urge Congress to amend the HMSA. Following the PETA investigation, The HSUS announced a campaign to lobby for the inclusion of poultry in the HMSA and offered a petition for individuals to sign asking Congress for this inclusion. As of mid-2005, more than eighty thousand signatures had been collected.

Despite the recent success in obtaining legislation addressing humane handling and slaughter of livestock, there is considerable room for improvement, not only in the legislative underpinnings of humane handling and slaughter but also in the enforcement of the existing but relatively rudimentary legislation dealing with farm animal protection (especially important given the 8 billion animals a year raised and slaughtered in the United States). Everybody can agree that animals should not be badly handled and tormented when they are transported and slaughtered. However, the law is still too narrowly focused (it does not cover religious slaughter and poultry, for example) and it has been enforced poorly from its implementation. For example, USDA stations its inspectors in slaughter facilities to inspect and certify that animals are slaughtered humanely, but these inspectors receive their USDA paychecks via the companies they inspect and are "embedded" in those companies in ways that make

it very difficult for them to take effective action if they see problems with the slaughter process.

Marine Mammal Protection Act: Assessment of Progress

In 1972 the Marine Mammal Protection Act (MMPA) was passed. This law imposed a moratorium on the "harassing, hunting, capturing, or killing" of all marine mammals. The Secretary of Commerce may grant permits to allow the taking and importation of marine mammals: (1) for scientific research or public display; (2) as incidental bycatch in commercial fishing; and (3) in accord with sound principles of resource protection and conservation (16 U.S.C. §§ 1361–1421h). In 1992 the Dolphin Conservation Act was added to the Marine Mammal Protection Act, banning certain tuna-harvesting practices that threatened dolphin populations. The law was amended again in 1994 to reduce the incidental taking of marine mammals during commercial fishing activities.

The MMPA is a relatively comprehensive law from the perspective of animal advocates, and the United States is one of the few countries with such a strong law. The law does include certain exemptions to the moratorium, however, such as capturing marine animals for public display, even when the educational value, the basis for the exemption, is in dispute. The law embodies de facto credibility for educational purposes; a marine mammal facility is not required to show how its exhibit is educational. Plus, there are no explicit standards for keeping such animals, and the standards that do exist are difficult to enforce. Furthermore, the law was weakened when it was reauthorized in 1994. Before 1994 one needed explicit permission to import or export a marine mam-

mal, but, after reauthorization, export permits were no longer necessary.

Animal Welfare Act: Assessment of Progress

Even before closing the HSA campaign in 1958, The HSUS had begun to turn its attention to the suffering of animals in research, testing, and education, joining the Animal Welfare Institute in a campaign to reform practices in the country's laboratories.

Generally speaking, the Animal Welfare Act (AWA), enforced by USDA, establishes the standards that govern the humane handling, care, treatment, and transportation of animals by dealers, research facilities, and exhibitors and also sets a standard by which animals are handled for transportation in commerce. While the law defines "animal" as any warm-blooded animal used for research, testing, experimentation, or exhibition purposes, or as a pet, it excludes horses not used for research purposes, farm animals, and birds, mice, and rats used in research (U.S.C. §§ 2131–2159). It also prohibits interstate transportation of animals, including live birds used for fighting purposes.

The Laboratory Animal Welfare Act was passed in 1966 "to provide humane standards for dogs, cats, primates, rabbits, hamsters, and guinea pigs in animal dealers' premises and in laboratories prior to experimental use of animals" (Animal Welfare Institute 1990, 77). It was later amended in 1970 (when it was renamed the Animal Welfare Act) and amended further in 1976, 1985, 1990, and 2002. In 1970 the amendments required that the humane standards must be applied not only before the experimental use of animals but also throughout the entire stay of animals in laboratories. The amended law applied to all warm-blooded

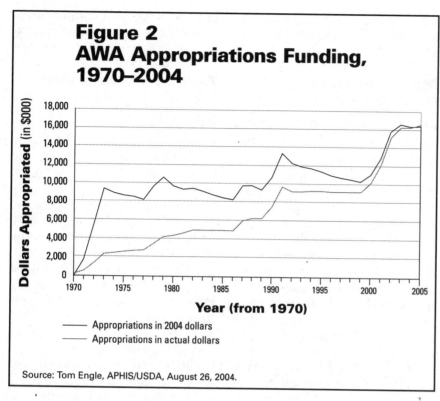

Figure 2
AWA Appropriations Funding, 1970–2004

Dollars Appropriated (in $000)

Year (from 1970)

—— Appropriations in 2004 dollars
—— Appropriations in actual dollars

Source: Tom Engle, APHIS/USDA, August 26, 2004.

animals determined by the Secretary of Agriculture as being used or intended for use in experimentation or exhibition except horses not used in research and farm animals used in food and fiber research.

In 1976 the law was amended to require research laboratories to pay similar fines as those for animal exhibitors and dealers who violated the standards set by the AWA. A provision was added to prohibit interstate transportation of dogs used for animal-fighting ventures. In 1985, in response to several public scandals about the mistreatment of laboratory animals in research projects, the guidelines regarding standards of care and alleviation of pain and distress were made more specific. (For example, the law required that the pain and distress suffered by laboratory animals be reduced, and that psychological well-being be enhanced by providing adequate exercise for dogs and an enriched physical environment for primates.) The AWA was amended again in 1990 to establish a holding period for dogs and cats at shelters and other holding facilities before sale

to dealers; in addition, dealers had to provide written certification to the recipient regarding each animal's background.

In 1989 The HSUS and the Animal Legal Defense Fund (ALDF) resorted to litigation to reverse USDA's administrative exclusion of rats, mice, and birds from regulatory coverage by the AWA. The litigation asked the U.S. District Court to force USDA to protect all warm-blooded animals used in research laboratories. Although the district court sided with the petitioners and found that exclusion of rats, mice, and birds from coverage was an arbitrary and capricious action by USDA, the appeals court later ruled that the animal protection groups did not have legal standing to sue in federal court to force USDA to change its decision.

In 1999 the American Anti-Vivisection Society (AAVS) filed a new lawsuit on the issue. One year later the court found that it had standing to sue for injunctive relief. At this point, USDA decided to negotiate with the AAVS and reportedly agreed to promulgate regulations

that would cover birds, rats, and mice used in research. This development caused considerable alarm among the medical research lobby, which was able to have a rider inserted into a federal appropriations bill that forbade USDA to use any federal funds to promulgate such regulations. In 2002 the particularly powerful senior senator from North Carolina, Jesse Helms, inserted an amendment into the farm bill that permanently excluded rats, mice, and birds used in research from AWA oversight. This development indicated that, although the animal protection movement has gained political influence and public support, the research lobby still has the ability to get a few key politicians to listen to its concerns. To date there are no indications that the movement will have sufficient influence to reverse this loss because the public is not that strongly moved by concern for the welfare of mice, rats, and birds.

In 2002 an amendment was added to prohibit interstate transportation of live birds for fighting purposes. This amendment was intended to hamper the illegal cockfighting industry as well as cockfighting activities in the last two U.S. states, Louisiana and New Mexico, where it remained legal as of mid-2005. Since the amendment was passed, several cockfighting pits have been shut down. But part of the original amendment that would have established felony jail penalties for engaging in an animal fight was dropped during the conference committee discussion of the 2002 farm bill (to which the cockfighting AWA amendment was attached). In 2003 and 2005, the animal protection movement continued its efforts on animal fighting, and the Animal Fighting Prohibition Act was introduced authorizing felony penalties for animal fighting as well as a ban on the interstate commerce of cockfighting implements.

The animal movement has argued that the AWA has not been enforced adequately since it was passed. Part of the problem has been a lack of resources. In the past ten to twenty years, an unlikely coalition of animal protection and research defense groups has been established to press for larger budgets for AWA enforcement. This is one of those areas where everybody perceives a benefit from more effective and more consistent enforcement. The AWA enforcement budget is shown in Figure 2 (the budget in actual dollars is provided on one line; the budget in inflation-adjusted dollars on the other line). The inflation-adjusted column indicates that real funding for AWA enforcement increased in two distinct periods. From 1989 to 1992 funding increased from about $9 million to $12 million, and from 2000 to 2003 funding increased again, from approximately $11 million to $16 million.

The 81 percent increase in actual dollars (or the 50 percent increase in inflation-adjusted dollars) appropriated for AWA enforcement from 1999 to 2003 has arguably led to more effective oversight by USDA inspectors of the approximately ten thousand sites (including research institutes, zoos, puppy mills, circuses and other exhibitors, and commercial breeders) because of the hiring of more than forty additional inspectors (HSUS 2004). However, the effectiveness of enforcement is not simply a measure of how many inspectors there are. From a perspective outside the Animal Care section in USDA/APHIS (Animal and Plant Health Inspection Service), it would appear that enforcement of the AWA (and the morale of the Animal Care staff) was more effective at the end of the 1990s than it is today. Certainly, the information mandated under the AWA is much less available today, despite expansion of the World Wide Web.

Thus, developments under the AWA represent a mixed outcome. The animal movement can point to changes that reflect broader coverage and more effective enforcement, but there have also been setbacks (such as the rats, mice, and birds issue). The movement still has ambitions to expand coverage of the AWA. There is no specific language in the AWA that addresses the practice of mass commercial breeding in puppy mills, for example, and guidelines for handling repeat violators of basic humane standards (e.g., adequate veterinary care, shelter, food, and sanitation) are inadequate. As a result, some puppy mills that have been cited more than once for AWA violations are still in business. The animal protection community lobbied (first in the 107th congressional session and again in the 108th session) for the introduction of the Puppy Protection Act. The Puppy Protection Act would reduce the number of times a female dog may be whelped during a twenty-four-month period, prevent females under one year old from being bred, and provide stricter penalties for puppy mills violating the AWA more than once in at least eight months.

Comparing the Political Impact of the Animal Movement

While the 1950s and 1960s were decades of growing political clout, Table 3 compares the legislative output on behalf of animals for the five-year period 1999–2003 with the five-year period 1979–1983. It is apparent that there has been more success in the most recent five-year period across most species groups, with the possible exception of wildlife. However, two of the four successes on behalf of wildlife from 1979 to 1983 are more accurately described as conservation rather than animal protection measures. While the accomplishments listed between 1979 and 1983 are exhaustive (not much occurred, even though debate on several critical issues from the welfare of laboratory animals to those of horses used in the racing industry could constitute what Mill defined as the "discussion" stage of a movement's development), the 1999–2003 accomplishments listed are, from a subjective viewpoint, not an exhaustive listing of legislative accomplishments. There are still more of them, however, than in the period in the early eighties.

It should be noted that a discrepancy remains among the recent federal accomplishments. Some accomplishments—the Animal Fighting Act and the additional funding for the AWA, both the result of the movement's determination—indicate that the animal protection movement is growing strong. But some accomplishments, such as the Veneman decision regarding downed animals or passage of the Captive Exotic Animal Protection Act (CEAPA), were driven by events that originated outside the movement's planned campaign activities. If mad cow disease had not spread to the United States, downers would likely have continued to be used in the food chain, despite the repeated efforts of animal protection lobbyists to stop the practice. In 2003 the captive exotic animal issue—where the animal movement sought to ban the keeping of exotic animals, such as lions, tigers, jaguars, and cougars as pets—gained national attention when Roy Horn, of the famous Las Vegas entertainment duo Siegfried and Roy, was mauled by one of his own tigers during a show. This event, reinforced when a private citizen was mauled by a pet tiger he was keeping in his small Harlem apartment, received heavy media coverage and stimulated passage of the CEAPA.

Table 3
Comparative Analysis of Federal Accomplishments

Major Federal Accomplishments

	1979–1983	1999–2003
Animal Welfare Act	• Provision on marine mammal care standards added	• USDA AWA enforcement budget boosted by ca. 50 percent • Interstate commerce in birds and dogs used in animal fighting prohibited
Companion Animals		• Banned dog and cat fur products
Cruelty Issues		• Banned "crush videos" (where small animals are tortured/crushed to death)
Farm Animals		• Obtained additional $6 million for enforcement of Humane Slaughter Act • Banned the use of downer cattle for human consumption • Obtained $703,000 for hoop barns for pig raising
Animals in Research		• Passed legislation authorizing the Interagency Coordinating Committee for the Validation of Alternative Methods (ICCVAM) • Passed legislation authorizing a national sanctuary system for retired laboratory chimpanzees
Wildlife	• Passed Alaska Lands bill—designating more than 100 million acres in Alaska as parks or wildlife refuges • Added Marine Mammal Protection Act regulations • National Park Service published final regulations banning trapping on some lands	• Banned commerce in big cats for the pet trade • Banned practice of cutting fins off sharks and discarding their bodies at sea while still alive

Source: Internal HSUS documents

State Legislation

While it is relatively simple to track the growth of animal protection legislation at the federal level (there are only two legislative bodies and one executive), tracking and evaluating legislative advances in fifty states is much more difficult and beyond our capacity for a detailed analysis in this relatively brief chapter. Therefore, we have chosen to focus on one particular area of animal protection legislation, the passage of felony-level penalties as part of state anti-cruelty laws.

For most of the twentieth century, only a handful of states included felony-level penalties in their anti-cruelty legislation. In the mid-1980s, animal protection organizations began to highlight the link between cruelty to animals and other forms of human violence (the name of the long-established HSUS program on this issue, "First Strike," reflects the idea that the animal is the first victim in a household to be abused). The fact that animal cruelty or abuse is a potential indicator of individual violent behavior (Lockwood and Ascione 1997) has driven considerable state legislative activity since 1985. As of the end of 2003, forty states and the District of Columbia included felony-level penalties in their anti-cruelty statutes (Table 4). Wisconsin, California, and Florida passed felony penalty upgrades in the 1980s (Table 5). From 1990 to 1994, six more states did so, followed by another eleven states from 1995 to 1999, and another sixteen from 2000 to 2003.

By any measure, these state legislative initiatives represent considerable progress for the animal protection movement over the last

Table 4
Tracking Passage of Felony Statutes

States with Felony Anti-cruelty Legislation

1986–89	7
1990–93	9
1994–97	18
1998–2001	34
2002–2003	40

Source: www.hsus.org: Legislation and Laws—Citizen Lobbyist Center.

twenty years. When most anticruelty statutes only carried misdemeanor penalties, animal organizations had trouble convincing the police and courts to spend any time on animal-cruelty crimes. Since felony-level penalties were established, the police and courts have taken a few egregious cases through the courts, which consequently administered significant penalties. Thus, in a notorious Iowa case, where three youths broke into a shelter and mutilated and killed a number of cats, the leader of the group received a two-year jail sentence (Bollinger 1998).

The Iowa case illustrates why states have agreed to institute felony-level penalties. There are some cases where it is clear that the perpetrator of the abuse could be a wider danger to society and where the courts need to administer more significant penalties than a few-hundred-dollar fine. A.N.R. (in Ascione and Arkow 1999) has argued that one may classify cases of animal suffering caused by humans in four basic categories: intentional cruelty, in which the perpetrator gains satisfaction from the animal suffering; abuse, in which the behavior is mainly a release of emotional energy and where the animal's suffering is a by-product rather than a necessary component for the perpetrator; neglect, in which the animal's suffering is caused by the ignorance or laziness of the perpetrator; and use, in which the animal may suffer but the activity is sanctioned by society (e.g., animal research, trapping, factory farming). Of these, the most serious is intentional cruelty because it predicts significant future (or current) sociopathic behavior against other humans and animals. Fortunately, intentional cruelty is rare, as is animal abuse. Most reported cases of animal cruelty fall into the neglect category. We were curious, therefore, to see how the felony-level upgrades dealt with issues of intentionality.

Favre and Loring (1983, 145) put forth four critical questions that must be asked when comparing state cruelty statutes: (1) Which animals are protected by the statute? (2) Which humans are held responsible? (3) What is the scope of care that is to be provided? (4) How is the duty (to provide certain care) qualified or exempted? With a large majority of states now having felony-level provisions, one must also consider (5) the circumstances that might lead to prosecution of a felony versus a misdemeanor. From the animal protection perspective, the *intent* of the perpetrator to cause deliberate and premeditated animal suffering or to engage in gratuitous-

Table 5
State Anti-cruelty Legislation with a Consideration for Language of Intent

Felony Legislation?	Language of Intent	No. of States	States
No Felony	No language of intent	0	
	Language of intent	9	Alaska, Ark., Hawaii, Idaho, Kans., Miss., N.D., S.C., Utah
Felony	No language of intent in either	3	Minn., Nev., S.D.
	Language of intent in felony but not misdemeanor	14	Calif., Conn., Del., D.C., Fla., Ill., Mass., Neb., N.H., N.J., N.M., Ohio, Okla., W.V.
	language of intent in misdemeanor but not felony	1	Mo.
	Language of intent in both	24	Ala., Ariz., Colo., Ga., Iowa, Ind., Ky., La., Md., Me., Mich., Mont., N.C., N.Y., Ore., Pa., R.I., Tenn., Tex., Va., Vt., Wash., Wis., Wyo.

Source: State felony laws that can be found on state websites or databases such as Lexis-Nexis.

ly abusive behavior would seem to be a relatively simple way to distinguish between animal-cruelty cases that fall under the felony provisions and those that remain misdemeanors. However, more careful examination of the laws that have been passed and the way in which they are implemented reveals that there is little underlying logic to the felony-penalty upgrades or to the way the courts apply the anti-cruelty statutes.

The legislative language of intent includes a variety of words in the definitions of animal cruelty: "intentionally," "willfully," "knowingly," "maliciously," and/or "purposefully." Comparing the definitions of these words in the widely used *Black's Law Dictionary* (Black et al. 1990), for example, provides little useful guidance on how these terms might be defined and distinguished. Lawyers might argue that state laws cannot be understood fully without looking at their implementation during court proceedings and case outcomes.

Favre and Loring (1983) separated animal-cruelty statutes into two different categories, those without any language of intent and those with such language. All fifty states and the District of Columbia have animal-cruelty statutes. Three states (Minnesota, Nevada, and South Dakota) do not use language of intent at all (Table 5). Of the forty states and the District of Columbia with felony provisions, seventeen[1] use the identical language in their felony and misdemeanor provisions (whether language of intent is included or not). Usually, offenders committing more than one offense "graduate" to receiving felony-level penalties in subsequent violations of the misdemeanor language. Connecticut, one of the seventeen states, is an exception: a violator of one portion of the animal-cruelty statute (containing no language of intent) may be subjected to either a misdemeanor or felony-level penalty. However, in another portion of the statute where language of intent is used, the offender, if convicted, must be charged with a felony (Table 5).

In statutes where the language differs between the felony and misdemeanor portions, those of nine states[2] and the District of Columbia use some form of language of intent in their felony portions but not in their misdemeanor portions. Generally, one could therefore determine that, for these statutes, evidence of intent surrounding an act of animal cruelty automatically amounts to a more serous violation of the law. Granted, the act of cruelty (e.g., mutilation versus general neglect) may factor into stricter penalties. However, there are nine examples where there is a correlation between intent and level of crime. All of the remaining states[3] without felony-level penalties already include language of intent in their misdemeanor provisions. If these weaker cruelty laws are eventually strengthened to include felony penalties, one might question how the felony language would be constructed and, in turn, differentiated from the current misdemeanor language.

One possibility looks at the type of cruelty associated with the language of intent. Alabama, Illinois, and Kentucky have misdemeanor and felony provisions that both use language of intent; however, the felony provisions only apply to companion animals. (In Pennsylvania the felony provision only applies to zoo animals.)

The four states identified in Table 6 (California, Florida, Illinois, and Oregon) exemplify different ways in which language of intent is positioned. California has inserted intent language in the felony provision, while the original misdemeanor language includes terms such as mutilation, torture, and killing of an animal. California's anti-cruelty statute seems especially strong for two critical reasons: if any evidence of intent is present, the offender must be convicted of a felony, but an offender may also be convicted of a felony even if intent is not present.

In Florida, as in California, the felony provision contains language of intent, but the misdemeanor language does not. The felony penalty does not include the misdemeanor language, and the acts under the felony penalty are seemingly more severe than those under the misdemeanor penalty.

Unlike other states that tend to lump cruel acts together, Illinois separates different types of cruelty into distinct categories. Basic animal cruelty (e.g., beating, starving, overworking, cruelly treating) falls into the misdemeanor category, while repeated offenses, "aggravated cruelty," and "animal torture" are categorized as felonies. Both aggravated cruelty and animal torture include language of intent. In the case of aggravated cruelty, the word "intentionally" is used; animal torture includes the terms "knowingly" and "intentionally." This raises the question of why certain language is used in parts of some statutes and not in others. The analysis of statute language raises questions about the consistency of the language of intent—what is used and why. In the Oregon statutes, "intentionally" and "knowing" precede all acts of animal cruelty marking a misdemeanor, but in the felony language, "maliciously" is used solely when an animal is killed, while "intentionally" and "knowingly" are linked to torture.

To assess the impact of one recent state felony anti-cruelty law, it is useful to look at the experience in Texas. The existing law was amended in 2001, producing several years of experience in the application of the felony penalty. In June 2004 Fikac (2004) reported the number of individuals convicted of a felony since 2001, based on data provided by the Texas Department of Criminal Justice (DCJ): twenty-one people had served state prison time since the 2001 law was enacted, with six of them still in prison at that time. The number excluded the people who were convicted of a felony but were given probation and those who were jailed on a misdemeanor conviction.

The authors were given the names of twenty of the convicted felons by Texas DCJ. A search was conducted in two databases: Lexis-Nexis and a database of news clippings on reported animal-cruelty cases throughout the country maintained by The HSUS. Using the Lexis-Nexis database, we were able to find the jail time served by fourteen of the twenty felons and the type of felony with which they were charged, but we were not given any

Table 6
Four-State Analysis of Language of Intent

State	Year Felony Law Passed/ Amended	Felony Language	Misdemeanor Language
Calif.	1988	Every person who **maliciously*** and **intentionally** maims, mutilates, tortures, or wounds a living animal, or **maliciously** and **intentionally** kills an animal. Language identical to a misdemeanor offense.	Every person who overdrives, overloads, drives when overloaded, overworks, tortures, torments, deprives of necessary sustenance, drink, or shelter, cruelly beats, mutilates, or cruelly kills any animal, or causes or procures any animal to be so overdriven, overloaded, driven when overloaded overworked, tortured, tormented, deprived of necessary sustenance, drink, shelter, or to be cruelly beaten, mutilated, or cruelly killed; and whoever, having the charge or custody of any animal, either as owner or otherwise, subjects any animal to needless suffering, or inflicts unnecessary cruelty upon the animal, or in any manner abuses any animal, or fails to provide the animal with proper food, drink, or shelter or protection from the weather, or who drives, rides, or otherwise uses the animal when unfit for labor.
Fla.	1989, 1999	A person who **intentionally** commits an act to any animal which results in the cruel death, or excessive or repeated infliction of unnecessary pain or suffering, or causes the same to be done.	A person who unnecessarily overloads, overdrives, torments, deprives of necessary sustenance or shelter, or unnecessarily mutilates, or kills any animal, or causes the same to be done, or carries in or upon any vehicle, or otherwise, any animal in a cruel or inhumane manner.
Ill.	1999	Cruel treatment or second or subsequent offense. Aggravated cruelty: **intentionally** commit an act that causes a companion animal to suffer serious injury or death. Animal torture: **Knowingly** or **intentionally** causes the infliction of or subjection to extreme physical pain, motivated by an **intent** to increase or prolong the pain, suffering or agony of the animal.	Cruel treatment: Beat, cruelly treat, starve, overwork, or otherwise abuse any animal.
Ore.	1995	A person commits the crime of aggravated animal abuse in the first degree if the person: **maliciously** kills an animal; or **intentionally** or knowingly tortures an animal.	A person commits the crime of animal abuse in the first degree if, except as otherwise authorized by law, the person intentionally, knowingly or recklessly: causes serious physical injury to an animal; or cruelly causes the death of an animal.

Source: State felony laws that can be found on state websites or databases such as Lexis-Nexis. *Emphasis added in boldface throughout.

information on the type of animal cruelty any had committed. The HSUS database of approximately 1,300 clippings a year found reports of only three of the twenty felons.

Those pushing for more effective animal-cruelty legislation should take steps to make sure that their state law: (1) applies to all animals; (2) applies to first-time offenders; (3) has large fines and lengthy prison time as penalties; (4) has no exemptions; (5) allows or requires convicted abusers to get counseling at their own expense; and (6) prohibits abusers from possessing animals or living where animals are present (*www.hsus.org*: Legislation and Laws/Citizen Lobbyist Center).

In 2005 animal advocates in Texas were working to strengthen their anti-cruelty law again. When news broke that a man used his lawnmower to run over his puppy, and that he could not be prosecuted because the current law only applies to harming another person's animal, the urgency to correct this loophole heightened. Not only would the introduced bill amend the current law to apply to those who abuse their own animal in a cruel manner, but it expands the definition of "animal" to include harming another person's livestock and the cruel killing of stray and wild animals (Fikac 2005).

This anecdotal analysis of anti-cruelty statutes and their enforcement indicates how idiosyncratic anti-cruelty legislation across the country is, how little logic is applied to developing language that clearly discriminates between types of animal abuse, and how difficult it is to follow up on how effective enforcement of both the misdemeanor and the felony provisions can be. Thus, one must conclude that the animal protection movement has made significant progress in upgrading anti-cruelty legislation, but the underlying logic of many of the changes is confusing, and how the laws are enforced (the most important measure of a successful outcome) is very difficult to measure.

Animal Protection Initiatives[4]

The animal protection movement has used state initiative petitions at various stages in the twentieth century but with limited success until fairly recently. Between 1940 and 1988, animal advocates qualified just a handful of animal protection initiatives, and only one of them passed—a 1972 measure in South Dakota to ban dove hunting, which was reversed eight years later. Voters in other states rejected a series of initiatives restricting the killing of wildlife. For instance, in 1983 Maine voters rejected a ban on moose hunting; Ohio and Oregon voters rejected anti-trapping initiatives in 1978 and 1980, respectively.

Since 1990, however, there has been a proliferation of animal protection initiatives (Tables 7a,b). Voters have approved seventeen of twenty-five animal protection ballot initiatives on subjects ranging from cockfighting to bear baiting, from horse slaughter to canned hunts and the factory farming of pigs. During this period, more than four million signatures of registered voters have been gathered, largely by animal advocates, to qualify the twenty-five initiatives. Most of the initiatives have been spearheaded by the organizing efforts of The HSUS and The Fund for Animals. They carefully identified winnable issues in demographically favorable states, and they organized volunteer petitioners, conducted public attitude surveys to guide the wording of the petitions, raised money, and persuaded voters to support the initiatives, primarily by airing emotionally compelling advertising showing direct harm to animals.

Since 1991 the animal movement's victories in the initiative process have been plentiful and diverse. For example, animal advocates have worked to place anti-trapping initiatives on seven ballots since 1995, prevailing in five instances. Six other initiatives dealt with hound hunting and baiting of predators, and animal advocates prevailed in four of them. One measure related to the shooting of captive animals, in so-called canned hunts, and two measures related to the airborne hunting of wolves in Alaska. Voters approved all three of these measures.

These victories have been built on a proven formula for predicting the success of an initiative. The animal issue must be selected carefully and must be "right" for that particular state. State residents must be polled to determine if there is enough support for an issue. The state must have people who can donate money for the initiative, newspapers and other media outlets must support the issue, and the initiative must address a long overdue reform. (For an example of the last of these, before the 2002 initiative that banned cockfighting, Oklahoma was one of only three states where cockfighting was still legal, and a ban of the blood sport was long overdue.)

The success of animal protection initiatives is even more impressive when considering that humane advocates have not been able to leverage huge financial advantages to secure victories. On the contrary, in some cases, including the 1994 measure in Oregon to ban bear baiting and hound hunting, animal protection groups have overcome the lopsided financial advantages enjoyed by their opponents. At the same time, hunting groups have been successful only in those cases where they amassed huge war chests that allowed them to blitz voters with their message and erode public support for animal protection initiatives. For example, hunting groups

Table 7a
Animal Protection Initiatives and Referendums—Wins

		Wins	Percentage Voting Yes	Percentage Voting No
1990	Calif.	**Proposition 117:** prohibits sport hunting of mountain lions	52	48
1992	Colo.	**Amendment 10:** prohibits spring, bait, and hound hunting of black bears	70	30
1994	Ariz.	**Proposition 201:** prohibits steel-jawed traps and other body-gripping traps	58	42
	Ore.	**Measure 18:** bans bear baiting and hound hunting of mountain lions	52	48
1996	Alaska	**Measure 3:** bans same-day airborne hunting of wolves and foxes	58	42
	Calif.	*Proposition 197*: allows trophy hunting of mountain lions*	42	58
	Colo.	**Amendment 14:** bans leghold traps and other body-gripping traps	52	48
	Mass.	**Question 1:** restricts steel-jawed traps and other body-gripping traps, bans hound hunting of bears and bobcats, and eliminates quota for hunters on Fisheries and Wildlife Board	64	36
	Ore.	*Measure 34*: repeals ban on bear baiting and hound hunting of bears and cougars*	42	58
	Wash.	**Initiative 655:** bans bear baiting and hound hunting of bears, cougars, bobcats, and lynx	63	37
1998	Ariz.	**Proposition 201:** prohibits cockfighting	68	32
	Calif.	**Proposition 4:** bans the use of cruel and indiscriminate traps and poisons	57	43
	Calif.	**Proposition 6:** prohibits slaughter of horses and sale of horse meat for human consumption	59	41
	Colo.	**Amendment 13:** *provides uniform regulations of livestock*	39	61
	Colo.	**Amendment 14:** regulates commercial hog factories	62	38
	Mo.	**Proposition A:** prohibits cockfighting	63	37
2000	Alaska	*Measure 1*: bans wildlife issues from ballot*	36	64
	Alaska	**Measure 6:** bans land-and-shoot wolf hunting	53	47
	Ariz.	*Proposition 102*: require two-thirds majority for wildlife issues*	38	62
	Mont.	**Initiative 143:** prohibits new game farm licenses	52	48
	Wash.	**Initiative 713:** restricts steel-jawed traps and certain poisons	55	45
2002	Ariz.	**Proposition 201:** *expands gambling at greyhound tracks*	20	80
	Fla.	**Amendment 10:** bans gestation crates for pigs	55	45
	Ga.	*Measure 6*: specialty license plate for spay/neuter*	71	29
	Okla.	**State Question 687:** bans cockfighting	56	44
	Okla.	*State Question 698*: increases signature requirement for animal issues*	46	54

Note: Italics indicate bad measures that were defeated. * Referendum (referred to ballot by state legislature).

Table 7b
Animal Protection Initiatives and Referendums—Losses

		Losses	Percentage Voting Yes	Percentage Voting No
1992	Ariz.	**Proposition 200:** bans steel-jawed traps and other body-gripping traps	38	62
1996	Idaho	**Proposition 2:** bans spring bait, and hound hunting of black bears	40	60
	Mich.	**Proposal D:** bans baiting and hounding of black bears	38	62
	Mich.	**Proposal G*:** exclusive authority over wildlife to National Resources Committee in Mich.	64	36
1998	Alaska	**Proposition 9:** bans wolf snare trapping	36	64
	Minn.	**Amendment 2:** constitutional recognition of hunting	77	23
	Ohio	**Issue 1:** restores ban on mourning dove hunting	40	60
	Utah	**Proposition 5*:** requires two-thirds majority for wildlife ballot issues	56	44
	Mass.	**Question 3:** bans greyhound racing	49	51
2000	N.D.	**Question 1:** constitutional recognition of hunting	77	23
	Ore.	**Measure 97:** restricts steel-jawed traps and certain poisons	59	41
	Va.	**Question 2*:** constitutional recognition of hunting	60	40
2002	Ark.	**Initiated Act 1:** increases penalties for animal cruelty	38	62

* Referendum (referred to ballot by state legislature).
Source: Internal HSUS document on ballot measures.

spent $1.8 million against an anti-trapping initiative in Arizona in 1992. They spent $2.5 million in Michigan and $750,000 in Idaho against initiatives to ban bear hunting, and $2.5 million against the dove hunting ban in Ohio. Hunting groups outspent animal advocates by margins of from four to one to ten to one in these campaigns.

Animal advocates have not used large amounts of cash to qualify measures for the ballots, either. Generally, they have deployed volunteer petitioners to collect signatures for ballot measures. Conventional wisdom is that initiative qualification in California requires a minimum of $1 million for signature collection, but in 1990, Proposition 117, the mountain lion initiative, relied exclusively on volunteer petitioners, and less than $500,000 was required to collect the neces-

sary signatures. In 1998 the California group Protect Pets and Wildlife, a coalition of humane organizations dedicated to banning the use of steel-jawed leghold traps, spent about $350,000 to amass more than 700,000 signatures, relying largely on seven thousand volunteer petitioners. In Massachusetts in 1995–96, animal advocates spent only $25,000 to gather nearly 200,000 signatures to add a measure to restrict trapping to the November ballot.

Not only have opponents tried to thwart efforts by animal advocates by outspending them, but they have also organized measures to make it more difficult to pass animal protection initiatives. They have tried to raise the standard for both qualification and voter approval of measures. In 1996 Idaho hunting groups soundly defeated

Proposition 2 to ban spring bear hunting and the use of dogs or bait to hunt bears. Their formula for success was a campaign targeting "out-of-state animal rights extremists" who, they charged, wanted to do away with "Idaho freedoms." They spent nearly $800,000 to defeat the measure, while proponents spent just a fraction of that amount in support of the measure. Hunting groups then succeeded in passing sweeping changes to the initiative process, drastically reducing the time allowed for petitioning and requiring that petitioners collect signatures dispersed throughout the state. For example, petitioners had to amass at least 6 percent of registered voters in twenty-two of the state's forty-four counties. Before that stipulation, there were no geographic distribution requirements.

Since many of the initiative victories affect hunting of wildlife, hunters have used either the initiative process or the state legislature to pass resolutions that recognize hunting as a constitutional right. Initiatives preserving the constitutional right to hunt have been passed in Alaska, North Dakota, and Virginia. Animal advocates, while not supporting such measures, have not been interested in pouring time and money into defeating them.

Overall, animal advocates have been victorious 67 percent of the time since 1991. While this may be a significant number in itself, it is crucial to weigh the significance of each ballot initiative in its own right. For example, one of the most important initiative wins for the animal protection movement was passage of the 1992 Colorado Amendment 10, which prohibited sport hunting of bears in the spring and the use of baits and/or hounding. The first of its kind to succeed in the initiative process, this measure set a precedent; Oregon, Massachusetts, and Washington later passed similar measures. The 2002 Florida initiative banning the use of gestation crates for pregnant sows was the first measure to be passed regarding animals involved in agribusiness. The success of this initiative has opened the door for animal advocates to consider using the initiative process in other states to effect further reforms on behalf of farm animals.

While animal advocates sustained occasional setbacks—each one produced by the substantial investment of dollars by opposition groups—the movement has used the initiative process carefully to obtain some basic protections for animals. The animal movement's victories have demonstrated that its values strike a chord with the public. These victories have also signaled to policy makers that animal protection demands cannot be summarily dismissed. The initiatives have provided another measure of confidence to animal advocates in the

political sphere, prompting additional investment not only in initiative campaigns, but also in traditional legislative campaigns.

Conclusion

From 1900 to 1950, the animal protection movement had relatively little political clout. In Moyer's model, the movement was in stage one and two. In the 1950s the movement began to have success passing new legislation, and it began to grow as new animal protection organizations were established. It steadily moved into Moyer's stage three. In the late '70s and early '80s, it moved into stage four as the media discovered "animal rights" and gave the movement significant exposure. In the 1990s media attention changed (Herzog 1995). While reference to animal issues and the movement itself became much more common in the media marketplace (e.g., several *Seinfeld* episodes involved animal rights issues), the cover stories that focused on the movement became much less common. Some in the movement saw this decline as a failure and resorted to more aggressive tactics, while others recognized that animal protection could now command a place in public policy discussions and took advantage of the openings presented.

Although the animal protection movement has been able to gain significant protection for animals in the past twenty years, much remains to be done. Moyer's movement model predicts that, as successes are gained and animal protection reforms are incorporated into the public agenda, the movement itself will wane. Such weakening is not inevitable. The movement's influence can continue to grow and expand; while protecting animals should always be the focus, this focus must be viewed in conjunction with appropriate goals to gain more measurable outcomes and thus more social acceptance

and political clout. The movement must continue working to correct earlier shortcomings and to push the envelope on behalf of animals to be resourceful and effective.

Notes

[1]California (lesser felony with identical language. No language of intent); Colorado (second or subsequent offense; knowingly); Connecticut (no language of intent); Iowa (second or subsequent offense; intentionally); Illinois (for cruel treatment; no language of intent); Indiana (second or subsequent offense, knowingly, intentionally); Minnesota: (second conviction w/in five years); North Carolina: (same language, intentionally); Nebraska (subsequent offenses); New Hampshire (second or subsequent offense); New Mexico (fourth or subsequent offense); Nevada (guilty after third offense); Ohio (for second offense only); Pennsylvania (subsequent offenses; willfully, maliciously); Tennessee (second or subsequent offense; intentionally, knowingly); Texas (third conviction; intentionally, knowingly); and Vermont (second offense).

[2]California, Delaware, Florida, Illinois, Massachusetts, Nebraska, New Hampshire, New Jersey, and New Mexico.

[3]Alaska; Arkansas; Hawaii; Idaho; Kansas; Mississippi (language of intent only when pertaining to dogs); North Dakota; South Carolina; and Utah.

[4]A significant portion of the data has been taken from Pacelle 2001 and 2003 with the permission of the author.

Literature Cited

Animal Welfare Institute. 1990. *Animals and their legal rights: A survey of American laws from 1641 to 1990.* 4h ed. Washington, D.C.: Animal Welfare Institute.

Ascione, F.R., and P. Arkow. 1999. *Child abuse, domestic violence, and animal abuse: Linking the circles of compassion for prevention and intervention.* West Lafayette, Ind.: Purdue University Press.

Black, H.C., J.R. Nolan, J.M. Nolan-Haley, M.J. Connolly, S.C. Hicks, and M.N. Alibrandi. 1990. *Black's law dictionary.* 6h ed. St. Paul: West Publishing Company.

Bollinger, V. 1998. One deadly night at Noah's Ark. *HSUS News,* 43(2): 36–40.

Favre, D.S., and M. Loring. 1983. *Animal law.* Westport, Conn.: Quorum Books.

Fikac P. 2004. Law rarely bites animal abusers: In its first three years, statute has put just 21 people in prison. *San Antonio Express-News*, June 1.

————. 2005. Animal cruelty crackdown touted. *San Antonio Express-News*, March 20.

Herzog, H.A. 1995. Has public interest in animal rights peaked? *American Psychologist* 50: 945–947.

The Humane Society of the United States (HSUS). 1956. Senate committee schedules April slaughter bill hearing. *HSUS News*, April, 1.

————. 2004. Internal document on federal legislative accomplishments. Washington, D.C.: HSUS.

————. 1994–2004. *The humane scorecard: 102nd–107th Congresses*. Washington, D.C.: HSUS.

Lockwood, R., and F.R. Ascione. 1997. *Cruelty to animals and interpersonal violence: Readings in research and application*. West Lafayette, Ind.: Purdue University Press.

Moyer, B. 1987. *The movement action plan: A strategic framework describing the eight stages of successful social movements*. San Francisco at *www.campus activism.org/displayresource. php?giRid=257& gsPhile=movement_action_plan.pdf&giPhid=4 19)*.

Pacelle, W. 2001. The animal protection movement: A modern-day model use of the initiative process. In *The battle over citizen lawmaking: The growing regulation of initiative and referendum: 2001*, ed. M.D. Waters, 109–119. Durham: Carolina Academic Press.

————. 2003. The animal protection movement and I and R. In *Initiative and referendum almanac: 2003*, ed. M.D. Waters, 482–484. Durham, N.C.: Carolina Academic Press.

Unti, B. 2004. *Protecting all animals: A fifty-year history of The Humane Society of the United States*. Washington, D.C.: Humane Society Press.

Unti, B., and A.N. Rowan. 2001. A social history of postwar animal protection. In *The State of the Animals: 2001*, ed. D.J. Salem and A.N. Rowan, 21–37. Washington, D.C.: Humane Society Press.

Warrick, J. 2001. They die piece by piece: In overtaxed plants, humane treatment of cattle is often a battle lost. *The Washington Post*, April 10.

Wiebers, M.S.W., A. Gillan, and D.W. Wiebers. 2000. *Souls like ourselves: Inspired thoughts for personal and planetary advancement*. Rochester, Minn.: Sojourn Press.

Competition between Marine Mammals and Fisheries: Food for Thought

CHAPTER

Kristin Kaschner and Daniel Pauly

This chapter is adapted from "Competition between Marine Mammals and Fisheries: Food for Thought" published by The Humane Society of the United States/Humane Society International.

Introduction

Marine mammals and humans have co-existed on this planet for several hundred thousand years. Both rely heavily on the exploitation of marine resources, though whales, dolphins, and pinnipeds have been doing so for much longer, roaming the oceans for millions of years, long before the emergence of modern humans (Hoelzel 2002). It is not surprising that, when there is a "new kid on the block," co-existence is not always very peaceful, and many of the encounters between humans and marine mammals result in a variety of conflicts.

Room for Conflict

Many species of marine mammals are affected and frequently threatened by fisheries and other human activities (Northridge 1991, 2002). In the past the main threats were large-scale whaling (Clapham and Baker 2002) and sealing operations (Gales and Burton 1989; Knox 1994; Rodríguez and Bastida 1998). These focused initially on the waters of northern Europe and Asia, but

soon extended all the way to Antarctica and reduced countless populations to small fractions of their former abundance (Perry, DeMaster, and Silber 1999) or wiped them out completely, as with the now-extinct Atlantic gray whale (Mitchell and Mead 1977) or the Caribbean monk seal (Kenyon 1977; Gilmartin and Forcada 2002). Today, humans adversely affect marine mammals mainly through incidental entanglement in fishing gear (Northridge 1991, 2002; Harwood et al. 1999; Kaschner 2003), chemical (Mossner and Ballschmiter 1997; Borrell and Reijnders 1999; Coombs 2004) and acoustical pollution (Johnston and Woodley 1998; Jepsen et al. 2003), and, in some cases, ship strikes (Clapham, Young, and Brownell 1999; Fujiwara and Caswell 2001). Some populations close to the point of extinction are the vaquita (D'Agrosa, Lennert-Cody, and Vidal 2000), the Mediterranean (Aguilar 1998; Ridoux 2001; Gucu, Gucu, and Orek 2004) and Hawaiian monk seals (Carretta et al. 2002), and the western North Atlantic right whale (Perry, DeMaster, and Silber 1999; Committee on the Status of Endan-

gered Wildlife in Canada 2003). On the other hand, there are examples of some marine mammals potentially adversely affecting fisheries. Controversial cases include damaging of gear (e.g., harbor seals vs. fish farms) (Johnston 1997; Fertl 2002), devaluation of catch through depredation (killer whales vs. longline fisheries in Alaska) (Dahlheim 1988; Fertl 2002), or, indirectly, through costs incurred by gear modifications that are required to reduce anthropogenic impacts on marine mammal species (e.g., dolphin-excluder devices, pingers) (Harwood 1999; Palka 2000; Read 2000; Culik et al. 2001).

Is Competition a Problem?

Competition between marine mammals and fisheries for available marine food resources has often been mentioned as another issue of concern (Beddington, Beverton, and Lavigne 1985; Harwood and Croxall 1988; Plagányi and Butterworth 2002). This is understandable, since many marine mammal species, in common with humans, operate near or at the top of the marine food web (Pauly et al. 1998b). In recent years, as the fisheries crisis has developed from a set of regional problems to a global concern (Pauly et al. 2002, 2003), and the animal protein that millions of people depend on is in increasingly shorter supply, there is a growing need to find scapegoats for the collapse of fisheries. Most marine mammals are large—suggesting that they must eat a great deal—and visible to us, at least in comparison with other marine top predators, such as piscivorous fish. Moreover, some species—notably various species of fur seals (Torres 1987; Wickens and York 1997)—have recovered from previous levels of high exploitation and their populations are increasing, although population levels of most species are still far below their pre-exploitation abundance (Torres 1987; Wickens and York 1997; Perry, DeMaster, and Silber 1999). For these reasons, whales, dolphins, and pinnipeds are likely culprits behind the problems various fisheries are facing. Thus the voices of countries and corporations with large fishing interests, requesting "holistic management" that includes "the utilization of marine mammals such as whales...to increase catch from the oceans" (Institute of Cetacean Research 2001a, n.p.), have been growing louder. As a consequence, much political pressure has been applied in recent years in various international fora concerned with the management of global marine resources to begin to address competition between marine mammals and fisheries on a global scale (van Zile 2000; Food and Agriculture Organization of the United Nations 2001; Holt 2004).

What Is Competition?

From an ecological perspective, competition is a situation where the simultaneous presence of two resource consumers is mutually disadvantageous (Plagánzi and Butterworth 2002). A rarely acknowledged but implicit assumption is that removal of one of the players would translate into direct benefits for the remaining player. In the context of the proposed competition between marine mammals and fisheries, competition occurs when both marine mammals and fisheries consume the same types of food in the same general geographical areas (and water depths). More important though, competition occurs only if the removal of either marine mammals or fisheries results in a direct increase in food available to the other (Cooke 2002; International Whaling Commission 2003).

Measuring Competition

Many studies have attempted to qualitatively and quantitatively assess the ecological role of marine mammals and the extent of their trophic competition or overlap with fisheries (Harwood and Croxall 1988; Sigurjónsson and Vikingsson 1992; Bowen 1997; Trites, Christensen, and Pauly 1997; Hammill and Stenson 2000; Thomson et al. 2000; Yodzis 2001; Boyd 2002). To address this question, various approaches have been applied to the problem of modeling marine mammal food consumption and the potential effects of this intake on fishery yields, reviewed in detail elsewhere (Cooke 2002; Harwood and MacLaren 2002; International Whaling Commission 2003). Existing approaches range from simple, static "who-eats-how-much-of-what" models to very sophisticated trophodynamic ecosystems models that consider, among other things, interactions among multiple species changing over time and in space (Bogstad, Hauge, and Ulltang 1997; International Council for the Exploration of the Sea 1997; Bogstad, Haug, and Mehl 2000; Christensen and Walters 2000; Livingston and Jurado-Molina 2000). The "who-eats-how-much" models generally are regarded as inadequate to investigate potential competition since they largely ignore important issues of uncertainty and food web interactions (Harwood and MacLaren 2002; International Whaling Commission 2003). However, the application of more complex models, such as those recommended by the United Nations Environment Programme to investigate proposals for marine mammal culls (1999), is often hampered by the lack of availability of necessary data (Tjelmeland 2001; Harwood and MacLaren 2002; International Whaling Commission 2003) and the degree of uncertainty associated with their parameters.

It has been suggested that an undesired consequence of the efforts to focus on the uncertainties and difficulties associated with the application of complex models has been an effective rejection of the "scientific approach" by politicians, administrators, fishers, and laypeople. Thus many people end up considering the simpler "who-eats-how-much-of-what" approach as a "commonsense" notion wherein fewer marine mammals must mean more fish for humans to catch (Holt 2004). As another side effect of their data requirements, most complex models focus on relatively small geographic areas (Stenson and Perry 2001; Bjørge et al. 2002; Garcia-Tiscar et al. 2003). Although this may suffice for some coastal species, such small scales may be inappropriate for species that are highly migratory and range globally or across large ocean basins. As a result, perception of the extent of the problem in terms of resource overlap between fisheries and marine mammal species is distorted by models that are restricted to areas that represent only a fraction of a species' distributional range.

We propose a different type of approach, allowing some perspective on the issue of potential competition between fisheries and marine mammals on a global scale. By developing further the "who-eats-how-much-of-what" approach, we can demonstrate that the application of some true common sense[1] may be sufficient to counter claims that culling marine mammals will help us alleviate the major problems the world's fisheries are facing today, and even world hunger.

What We Do

In this essay we summarize the major flaws in the case for culling, put forward at international fora with increasing insistence, which blames marine mammals for the world's fisheries crisis and promotes the pre-emptive removal of marine mammals as a solution to problems such as globally dwindling fish stocks and world hunger. More important, however, we show that, even though this group of predators does collectively consume a large quantity of marine resources as part of its natural role in marine ecosystems, there is likely very little actual competition between "them" and "us," mainly because marine mammals, to a large extent, consume food items that humans do not catch and/or consume them in places where fisheries do not operate.

Who Eats How MUCH?

The Naïve Approach

Substantial political pressure has been applied in recent years to promote the claim that competition between marine mammals and fisheries is a serious global issue that needs to be addressed in the context of world hunger in general and dwindling fish stocks specifically (van Zile 2000; Food and Agriculture Organization of the United Nations 2001; Holt 2004). These claims are based on very simplistic food consumption models—crude so-called surplus yield calculations (Harwood and MacLaren 2002)—

and are referred to here as the "naïve" approach. These models calculate the quantity of prey taken by marine mammal species by simply estimating the amount of food consumed by one animal of a specific species based on its estimated mean weight, multiplying this amount by the total estimated number of animals of this species, and then summing this estimate of food intake for all or major subgroups of marine mammal species. Estimates thus derived put the total amount consumed by cetaceans worldwide, for instance, at three to six times the global marine commercial fisheries catch (Institute of Cetacean Research 2001b; Tamura 2003). As a result it is often implied that a reduction in the predator population will translate directly into a corresponding increase in prey (Kenney et al. 1997; Sigurjónsson and Vikingsoon 1997; MacLaren et al. 2002; Tamura 2003) and that this increase would then be available for fisheries exploitation.

Problems with the Naïve Approach

There are many problems associated with the naïve approach—so many that the scientific community has effectively refused even to consider a discussion about culling marine mammal species based on these simple estimates (International Whaling Commission 2003). One problem is that reliable and comprehensive abundance estimates are still lacking for the majority of marine mammal species throughout much of their distributional ranges—most global estimates represent only guesstimates at best. Moreover, since we cannot directly measure the amount of food consumed by the animals, our estimates of food intake rely on physiological models that are largely based on what we know about the relationship between the amount an animal must eat to sustain itself given a certain

body mass (Boyd 2002; Leaper and Lavigne 2002). However, we still know very little about the factors that influence this relationship, and the naïve approach effectively ignores the large variations among individuals and species associated with differences in age and seasons, and the proportion of time spent on different activities, to mention only a few. More important, the naïve approach completely ignores the complex range of dynamic factors that affect how removal of high-level predators affects ecosystems (Parsons 1992), some of which we discuss later. For all of these reasons, gross estimates of the total amount of fish consumed by marine mammals, by themselves, provide little or no information about the net "gain" in fisheries catches that might result from a reduction in numbers of any marine mammal population.

But for the Sake of Argument...

It may seem intuitive that, because whales and other marine mammals are big and eat a great deal, having fewer of them should result in more fish being available for human consumption. There is as yet no model that is detailed enough and meets sufficiently stringent scientific requirements that would allow us to reliably investigate the effects, positive or negative, that reduction of marine mammal populations might have on net fisheries catches. Indeed, such a model may never be developed. Therefore, rather than focusing our efforts on attempting to do what probably cannot be done, we instead show the flaws in the arguments that favor resumption of whaling using the naïve approach—based on commonsense considerations and a few additional parameters.

We used a simple food consumption model, outlined briefly in the sidebar on page 98, to estimate global annual food consumption of

Basic Food Consumption Model: Who Is Eating How Much of What?

We generated estimates of annual food consumption during the 1990s for each marine mammal species using a simple food consumption model[17] (Trites, Christensen, and Pauly 1997) and syntheses of recently published information about the population abundances, sex ratios, sex-specific mean weights, and weight-specific feeding rates extracted from more than three thousand sources of primary and secondary literature compiled into a global database. To convey the extent of uncertainty associated with this total estimate of marine mammal food consumption, we generated minimum and maximum estimates by running the model with different feeding rates but ignoring effects such as seasonal differences in food intake (Kaschner 2004). Corresponding mean global fisheries catches for the 1990s were taken from the global fisheries catch database developed and maintained by the Sea Around Us Project at the Fisheries Centre (University of British Columbia, Canada) (sidebar on page 100) and averaged over the last decade. Note that this is an estimate of only the reported catches and that total takes by fish-

eries are probably closer to 150 million tons per year, if illegal, unreported, or unregulated (IUU) catches are taken into account (Pauly et al 2002) (Figure 1). The percentages of different food types in total marine mammal consumption were estimated based on the diet composition standardized across species, itself based on two hundred published qualitative and quantitative studies of species-specific feeding habits (Pauly et al. 1998a). The proportions of different food types represented in fisheries catches were obtained by assigning individual target species/taxa to the appropriate food type category based on life history, size, and habitat preferences of the target species or taxa. Food types included benthic invertebrates (BI), large zooplankton (LZ), small squid (SS), large squid (LS), small pelagic fishes (SP), mesopelagic fish (MP), miscellaneous fish (MF), higher vertebrates (HV), and an additional food type containing all catches of species targeted only by fisheries, such as large tuna, which we called non-marine mammal fishes (NM) (Figure 2).

different groups of marine mammals to compare them with catches taken by world fisheries (Figure 1). Mean estimates for all groups are indeed almost as high as or slightly higher than global reported fisheries catches (although it should be noted that total fisheries catches are likely underestimated (Pauly et al. 2002). To convey—at least to some extent—the degree of uncertainty associated with these estimates, we have also included minimum and maximum

estimates generated by the model, which illustrate the wide margin for error that must be considered before attempting to use such estimates in a management context.

We arrive at maximum estimates of global mean food intake for baleen whales that are similar to those published previously (Institute of Cetacean Research 2001a; Tamura 2003). Although there are comparatively few of this species[2] baleen whales do, indeed, take the bulk of the total food consumed by

all marine mammals due to their large size. However, in terms of the type of food targeted also by fisheries (shown in red in Figure 1; mostly small pelagics, benthic invertebrates, and a group we have dubbed "miscellaneous fishes," which mainly includes medium-sized groundfish and pelagic fish species), baleen whales likely consume less or at least no more than fisheries do every year. The majority of what baleen whales (as well as toothed whales and pinnipeds) eat consists of food types that, for reasons of taste and accessibility, are of little interest to commercial fisheries. We expand on this important consideration of *what* is being eaten in the next section.

Who Eats How Much of What?

Different Species, Different Strokes

During their foraging dives, many marine mammal species regularly venture to depths of more than a thousand meters (Campagna et al. 1998; Hooker and Baird 1999; Hindell et al. 2002; Laidre et al. 2003) and far under the pack ice (Davis et al. 2003), into areas rarely if ever visited by humans. There, they feed on organisms about whose existence we often know only indirectly based on specimens collected from the stomachs of marine mammal species (Fiscus and Rice 1974; Clarke 1996).

Along similar lines, at least some of our favorite seafood delicacies, such as tuna, are rarely if ever consumed by marine mammals. In light of these and many other differences in taste and accessibility, the distinction between which food types are targeted by marine mammals and which by fisheries warrants serious attention. Based on the approach described in the sidebar at left, we specified the relative amount of nine different food types

Figure 1
Who Eats How Much?

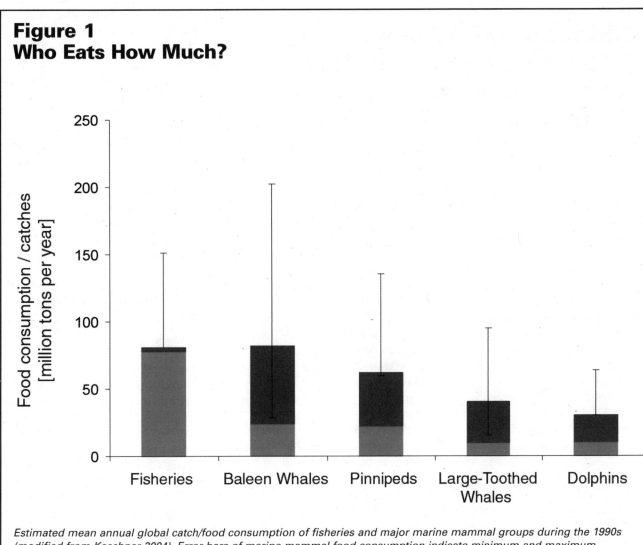

Estimated mean annual global catch/food consumption of fisheries and major marine mammal groups during the 1990s (modified from Kaschner 2004). Error bars of marine mammal food consumption indicate minimum and maximum estimates based on different feeding rates (Leaper and Lavigne 2002). Total fisheries catches are probably closer to 150 million tons per year if illegal, unreported, and unregulated catches are taken into account (Pauly et al. 2002). Marine mammals' food intake consisting of prey types that are also major groups targeted by fisheries are presented in red (mainly small pelagic fishes, miscellaneous fishes, and benthic invertebrates). Note that, although mean global food consumption of all marine mammals combined is estimated to be several times higher than total fisheries catches, the majority of food types the various marine mammal groups consume are not targeted by fisheries.

consumed by major marine mammal groups and fisheries (Figure 2). The majority of all food consumed by any marine mammal group consists of food types that are of little interest to commercial fisheries. Diets of pinnipeds and dolphins appear to be most similar to global fisheries catch composition, while the diet of large toothed whales, which feed predominantly on large, deep-sea squid species not targeted by fisheries (Clarke, Martins, and Pascoe 1993), shows the least similarity.

Size—among Other Things—Matters

Like all other parameters in the basic food consumption model, the marine mammal diet composition is affected by uncertainties. Problems arise due to the difficulties associated with obtaining diet information from sufficient sample sizes in the wild (Barros and Clarke 2002). Diet composition estimates based on stomach content analyses tend to be biased toward cephalopods, as their hard parts are less

readily digested than those of other prey groups (Zeppelin et al. 2004). Such biases may be addressed by applying correction factors that compensate for differential effects of digestion on different prey types (Tollit et al. 1997, 2003). More serious biases are introduced by the predominance of stranded animals in the overall sample. Such animals may not be representative of the rest of the population, as they are often sick and/or their stomach contents over-represent the coastal components of their diet (Barros

Modeling and Mapping of Global Fisheries Catches— You Couldn't Have Caught That There!

Until recently, the exact origin of fisheries catches of the world was mostly unknown. The reasons were many, and where fisheries landing statistics exist (and they do, in some form, for the overwhelming majority of the world's fisheries), they usually suffer from a number of deficiencies. Ignoring typical problems of missing/incomplete data and inconsistent units of measure, one of their most common weaknesses is that they are often quite vague, particularly about the identity of the harvested taxa as well as the exact location where they were caught. To overcome this problem, over the past four years, the Sea Around Us Project has developed a spatial allocation process that relies on what might be called the application of common sense (in conjunction with very large amounts of related data stored in supporting databases) to assign the coarse-scale reported landings from large statistical areas into the most probable distribution within a global grid system with 0.5° latitude by 0.5° longitude cell dimensions (approximately 180,000 ocean cells). The basic assumptions are that catches of a particular fish species (or other harvested taxa) by a specific country cannot occur where the reported species does not occur, and that they cannot stem from areas where the country in question is not allowed to fish. Therefore, information about species distributions and fishing access agreements

can serve to limit the available area where reported catches can be made within the large statistical area. We developed and used a global database of species distributions based on published maps of occurrence (where available) or by using other sources of information to help restrict the range of exploited taxa, notably water depth (for non-pelagic species), latitudinal limits, statistical areas, proximity to critical habitats (such as seamounts, mangroves, or coral reefs), ice coverage, and historical records. In addition, we compiled large amounts of information describing the access agreements between fishing nations to the fisheries resources of other coastal countries based on formal bilateral agreements, existing joint ventures between governments and private companies and/or associations, and the documented history of fishing before the declaration of exclusive economic zones by various countries and other observations. The intersection of these databases with reported catches by countries from large statistical fishing areas allows the allocation of fine-scale fisheries catches to individual spatial cells. Predicted catch and biomass distributions of taxa exploited by fisheries of the world can be viewed online at *www.seaaroundus.org,* and average catch distribution for the 1990s is shown in Figure 3. (This sidebar is generally adapted from Watson et al. 2004.)

sonal variation in the diet composition of marine mammal species (Haug et al. 1995; Nilssen 1995; Tamura 2001).

The standardized diet composition used here may be fairly robust to these sources of bias/uncertainty, as the food type categories are very broad.[3] However, due to these biases, the similarity in food types exploited by fisheries and marine mammals shown in Figure 2 is likely to be even lower than suggested here,[4] especially if other aspects, such as differences in prey size, are taken into consideration as well.

Who Eats How Much of What WHERE?

The spatial overlap of resource exploitation is necessary for competition to occur. In this section, we assess the degree of overlap between marine mammal food consumption and fisheries by comparing on a global scale the areas where marine mammals are likely to feed to the areas in which most fishing activities occur.

Where Are Fisheries?

To illustrate where most human fishing activities occur, we used the mapped distribution of global fisheries for an average year during the 1990s (Figure 3) using a modeling process described briefly in the sidebar at left. As can be seen, the vast majority of fisheries catches is taken along the continental shelves of Europe, North America, Southeast Asia, and the west coast of South America. Highest catches occur where continental shelves are wide, such as the Bering, East China, and North seas, or in highly productive upwelling systems, such as those that can be found along the west coasts of South America and South Africa. However, despite the distant water fleets roaming the oceans and the development of deep-sea fisheries operating far off-

and Clarke 2002). Other, newer molecular methods, including stable isotope (Best and Schell 1996; Hooker et al. 2001; Das et al. 2003) and fatty acid (Iverson 1993; Hook-

er et al. 2001; Lea et al. 2002; Grahl-Nielsen et al. 2003) analyses, also have biases (Smith, Iverson, and Bowen 1997). Finally, there is substantial geographical and sea-

Figure 2
Who Eats How Much of What?

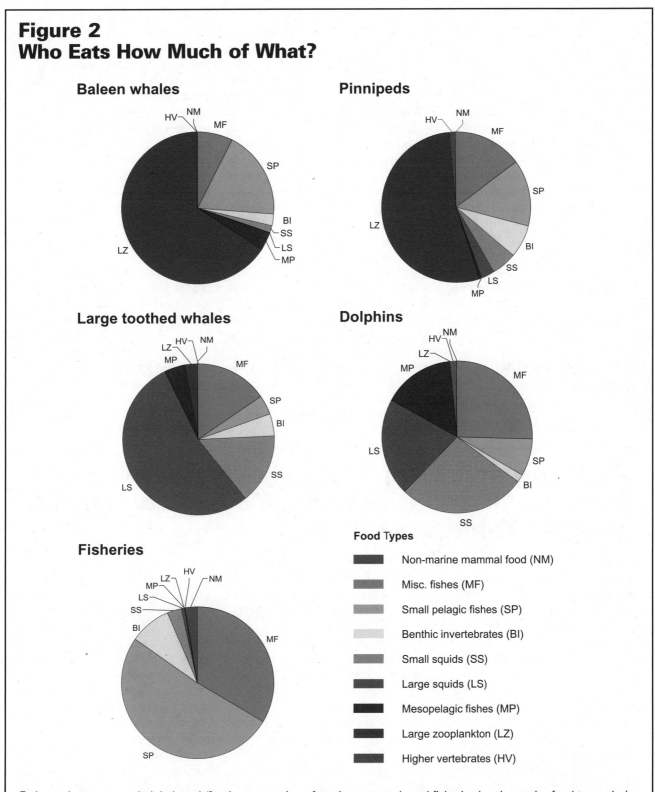

Baleen whales

Pinnipeds

Large toothed whales

Dolphins

Fisheries

Food Types

Non-marine mammal food (NM)

Misc. fishes (MF)

Small pelagic fishes (SP)

Benthic invertebrates (BI)

Small squids (SS)

Large squids (LS)

Mesopelagic fishes (MP)

Large zooplankton (LZ)

Higher vertebrates (HV)

Estimated mean annual global catch/food consumption of marine mammals and fisheries by nine major food types during an average year in the 1990s expressed as proportions of total (from Kaschner 2004). The percentages of different food types in marine mammal consumption were computed based on diet composition standardized across species (Bonfil et al. 1998). Corresponding percentages of different food types in fisheries catches were obtained by assigning individual target species/taxa to the appropriate food type category based on life history, size, and habitat preferences of the target species or taxa. Food types mainly consumed by marine mammals are presented in hues of blue and green, and food types that are major fisheries target groups are presented in yellows and reds. Note that food types primarily targeted by fisheries represent only a small proportion of the diet of any marine mammal group.

shore, major fishing grounds generally lie in close proximity to areas with high human populations, off the coasts of industrial fishing nations. It is noteworthy that comparatively little catch is taken off the coasts of developing countries, such as in East Africa or even the Indian subcontinent, where fish, caught mostly by small-scale fishers, still represents a major form of sustenance and is often the only source of animal protein (Delgado et al. 2003). Moreover, the majority of catches that are taken along the coasts of developing countries (e.g., along the coast of northwest Africa) are not harvested by local fishers, but rather by the large trawlers of distant water fleets of industrial nations (Bonfil et al. 1998).

Where Are Marine Mammals?

Unlike humans, marine mammals are true creatures of the sea and spend the majority, if not all, of their time living and feeding in the oceans. Except for a few species that haul out on land during reproductive seasons or have very small coastal ranges, distribution of marine mammals is not restricted by the distance to the nearest landmass or the climatic conditions that largely influence the locations of fishing grounds and major human settlements. Conversely, many species occur predominantly in geographic areas still largely inaccessible and/or rarely frequented by humans, such as the ice-breeding seals of the Northern and Southern hemispheres or many of the dolphin or whale species predominantly occurring in tropical offshore waters. Because of the vastness of the oceans and the elusiveness of many species, it is difficult to determine accurately where they occur and feed.

Here we have used a novel habitat suitability modeling approach, outlined in the sidebar below, to map the likely occurrence of marine mammal species based on the relative suitability of the environment, given what is known about their habitat preferences. Based on our predictions, most of the food that marine mammals consume is taken far offshore, in areas where the majority of fishing boats rarely venture. Often cosmopolitan in their distributions, the baleen and large toothed whale species, for example, likely are feeding mostly in the open oceans. Due to the sheer size of the feeding ranges of these species, consumption densities (annual food intake per km[2]) are comparatively low and fairly homogeneous across large areas. Food intake of the smaller dolphin species is even lower and appears to be concentrated in temperate waters. Pinniped food consumption, in contrast, tends to be associated more closely

Modeling and Mapping Large-Scale Marine Mammal Distributions: We May Know More than We Think We Know...

Delineation of marine mammal distributions is greatly hampered by the vastness of the marine environment and the low densities of many species. Since marine mammals spend the majority of their lives under water and roam widely throughout oceans, it is difficult to determine whether a species fails to occur in a particular area or whether we have not spent enough time looking for it or simply missed it when we did look there. All of these factors contribute to the difficulties we encounter when trying to map distributions of any whale, dolphin, or pinniped species. Consequently, most published maps of distribution are tentative, often consisting only of outlines, sketched by experts who represent what they believe to be the maximum boundaries of a given species' occurrence. We have developed a rule-based approach to map the distributions of 115 marine mammal species in a more objective way by exploiting various types of quantitative and qualitative ecological information, including (but not limited to) expert knowledge and general observations (Kaschner 2004). Within a global grid (described in the sidebar on page 100) we used our model to relate quantitatively what is known about a species' general habitat preferences to the environmental conditions in an area, thus effectively showing where the environment may be suitable for a particular whale, dolphin, or pinniped species, given what we know about the types of habitat they tend to prefer. Or put differently, the model rigorously defines the geographic regions that experts describe when they talk about a "coastal, tropical species" (e.g., the Atlantic humpbacked dolphin) or a species that "prefers offshore, polar waters" (e.g., the hooded seal). Although the actual occurrence of a species will depend on a number of additional factors, extensive testing of the model shows that it can already describe, even in its present simple form, known patterns of species occurrence quite well (Kaschner et al. in review; Kaschner et al. in prep.). The predicted distributions for the 115 marine mammal species considered here can be viewed online at *www.seaaroundus.org*.

Figure 3
Where Are Fisheries?

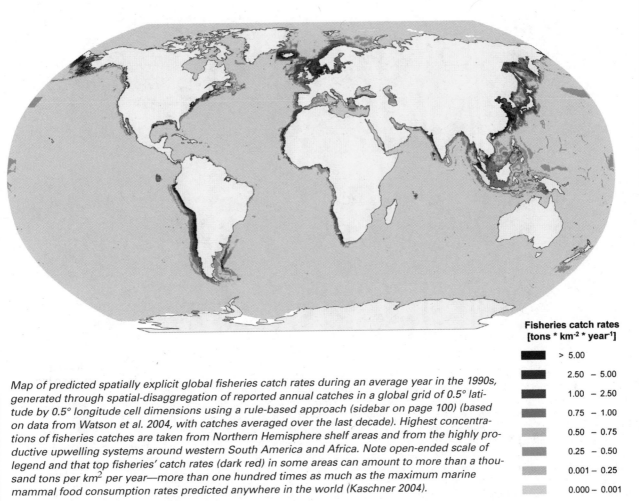

Fisheries catch rates
[tons * km⁻² * year⁻¹]

⬛	> 5.00
⬛	2.50 – 5.00
⬛	1.00 – 2.50
⬛	0.75 – 1.00
⬛	0.50 – 0.75
⬛	0.25 – 0.50
⬛	0.001 – 0.25
⬜	0.000 – 0.001

Map of predicted spatially explicit global fisheries catch rates during an average year in the 1990s, generated through spatial-disaggregation of reported annual catches in a global grid of 0.5° latitude by 0.5° longitude cell dimensions using a rule-based approach (sidebar on page 100) (based on data from Watson et al. 2004, with catches averaged over the last decade). Highest concentrations of fisheries catches are taken from Northern Hemisphere shelf areas and from the highly productive upwelling systems around western South America and Africa. Note open-ended scale of legend and that top fisheries' catch rates (dark red) in some areas can amount to more than a thousand tons per km² per year—more than one hundred times as much as the maximum marine mammal food consumption rates predicted anywhere in the world (Kaschner 2004).

with coasts and shelf areas, with feeding taking place mostly in the polar waters of both hemispheres and the restriction to smaller areas in combination with high abundances of most species results in much higher, locally concentrated feeding densities.

Overall, the concentration of food intake in the higher latitude, polar waters would be even more pronounced if seasonal migrations and feeding patterns of different species were incorporated into our model, particularly those of baleen whales. We also need to stress that some areas of apparent high consumption, such as the South and East China seas for the baleen whales, represent overestimates of

food intake rates that are related to a specific feature of our modeling approach, which relies on global abundance estimates to generate local densities and which currently ignores, for example, the effects of population structure and differences in the recovery status or relative abundance between individual subpopulations.[5]

Where They Meet

Using the predicted geographic distributions of marine mammal food consumption and fisheries catches, we now investigate the extent to which they overlap. Again, however, to address the issue of potential competition, we

must consider not only how much both players take where, but also what they take. To assess this, we produced global maps showing the overlap in resource exploitation between the major marine mammal groups and fisheries (Figure 4), using an approach that considers not only the extent of spatial and dietary overlap, but also the relative importance of a given area to either group (sidebar on page 105). Areas of overlap between fisheries and marine mammal groups are mostly concentrated in the Northern Hemisphere and appear to occur primarily between pinnipeds and fisheries. In contrast, fisheries' overlap with baleen whales is relatively low, and pre-

Figure 4
Where Do They Meet?

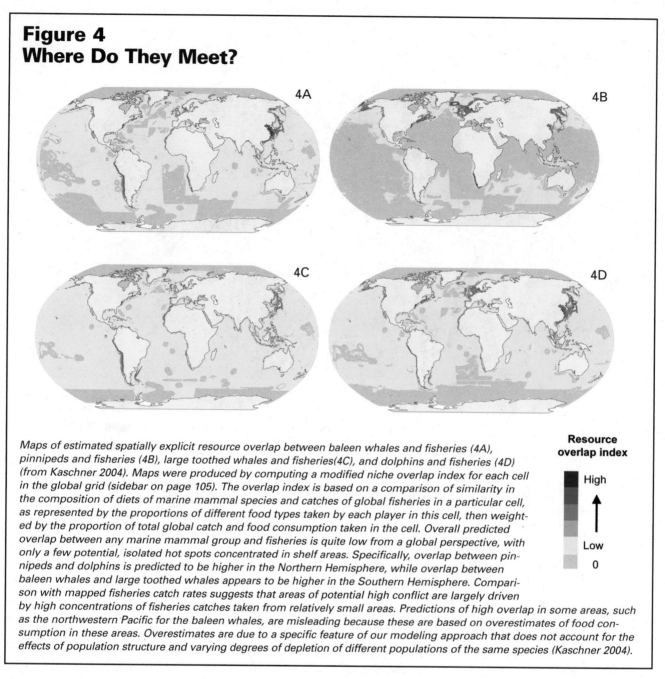

Maps of estimated spatially explicit resource overlap between baleen whales and fisheries (4A), pinnipeds and fisheries (4B), large toothed whales and fisheries(4C), and dolphins and fisheries (4D) (from Kaschner 2004). Maps were produced by computing a modified niche overlap index for each cell in the global grid (sidebar on page 105). The overlap index is based on a comparison of similarity in the composition of diets of marine mammal species and catches of global fisheries in a particular cell, as represented by the proportions of different food types taken by each player in this cell, then weighted by the proportion of total global catch and food consumption taken in the cell. Overall predicted overlap between any marine mammal group and fisheries is quite low from a global perspective, with only a few potential, isolated hot spots concentrated in shelf areas. Specifically, overlap between pinnipeds and dolphins is predicted to be higher in the Northern Hemisphere, while overlap between baleen whales and large toothed whales appears to be higher in the Southern Hemisphere. Comparison with mapped fisheries catch rates suggests that areas of potential high conflict are largely driven by high concentrations of fisheries catches taken from relatively small areas. Predictions of high overlap in some areas, such as the northwestern Pacific for the baleen whales, are misleading because these are based on overestimates of food consumption in these areas. Overestimates are due to a specific feature of our modeling approach that does not account for the effects of population structure and varying degrees of depletion of different populations of the same species (Kaschner 2004).

dicted hot spots in the western North Pacific are largely due to the biases associated with determining food consumption discussed in the previous section. Partially due to dolphins' comparatively low total food intake, the overlap between fisheries and this group is quite low and again mostly concentrated in the Northern Hemisphere. Not surprising, the lowest overlap occurs between fisheries and deep-diving, large toothed whales, whose diets primarily consist of large squid species and mesopelagic fish, not currently exploited by fisheries.

How Big of a Problem Is That?

Overlap between marine mammal groups and fisheries is probably not a global issue but is restricted to a few relatively small geographic regions and a few species.

The skewed perception of this problem by nations in close vicinity to these hot spots of interaction becomes understandable, if still somewhat myopic. However, to put the size of the potential overlap problem into perspective, we calculated the proportion of food consumption that stems from areas of predicted high overlap (Figure 5). In the 1990s, on average, only about 1 percent of all food taken by any marine mammal group was consumed in areas with significant spatial and/or dietary overlap with fisheries catches, indicating that both players should be able to co-exist quite peacefully in most of the world's oceans.[6]

The 10–20 percent of global fisheries catches taken in areas of potential high overlap represents a relatively significant amount, of course. Recall, however, that overlap does not automatically equal competition, and our results likely over- rather than underestimate overlap for the reasons outlined in the previous sections. Moreover, as shown by comparing the maps of food consumption and fisheries catches, areas of high overlap appear to be associated largely with areas of extreme concentrations of fisheries extractions, rather than locally concentrated food intake by marine mammals. It is therefore more likely for fisheries to affect marine mammal species adversely in these areas of intense fishing than vice versa, as has already been suggested elsewhere (DeMaster et al. 2001). For species with large distributional ranges, such as the minke whale, the reaction to any potential local depletion of prey species by fisheries may only be to shift to alternate feeding grounds. For those species with very restricted ranges, such as the vaquita in the Gulf of California or South Africa's Heaviside's dolphins, such local depletions of food resources by intensive fisheries may pose serious threats to the survival of the species.

Overall, our analysis indicates that potential competition may be addressed better at a local level. We also note that most of the potential hot spots highlighted by our approach are in areas that have been the focal point of much debate about marine mammal-fisheries interactions, such as in the Bering Sea, with the potential negative effects of U.S. groundfish fisheries on the endangered western population of Steller sea lions (Fritz, Ferrero, and Berg 1995; Loughlin and York 2000) or the Benguela system off southwest Africa, with the potential effects of the increasing population of South African fur seals on the hake stocks in this area (Wickens et al. 1992; Punt and Butterworth 2001). These and other hot spots will require much more detailed investigation to establish the true extent of the problem at hand.

Biological Complications

It is generally agreed that far more complex models are needed, incorporating many additional parameters and requiring more, often still unavailable data (DeMaster et al. 2001; Harwood 2001; International Whaling Commission 2003) to

Spatial Overlap of Marine Mammal Food Consumption and Fisheries Catches: Where They Meet

In assessing potential competition between top predators in marine ecosystems, such as humans and many marine mammals, the question of who is eating/catching what where is very important, as this greatly determines the degree of overlap between the two. This question could not be addressed—at least not on a large scale—before the development of mapping techniques for marine mammal distributions and fisheries catches, such as those described in the sidebars on pages 100 and 102. Thanks to our novel approach for mapping large-scale distributions of marine mammal species, we were able to produce global maps showing where specific species are likely to feed by linking our predictions about the likely occurrence of individual species (sidebar on page 102) to the outputs from the basic food consumption model (sidebar on page 98). Food consumption maps for groups of species were then generated by totaling food consumption rates across all species within each group of marine mammals. To assess the degree to which there may be conflict between fisheries and marine mammals, we quantitatively compared "who is likely taking what where" by computing an index of resource exploitation overlap for each individual cell in our global raster with 0.5° latitude by 0.5° longitude cell dimensions. The index is a modified version of one developed initially to investigate the overlap in ecological niches between two species (MacArthur and Levins 1967), based on the comparison of similarity in resource exploitation of both species. Here, we compared the similarity in the composition of diets of marine mammal groups and catches of global fisheries in a particular cell represented by the proportions of different food types taken by each player in this cell, then weighted the qualitative index of diet similarity by the proportion of total global catch and food consumption taken in this cell to get a sense of the relative contribution of each cell to either total marine mammal food consumption or fisheries catches (MacArthur and Levins 1967; Trites, Christensen, and Pauly 1997; Kaschner 2004)[18]. The resulting maps (Figure 4) represent the area where conflicts between specific groups of marine mammals and fisheries may occur: both players potentially are taking comparatively large amounts of similar food types in the same geographic region.

adequately address interactions between marine mammals and fisheries—and the potential far-reaching effects of the removal of top predators from marine ecosystems (Ray 1981; Parsons 1992; Pauly et al. 1998b; DeMaster et al. 2001) in those areas where competition may occur. The assumptions, structures, and data needed for such models have been reviewed extensively elsewhere (DeMaster et al. 2001; Harwood 2001; International Whaling Commission 2003). However, here we highlight the problems associated with attempts to increase fisheries catches by culling marine mammals in those areas where competition is most likely.

Beneficial Predation: We May Be in for Surprises

Although the term food chain is often used when describing the feeding interactions underlying marine ecosystem structure, we should speak of "food webs."[7] Finely patterned food webs do not function as efficiently as a simple food chain would: much of the biomass synthesized by phytoplankton fails to reach higher trophic levels and is diverted instead into unproductive pathways, notably the so-called microbial loop. On the other hand, this diversity of pathways protects predators against the disappearance of any of their favorite prey species (Neutel, Heesterbeek, and de Ruiter 2002). It is not surprising therefore that higher-level predators, such as sharks or dol-

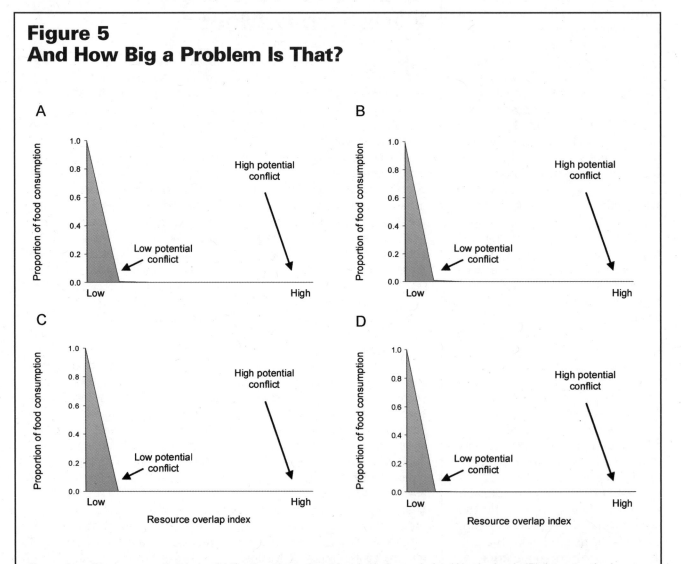

Figure 5
And How Big a Problem Is That?

Proportion of mean annual global catch/food consumption taken by baleen whales (A), pinnipeds (B), large toothed whales (C), and dolphins (D) in the 1990s in areas of predicted high or low resource overlap, respectively (from Kaschner, 2004). Note that in all cases more than 99 percent of all marine mammal food consumption stems from areas of very low overlap. Similarly, more than 85 percent of all fisheries catches are taken in areas of very low overlap (Kaschner 2004).

Figure 6
We May Be in for Surprises

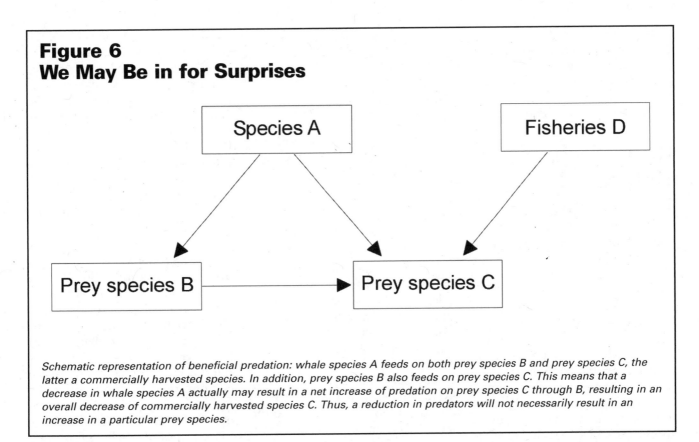

Schematic representation of beneficial predation: whale species A feeds on both prey species B and prey species C, the latter a commercially harvested species. In addition, prey species B also feeds on prey species C. This means that a decrease in whale species A actually may result in a net increase of predation on prey species C through B, resulting in an overall decrease of commercially harvested species C. Thus, a reduction in predators will not necessarily result in an increase in a particular prey species.

phins, consume a wide range of prey and concentrate on distinct species only in certain places or at certain times of the year. This feature of marine food webs is also the reason why removing a higher-level predator does not necessarily lead to an increase of what, at certain times and places, appears to be its "preferred" prey (Parsons 1992; Cooke 2002). Basically, predators not only consume their favorite prey but also the competitors and, in many cases, the predators of their prey (Parsons 1992; Punt and Butterworth 2001; Cooke 2002). This is illustrated schematically in Figure 6 in the form of a feeding triangle, representing a ubiquitous feature of marine food webs. Here, a high-level predator, represented by a toothed whale (A), feeds on two species (B and C), with C being the preferred prey, which is also exploited by commercial fisheries (D). B, however, also preys on C (and other organisms—E, F, and so on—of no concern here). In such cases, removing species A will not necessarily make it possible for

the biomass of C to increase or even for its production to become available to a fishery. Rather, it is more likely that B (whose numbers were also depressed by A) will increase and consume more of C (Walters and Kitchell 2001). If B happens to be a species that fisheries do not exploit, this will result in the production of C being wasted from the standpoint of fishery D. Indeed, to acquire the production of C, we would have to cull B as well and so on ad infinitum. This conundrum has caused ecologists to coin the term "beneficial predation"—that is, a form of predation wherein the predator (here, A) enhances the production of its prey (here, C) by suppressing potential competitors or predators (here, B). This effect is very common in marine food webs. Indeed, essentially all marine food webs can be conceived as composed of interlinked sets of feeding triangles shown schematically in Figure 6. Removing what appears to be a top predator in such cases only creates new top predators, and the would-

be fishery enhancer will find himself ultimately culling 20-centimeter fish so that he can catch more 5-centimeter fish, thus competing with birds, squids, and jellyfish.

Beneficial predation is not an ad hoc concept invented to discourage would-be cullers of marine mammals. Rather, counterintuitive results of removing high-level predators from ecosystems have been well demonstrated in various cases, based on a number of modeling approaches (Parsons 1992; Caddy and Rodhouse 1998; Yodzis 1998, 2001; Crooks and Soulé 1999; Pauly, Christensen, and Walters 2000; Punt and Butterworth 2001, Bjørge et al. 2002; Okey et al. 2004; Morisette, Hammill, and Savenkoff, submitted for publication).[8] In fact, it has been proposed as one reason for a stagnation in global groundfish landings since the 1970s, as it is possible that the reduction of toothed whales and other high-level predators that feed on desirable fish species but also on various squids, which in turn feed on juvenile groundfish, has contributed indirectly—through an increase of cephalopod consumption of juvenile fish—to the inhibition of finfish population recovery (Caddy and Rodhouse 1998; Piatkowski, Pierce, and Morais da Cunha 2001).

How Much Culling—If Any— Is Enough?

One important assumption in the context of competition is that marine mammal food consumption increases directly with marine mammal abundance. Though this is obviously true in general,[9] other factors, such as the vulnerability of prey species to predation (Mackinson et al. 2003), the ability of the predator to switch between prey species, and movements of animals between different areas, greatly influences how much a given species eats in a specific area. The flip side of this, then, is that it may be impossible to determine exactly how many animals would need to be culled to achieve the desired increase in fisheries catches. A study investigating this showed that, even for a very simple food web, many likely scenarios existed in which consumption of a given prey species by a marine mammal species would only decrease noticeably if the predator population was reduced by more than 50 percent (Cooke 2002). Given the wide-ranging movements of most species and the fact that fish and marine mammals tend not to respect human management boundaries, it is highly questionable that we would ever be able to manage marine mammal populations in a manner guaranteed to produce a measurable, long-term increase in fisheries catches.

Other Legitimate Questions

Who Would Get the Fish?

Although this may seem beside the point, we must highlight the questionable use of world hunger as a justification for culling marine mammals and subsequently targeting their prey.[10]

Though an estimated 950 million people worldwide currently rely on fish and shellfish for more than one-third of their animal protein (Plagánzi and Butterworth 2002), the per capita supply of wild-caught fish for human consumption has been declining since the mid-1980s, particularly in developing countries.[11] This is due in part to overfishing, which has led to the decline of global catches since the late 1980s (Watson and Pauly 2001; Pauly et al. 2002, 2003), but also to human population growth. Indeed, no natural resource, including wild-caught fish, could ever meet our ever-growing demand. We will not elaborate on the fact that of the 120–150 million or so tons of fish and invertebrates killed annually by fisheries, only about half is actually eaten by people: about thirty million tons of bycatch are discarded or killed by lost gear (ghost fishing), while a huge amount is lost to spoilage (Ward and Jeffries 2000) and during processing (e.g., gutting, filleting) (Bykov 1983) or left uneaten, in richer countries, at the edge of consumers' plates. Another thirty million tons, however, are fed to various livestock (Pauly et al. 2002) and carnivorous fish—notably salmon, sea bass, groupers, and tuna—in fish farming industries, which are one of the driving factors behind the increased fish exports from developing to developed countries, especially to the United States, the European Union, and Japan (Naylor 2000; Alder and Watson, in prep.).

Contrary to popular opinion, the herrings, sardines, mackerels, and other species ground up to produce the fish meal that is fed to carnivorous fish are, when suitably handled, perfectly edible by humans and are indeed appreciated in many parts of the world. These fish are increasingly hard to find in the markets of developing countries, in areas such as West Africa, where, being relatively cheap, they represented the major source of animal protein for poor people (Naylor 2000).[12] Given these trends, and increasing fish exports from developing to developed countries, it would be completely unrealistic to assume, and disingenuous to claim, that the meat of culled marine mammals or that of their former prey would become a substitute for the fish that is now exported from countries where people "do not have adequate food" (Institute of Cetacean Research 2001b). Indeed, it is precisely the low purchasing power of the people in these countries that prevents them from competing successfully with fish meal producers and fish feedlot operators.

Are We Simply Looking for Scapegoats?

Unlike earlier fisheries declines, which passed mostly unnoticed by the general public, the massive fisheries collapses of the last decades had a broad public impact, so they have generated widespread calls for mitigation (Food and Agricultural Organization of the United Nations 1995). In particular, people have noted that fisheries management has tended so far to focus on single stocks, thus neglecting feeding and other interactions among different species/stocks and their dependence on the health of their ecosystems. There have been, as a result, increasing demands for ecosystem-based fisheries management, or even "ecosystem management."[13] The scientific community has accepted this challenge, and, for the last few years, a lively scientific debate has been conducted in many national and international arenas on this topic. The principal questions asked deal with how to implement such a broad form of management and how to identify suitable indicators and formulate fisheries target and reference points within an ecosystem context.[14] This includes the challenge of achieving set conservation objectives for predators of species targeted by fisheries (Constable 2001).

Those who advocate a broad-based attack on marine mammals, on the other hand, behave as if they already have the answers. Because most fish stocks of the world have been overexploited (including those on which marine mammals rely), the mantra coming from this latter group is that all we have to do is remove marine mammals until the original balance is re-established. Here is a quote to that effect: "When a single species is protected, ignoring its role in the ecosystem, the balance in the ecosystem is disrupted" (Institute of Cetacean Research 2001b, n.p.). Albert Einstein is supposed to have noted that "all complex problems have one simple solution; however, it happens to be completely wrong." Here, not only have the fish been overexploited, but so have the marine mammals. Given reduced fishing pressure, fish can be expected to recover faster[15] than marine mammals (Best 1993; Trites et al. 1999), given their respective reproductive abilities. Indeed, all recent evidence confirms that baleen whales are far less abundant than they were historically (Brownell, Best, and Prescott 1983; Perry, DeMaster, and Silber 1999; Clapham, Young, and Brownell 1999; Clapham and Baker 2002; Holt 2002). Re-establishing the disrupted balance of ecosystems is therefore hardly a simple matter of reducing whale numbers.

What we have is an attempt to find a convenient scapegoat for the mismanagement of fisheries (Holt 2004) and the reduction of catches caused by excess fishing effort throughout the world. This puts the following quotation in context:

> The FAO considers that we cannot increase the harvest from the ocean if we continue present practices. To increase the catch from the ocean, holistic management and sustainable utilization of marine resources including marine mammals, such as whales, is essential. (Institute of Cetacean Research 2001a, n.p.)

This, indeed, is a beautiful example of a non sequitur: yes, we cannot increase landings "if we continue present practices." But the present practices are characterized by waste (e.g., bycatch [Northridge 1984, 1991; Alverson et al. 1994], discarding [Alverson et al. 1994] ghost fishing [Breen 1990]), and pathological management structures (e.g., excess fishing capacity [Mace 1997] and subsidies [Munro and Sumaila 2002]), and these are the practices that, all experts agree, must be overcome, rather than killing more whales, even if we think holistically.

And How about the Birds?

No one has proposed (so far!) killing all seabirds to increase fish available for human consumption. There are millions of seabirds in the world, consuming massive amounts of fish, squid, and other valuable invertebrates. Although birds tend to weigh little individually, their high metabolic rate leads to very high food consumption rates (Ellis and Gabrielsen 2002). Thus, in the aggregate, seabirds have been estimated to consume 50 to 80 million tons of fish and invertebrates per year (de L. Brooke 2004), at least half of what humans kill annually. Yet no one has proposed that seabirds be culled, and, indeed, saving seabirds from death (e.g., by entanglement in fishing gear) is one of the few conservation-related activities that is never disparaged in public, even though it greatly affects the manner in which some fisheries operations are conducted.

Clearly, if those proposing a global attack on marine mammals were consistent, they also should propose that we go after the seabirds. More important, we should eliminate all large fish as well, since they eat immense numbers of other fish, shrimps, and squids, generally far more than taken by marine mammals and seabirds (Livingston 1993; Trites, Christensen, and Pauly 1997). Indeed, the greatest predators of fish are other fish (Trites, Christensen, and Pauly 1997; Furness 2002). But again we are eliminating large predatory fish anyway, as we fish down marine food webs, reducing high-level predator biomasses as we go along (Pauly et al. 1998b; Christensen et al. 2003; Myers and Worm 2003). Nevertheless, overall catches are decreasing,[16] notably because, in the process, we are eliminating beneficial predation.

Conclusions

We have shown that, even though marine mammals consume a large quantity of marine resources as a whole, there is likely relatively little actual competition between "them" and "us" from a global perspective, mainly because they, to a large extent, consume food items that we do not catch in places where our fisheries do not operate. This is not to say that there may not be potential for conflict in the small geographic regions in which marine mammal food consumption overlaps with fisheries. These areas warrant further investigation. But even in these cases, it seems likely that the most common type of competitive interaction will be one where fisheries have an adverse impact on marine mammal species, especially those with small, restricted distributional ranges (DeMaster et al. 2001; Holmes 2004; Kaschner 2004). Our analysis clearly shows that these are isolated, regional issues to be addressed at the appropriate scale, and that there is no evidence that food competition between marine mammals and fisheries is a global problem, even when the uncertainties associated with the available information are considered. Thus, there is little basis to blame marine mammals for the crisis world fisheries are facing today. There is even less support for the suggestion that we could solve any of these urgent global problems, caused by a long history of mismanagement of fisheries and other resources, by reducing marine mammal populations. We may spend some time, however, thinking about the fact that marine mammals—and other top predators—have been managing marine resources successfully, consuming larger amounts than those taken by global fishing operations today, for millennia. Unlike us, they appear to have done so sustainably, without causing their prey species to collapse. Perhaps we could learn something from them. It's food for thought.

Acknowledgments

We acknowledge funding provided for this report by The Humane Society of the United States (HSUS). The underlying research was conducted as part of the "Sea Around Us" Project, with funding provided by the Pew Charitable Trusts of Philadelphia, Pennsylvania, and via Daniel Pauly by the National Science and Engineering Research Council of Canada. Additional support for Kristin Kaschner was provided by a "Li Tze Fong" graduate fellowship and a partial university graduate fellowship from the University of British Columbia.

Notes

[1]Granted, in combination with some fairly sophisticated spatial modeling techniques (Kaschner 2004; Kaschner et al. in review; Kaschner in prep.; Watson et al. 2004).

[2] We estimated only about 1 million baleen whales worldwide, versus about 35 million pinnipeds and 16 million dolphins (Kaschner 2004).

[3]That is, the effects of a species switching between feeding on 50 percent herring and 50 percent capelin in different seasons or in different areas of its range can be ignored, because it would still have a proportional diet composition consisting of 50 percent of the "small pelagics" food type.

[4]For example, though the "diet" of both a fishery and a marine mammal species may consist of 50 percent "small pelagics," the fishery may be targeting different small pelagic species from those consumed by the marine mammal.

[5]As a result, in the North Pacific, for example, the healthy and growing Eastern subpopulation of eighteen to twenty thousand gray whales that feeds and breeds along the Pacific coast of North America (Angliss and Lodge 2002; Perryman et al. 2002; Wade 2002) effectively "subsidizes" the highly depleted Western subpopulation. This latter subpopulation historically occurred all along the coasts of Russia and Japan and probably as far down as the East China Sea, but is now on the brink of extinction, reduced to barely a hundred animals concentrated in the Sea of Okhotsk (Weller et al. 2002a,b).

[6]When viewed from the perspective of fisheries, the overlap is slightly more pronounced, with less than 15 percent of all fisheries catches likely being caught in the areas that show up as hot spots on our maps (Kaschner 2004).

[7]Thus, the basic food produced at the bottom of marine food webs, mainly by minute phytoplankton, is consumed by herbivores of various sizes, some with a narrow range of preferred algal species, while others, facultative herbivores, also consume fellow zooplankters. From there, the pathways that biomass can follow along the food web branch even further, leading to small fish or large zooplankton, both consumed by larger fish or invertebrates, themselves consumed by a wide array of higher-order predators.

[8]Incidentally, the trophic dynamic software package Ecopath & Ecosim, widely applied to construct, balance, and analyze marine food webs and often used to investigate the effects of beneficial predation, was also used recently by ardent advocates of massive culls based at Japan's Institute of Cetacean Research. They conveniently failed to notice this feature of the software, however.

[9]That is, many whales will eat more than no whales at all.

[10]An example of a quotation: "Whaling can contribute to the world food shortage and environmental protection in several ways. [...] whaling is a means of obtaining high quality food from the sea without diminishing biodiversity and,[...] may allow more fish to be directed to human use" (Institute of Cetacean Research 2001a).

[11]Available at: *www.fao.org/fi/statist/ nature_china/30jan02.asp.* .

[12]Another example: Chilean sardine, once a staple food, is now scarce on Chilean markets, because most of the catch is ground up into fish meal to feed an export-oriented salmon industry so huge that it has consumed the bulk of the stocks of small pelagic fish once available in the rich waters of that country (Fulton 2003). Our last example is the rapid development in several Mediterranean countries of massive tuna feedlot operations in which immense quantities of the sardine and other small fish much appreciated around the Mediterranean are used to fatten tuna, which are then flown to Japan, where, like salmon, they enter a developed-country luxury market (Aguis 2002).

[13]For example, at the World Summit on Sustainable Development held in Johannesburg, South Africa, in 2002, organized by the United Nations Commission on Sustainable Development (*www.johannesburgsummit.org*).

[14]For example, at the Quantitative Ecosystem Indicators for Fisheries Management symposium, Paris, 2004, organized by the IOC International Ocean Commission/Committee at UNESCO headquarters (*www.ecosystemindicators.org*).

[15]As they did, for example, during World War II in the North Sea, which was mined and too dangerous to fish (Beverton and Holt 1957).

[16]Given that biological production is greater at lower than at higher trophic levels (TL), fisheries catches, initially at least, will tend to increase when TL decline (i.e., when the fisheries target species is lower in the food web) (Pauly et al. 1998b). This led to the suggestion of an FiB index, which, given an estimate of the biomass (or energy) transfer efficiency (TE; often set at 0.1[Pauly and Christensen 1995]) between TL, maintains a value of zero when a decrease in TL is matched by an appropriate catch increase (and conversely when TL increase) and deviates from zero otherwise. The FiB index is defined, for any year y, by

$$\text{FiBy} = \log\{[Yy \cdot (1/TE)TLy] \,/\, [Yo \cdot (1/TE)TLo]\}$$

where Yy is the catch at year y; TLy is the mean trophic level of the catch at year y; Yo is the catch and TLo is the mean trophic level of the catch at the start of the series being analyzed (Pauly et al. 1998b). Note that the FiB index is designed so that it does not vary during those periods when changes in TL are matched by catch changes in the opposite direction, that is, periods within a time series where the FiB index does not appear to change. Conversely, an increase of the FiB index indicates that the underlying fishery is expanding beyond its traditional fishing area (or ecosystem), while a decrease indicates a geographic contraction, or a collapse of the underlying food web, leading to "backward-bending" plots of TL vs. catch (Pauly et al. 1998b). All applications done so far of the FiB index indicate that once an area is extensively fished, "fishing down" (i.e., removing predators) does not increase catches as much as would be predicted from the higher production at lower trophic levels, so, based on the FiB index as well, removing top predators from marine food webs appears not to be an efficient strategy for increasing fisheries catches in a sustainable fashion.

[17]$Q_i = \sum N_{is} * W_{is} * R_{is}$, where Q represents the estimated food consumption of species i, which is calculated based on the abundance N, mean body mass W and daily ration consumed R, by both sexes s of the species (Trites, Christensen, and Pauly 1997).

[18]$$a_{lj} = \left(\frac{2\sum_k p_{lk} p_{jk}}{2\sum_k p_{lk}^2 + p_{jk}^2}\right) * (pQ_l * pC_j),$$ where for each cell the resource overlap index a between marine mammal species group l and fisheries j is calculated based on the proportion of resource k in the total diet or catch of the species group or fisheries and weighted by the proportion of total catch and food consumption summed across all species (MacArthur and Levins 1967; Trites, Christensen, and Pauly 1997; Kaschner 2004).

Literature Cited

Aguilar, A. 1998. Current status of Mediterranean monk seal (*Monachus monachus*) populations. Gland, Switzerland: IUCN.

Aguis, C. 2002. Tuna farming in the Mediterranean. *Infofish International* 5: 28–32.

Alder, J., and R. Watson. In prep. Fair trade or piracy in globalization: Effects on fisheries resources. In *Fisheries globalization,* ed. W.W. Taylor, M.G. Schechter, and L.G. Wolfson. New York: Cambridge University Press.

Alverson, D.L., M.H. Freeberg, J.G. Pope, and S.A. Murawski. 1994. *A global assessment of fisheries by catch and discards.* 233. Rome: Food and Agriculture Organization of the United Nations.

Angliss, R.P., and K.L. Lodge. 2002. U.S. Alaska Marine Mammal Stock Assessments—2002. 224. U.S. Department of Commerce.

Barros, N.B., and M.R. Clarke. 2002. Diet. In *Encyclopedia of marine mammals,* ed. W.F. Perrin, B. Würsig, and J.G.M. Thewissen, 323–327. San Diego: Academic Press.

Beddington, J.R., R.J.H. Beverton, and D.M. Lavigne, eds. 1985. *Marine mammals and fisheries.* London: George Allen and Unwin.

Best, P.B. 1993. Increase rates in severely depleted stocks of baleen whales. *ICES Journal of Marine Science* 50: 169–186.

Best, P.B., and D.M. Schell. 1996. Stable isotopes in southern right whale (*Eubalaena australis*) baleen as indicators of seasonal movements, feeding and growth. *Marine Biology* (Berlin) 124: 483–494.

Beverton, R.J.H., and S.J. Holt. 1957. *On the dynamics of exploited fish populations.* London: Chapman and Hall.

Bjørge, A., T. Bekkby, V. Bakkestuen, and E. Framstad. 2002. Interactions between harbour seals, *Phoca vitulina,* and fisheries in complex coastal waters explored by combined Geographic Information System (GIS) and energetics modelling. *ICES Journal of Marine Science* 59: 29–42.

Bogstad, B., K.H. Hauge, and Ø. Ulltang. 1997. MULTSPEC—A multi-species model for fish and marine mammals in the Bering Sea. *Journal of Northwest Atlantic Fishery Science* 22: 317–342.

Bogstad, B., T. Haug, and S. Mehl. 2000. Who eats whom in the Barents Sea? In *Minke whales, harp and hooded seals: Major predators in the North Atlantic ecosystem,* ed. G.A. Vikingsson and F.O. Kapel, 98–119. Tromsø, Norway: NAAMCO Scientific Publications.

Bonfil, R., G. Munro, U. Sumaila, U. Rashid, H. Valtysson, M. Wright, T.J. Pitcher, D. Preikshot, N. Haggan, and D. Pauly. 1998. Impacts of distant water fleets: An ecological, economic, and social assessment. 11–111. Godalming, Surrey, England: Endangered Species Campaign, World Wildlife Federation International.

Borrell, A., and P.J.H. Reijnders. 1999. Summary of temporal trends in pollutant levels observed in marine mammals. *Journal of Cetacean Research and Management* (Special Issue) 1: 145–155.

Bowen, W.D. 1997. Role of marine mammals in aquatic ecosystems. *Marine Ecology Progress Series* 158: 267–274.

Boyd, I.L. 2002. Estimating food consumption of marine predators: Antarctic fur seals and macaroni penguins. *Journal of Applied Ecology* 39: 103–119.

Breen, P.A. 1990. A review of ghost fishing by traps and gillnets. In *Proceedings of the Second International Conference on Marine Debris,* ed. R.S. Shomura and M.L. Godfrey, 571–599. Honolulu: National Oceanic and Atmospheric Administration.

Brownell, R.L.J., P.B. Best, and J.H. Prescott, eds. 1983. *Right whales—Past and present status: Reports of the International Whaling Commission* (special issue 10).

Bykov, V.P. 1983. *Marine fishes: Chemical composition and processing properties.* New Delhi: Amerind Publishing Company.

Caddy, J.F., and P.G. Rodhouse. 1998. Cephalopod and groundfish landings: Evidence for ecological change in global fisheries? *Reviews in Fish Biology and Fisheries* 8: 431–444.

Campagna, C., F. Quintana, B.B.J. Le, S. Blackwell, and D.E. Crocker. 1998. Diving behaviour and foraging ecology of female southern elephant seals from Patagonia. *Aquatic Mammals* 24: 1–11.

Carretta, J.V., M.M. Muto, J. Barlow, K. Baker, A. Forney, and M. Lowry. 2002. U.S. Pacific marine mammal stock assessments: 2002. 290. U.S. Department of Commerce.

Christensen, V., and C. Walters. 2000. Ecopath with ecosim: Methods, capabilities, and limitations. In *Methods for evaluating the impacts of fisheries on North Atlantic ecosystems*, ed. D. Pauly and T.J. Pitcher. FCRR 8(2): 79–105. Vancouver: Fisheries Centre, UBC.

Christensen, V., S. Guénette, J. Heymans, C. Walters, R. Watson, D. Zeller, and D. Pauly. 2003. Hundred year decline of North Atlantic predatory fishes. *Fish and Fisheries* 4: 1–24.

Clapham, P.J., and C.S. Baker. 2002. Modern whaling. In *Encyclopedia of marine mammals*, ed. W.F. Perrin, B. Würsig, and J.G.M. Thewissen, 1328–1329. San Diego: Academic Press.

Clapham, P.J., S. Young, and R.L.J. Brownell. 1999. Baleen whales: Conservation issues and the status of the most endangered populations. *Mammal Review* 29: 35–60.

Clarke, M.D. 1996. The role of cephalopods in the world's oceans: General conclusions and the future. *Philosophical Transactions of the Royal Society of London (Series B)* 351: 1105–1112.

Clarke, M.R., H.R. Martins, and P.L. Pascoe. 1993. The diet of sperm whale *(Physeter macrocephalus)* off the Azores. *Philosophical Transactions of the Royal Society of London* (Series B) 339: 67–82.

Committee on the Status of Endangered Wildlife in Canada. 2003. *COSEWIC assessment and update status report on the North Atlantic right whale* Eubalaena glacialis *in Canada*. Ottawa: COSEWIC.

Constable, A.J. 2001. The ecosystem approach to managing fisheries: Achieving conservation objectives for predators of fished species. *CCAMLR Science* 8: 37–64.

Cooke, J.G. 2002. Some aspects of the modelling of effects of changing cetacean abundance on fishery yields (SC/J02/FW10).

In International Whaling Commission: Modelling Workshop on Cetacean-Fishery Competition, 1–28. La Jolla, Calif. Unpublished.

Coombs, A.P. 2004. Marine mammals and human health in the eastern Bering Sea: Using an ecosystem-based food web model to track PCBs. Master's thesis. University of British Columbia.

Crooks, K.R., and M.E. Soulé. 1999. Mesopredator release and avifaunal extinctions in a fragmented system. *Nature* 400: 563–566.

Culik, B.M., S. Koschinski, N. Tregenza, and G.M. Ellis. 2001. Reactions of harbor porpoises *Phocoena phocoena* and herring *Clupea harengus* to acoustic alarms. *Marine Ecology Progress Series* 211: 255–260.

D'Agrosa, C., C.E. Lennert-Cody, and O. Vidal. 2000. Vaquita bycatch in Mexico's artisanal gillnet fisheries: Driving a small population to extinction. *Conservation Biology* 14: 1110–1119.

Dahlheim, M.E. 1988. Killer whale *(Orcinus orca)* depredation on longline catches of sablefish *(Anoplopoma fimbria)* in Alaskan waters. 14. Seattle, Wash.: Northwest and Alaskan Fisheries Center–NMFS.

Das, K., C. Beans, L. Holsbeek, G. Mauger, S.D. Berrow, E. Rogan, and J.M. Bouquegneau. 2003. Marine mammals from northeast Atlantic: Relationship between their trophic status as determined by $\delta13C$ and $\delta15N$ measurements and their trace metal concentrations. *Marine Environmental Research* 56: 349–365.

Davis, R.W., L.A. Fuiman, T.M. Williams, M. Horning, and W. Hagey. 2003. Classification of Weddell seal dives based on 3-dimensional movements and video-recorded observations. *Marine Ecology Progress Series* 264: 109–122.

de L. Brooke, M. 2004. The food

consumption of the world's seabirds. *Biology Letters* 271: S246–S248.

Delgado, C.L., N. Wada, M.W. Rosegrant, S. Meijer, and M. Ahmed. 2003. *Fish to 2020: Supply and demand in changing global markets*. Washington, D.C., and Penang, Malaysia: International Food Policy Research Centre and WorldFish Center.

DeMaster, D.P., C.W. Fowler, S.L. Perry, and M.F. Richlin. 2001. Predation and competition: The impact of fisheries on marine-mammal populations over the next one hundred years. *Journal of Mammalogy* 82: 641–651.

Ellis, H.I., and G.W. Gabrielsen. 2002. Energetics of free-ranging seabirds. In *Biology of marine birds,* ed. E.A. Schreiber and J. Burger, 359–407. Boca Raton, Fla.: CRC Press.

Fertl, D. 2002. Interference with fisheries. In *Encyclopedia of marine mammals,* ed. W.F. Perrin, B. Wursig, and H.G.M. Thewissen, 438–442. San Diego: Academic Press.

Fiscus, C.H., and D.W. Rice. 1974. Giant squids, *Architeuthis sp.,* from stomachs of sperm whales, captured off California. *California Fish & Game* 60: 91–93.

Food and Agriculture Organization of the United Nations (FAO). 1995. Code of conduct for responsible fisheries. Rome: FAO.

———. 2001. Report of the Reykjavik conference on responsible fisheries in the marine ecosystem. In *FAO Fisheries Report,* Reykjavik, Iceland.

Fritz, L.W., R.C. Ferrero, and R.J. Berg. 1995. The threatened status of the Steller sea lion, *Eumetopias jubatus,* under the Endangered Species Act: Effects on Alaska groundfish management. *Marine Fisheries Review* 57: 14–27.

Fujiwara, M., and H. Caswell. 2001. Demography of the endangered

North Atlantic right whale. *Nature* (London) 414: 537–541.

Fulton, J. 2003. Salmon farming in Chile. *Sea Around Us Newsletter* 18: 4–6.

Furness, R.W. 2002. Management implications of interactions between fisheries and sandeel-dependent seabirds and seals in the North Sea. *ICES Journal of Marine Science* 59: 261–269.

Gales, N.J., and H.R. Burton. 1989. The past and present status of the southern elephant seal *Mirounga leonina* Linn. in greater Antarctica. *Mammalia* 53: 35–48.

García-Tiscar, S., R. Sagarminaga, P.S. Hammond, and A. Cañadas. 2003. Using habitat selection models to assess spatial interaction between bottlenose dolphins (*Tursiops truncatus*) and fisheries in south-east Spain (abstract). In *Proceedings of the Fifteenth Biennial Conference on the Biology of Marine Mammals* 58. Greensboro, N.C.: Society of Marine Mammalogy.

Gilmartin, W.G., and J. Forcada. 2002. Monk seals—*Monachus monachus, M. tropicalis,* and *M. schauinslandi.* In *Encyclopedia of marine mammals,* ed. W.F. Perrin, B. Wursig, and H.G.M. Thewissen, 756–759. San Diego: Academic Press.

Grahl-Nielsen, O., M. Andersen, A.E. Derocher, C. Lydersen, Ø. Wiig, and K.M. Kovacs. 2003. Fatty acid composition of the adipose tissue of polar bears and of their prey: Ringed seals, bearded seals and harp seals. *Marine Ecology Progress Series* 265: 275–282.

Gucu, A.C., G. Gucu, and H. Orek. 2004. Habitat use and preliminary demographic evaluation of the critically endangered Mediterranean monk seal (*Monachus monachus*) in the Cilician Basin (Eastern Mediterranean). *Biological Conservation* 116: 417–431.

Hammill, M.O., and G.B. Stenson. 2000. Estimated prey consumption by harp seals (*Phoca groenlandica*), hooded seals (*Cystophora cristata*), grey seals (*Halichoerus grypus*), and harbour seals (*Phoca vitulina*) in Atlantic Canada. *Journal of Northwest Atlantic Fishery Science* 26: 1–23.

Harwood, J. 1999. A risk assessment framework for the reduction of cetacean by-catches. *Aquatic Conservation: Marine and Freshwater Ecosystems* 9: 593–599.

———. 2001. Marine mammals and their environment in the twenty-first century. *Journal of Mammalogy* 82: 630–640.

Harwood, J., and J.P. Croxall. 1988. The assessment of competition between seals and commercial fisheries in the North Sea and the Antarctic. *Marine Mammal Science* 4: 13–33.

Harwood, J., and I. MacLaren. 2002. Modelling interactions between seals and fisheries: Model structures, assumptions and data requirements (SC/J02/FW4). In International Whaling Commission—Modelling Workshop on Cetacean-Fishery Competition, 1–9. La Jolla, Calif. Unpublished.

Harwood, J., L.W. Andersen, P. Berggren, J. Carlström, C.C. Kinze, J. McGlade, K. Metuzals, F. Larsen, C.H. Lockyer, S.P. Northridge, E. Rogan, M. Vinther, and M. Walton. 1999. Assessment and reduction of the bycatch of small cetaceans in European waters (BY-CARE)—Executive summary. St. Andrews, Scotland: NERC Sea Mammal Research Unit.

Haug, T., H. Gjøsæter, U. Lindstrøm, K.T. Nilssen, and I. Røttingen. 1995. Spatial and temporal variations in northeast Atlantic minke whale *Balaenoptera acutorostrata* feeding habits. In *Whales, seals, fish and man: Proceedings of the International Symposium on the Biology of Marine Mammals in the North East Atlantic,* ed. A.S. Blix, L. Walløe, and Ø Ulltang, 225–239. Tromsø, Norway, November 29–December 1. Amsterdam: Elsevier.

Hindell, M.A., R. Harcourt, J.R. Waas, and D. Thompson. 2002. Fine-scale three-dimensional spatial use by diving, lactating female Weddell seals *Leptonychotes weddellii. Marine Ecology Progress Series* 242: 285–294.

Hoelzel, A.R., ed. 2002. *Marine mammal biology: An evolutionary approach.* Oxford, England: Blackwell Science Ltd.

Holmes, B. 2004. Whales, seals or men? Who stole all the fish? *New Scientist,* May 15.

Holt, R.S. 2002. Whaling and whale conservation. *Marine Pollution Bulletin* 44: 715–717.

Holt, S. 2004. Sharing our seas with whales and dolphins. *FINS—Newsletter of ACCOBAMS* 1: 2–4.

Hooker, S.K., and R.W. Baird. 1999. Deep-diving behaviour of the Northern bottlenose whale, *Hyperoodon ampullatus* (Cetacea: Ziphiidae). Proceedings of the Royal Society of London (Series B): *Biological Sciences* 266: 671–676.

Hooker, S.K., S.J. Iverson, P. Ostrom, and S.C. Smith. 2001. Diet of Northern bottlenose whales inferred from fatty acid and stable isotope analyses of biopsy samples. *Canadian Journal of Zoology* 79: 1442–1454.

Institute of Cetacean Research. 2001a. *What can we do for the coming food crisis in the 21st century?* Tokyo: Institute of Cetacean Research.

———. 2001b. *Didn't we forget something? Cetaceans and food for humankind.* Tokyo: Institute of Cetacean Research.

International Council for the Exploration of the Sea (ICES). 1997. Report of the Multispecies

Assessment Working Group (CM 1997/Assess: 16).

International Whaling Commission. 2003. Report of the modelling workshop on cetacean-fishery competition (SC/55/Rep 1). In International Whaling Commission: Modelling Workshop on Cetacean-Fishery Competition, 1–28. La Jolla, Calif. Unpublished.

Iverson, S.J. 1993. Milk secretion in marine mammals in relation to foraging: Can milk fatty acids predict diet. In *Marine mammals: Advances in behavioural and population biology,* ed. I.L. Boyd, 263–291. Oxford: The Zoological Society of London, Clarendon Press.

Jepson, P.D., M. Arbelo, R. Deaville, I.A.P. Patterson, P. Castro, J.R. Baker, E. Degollada, H.M. Ross, P. Herráez, A.M. Pocknell, F. Rodríguez, F.E. Howie, A. Espinosa, R.J. Reid, J.R. Jaber, V. Martin, A.A. Cunningham, and A. Fernández. 2003. Gas-bubble lesions in stranded cetaceans: Was sonar responsible for a spate of whale deaths after an Atlantic military exercise? (Brief communication). *Nature* 425: 575–576.

Johnston, D.W. 1997. Acoustic harassment device use at salmon aquaculture sites in the Bay of Fundy, Canada: Noise pollution and potential effects on marine mammals. *Canadian Technical Report of Fisheries and Aquatic Sciences* 2192: 12.

Johnston, D.W., and T.H. Woodley. 1998. A survey of acoustic harassment device (AHD) use in the Bay of Fundy, NB, Canada. *Aquatic Mammals* 24: 51–61.

Kaschner, K. 2003. *Review of small cetacean bycatch in the ASCOBANS area and adjacent waters: Current status and suggested future actions.* 123. Bonn, Germany: ASCOBANS-UN.

————. 2004. Modelling and mapping of resource overlap between marine mammals and fisheries on a global scale. Ph.D. diss., University of British Columbia.

Kaschner, K., R. Watson, C.D. MacLeod, and D. Pauly. In prep. Mapping worldwide distributions of data deficient marine mammals: A test using stranding data for beaked whales. *Journal of Applied Ecology.*

Kaschner, K., R. Watson, A.W. Trites, and D. Pauly. In review. Mapping worldwide distributions of marine mammals using a Relative Environmental Suitability (RES) model. *Marine Ecology Progress Series.*

Kenney, R.D., G.P. Scott, T.J. Thompson, and H.E. Winn. 1997. Estimates of prey consumption and trophic impacts of cetaceans in the USA northeast continental shelf ecosystem. *Journal of Northwest Atlantic Fishery Science* 22: 155–171.

Kenyon, K.W. 1977. Caribbean monk seal extinct. *Journal of Mammalogy* 58: 97–98.

Knox, G.A. 1994. Whales. In *The biology of the Southern Ocean,* ed. G.A. Knox, 141–160. Cambridge: Cambridge University Press.

Laidre, K.L., M.P. Heide-Jørgensen, R. Dietz, R.C. Hobbs, and O.A. Jørgensen. 2003. Deep-diving by narwhals *Monodon monoceros:* Differences in foraging behavior between wintering areas? *Marine Ecology Progress Series* 261: 269–281.

Lea, M.-A., Y. Cherel, C. Guinet, and P.D. Nichols. 2002. Antarctic fur seals foraging in the Polar Frontal Zone: Inter-annual shifts in diet as shown from fecal and fatty acid analyses. *Marine Ecology Progress Series* 245: 281–297.

Leaper, R., and D. Lavigne. 2002. Scaling prey consumption to body mass in cetaceans (SC/J02/FW2). In International Whaling Commission—Modelling Workshop on Cetacean-Fishery Competition, 1–12. La Jolla, Calif. Unpublished.

Livingston, P.A. 1993. Importance of predation by groundfish, marine mammals and birds on walleye pollock *Theragra chalcogramma* and Pacific herring *Clupea pallasi* in the eastern Bering Sea. *Marine Ecology Progress Series* 102: 205–215.

Livingston, P.A., and J. Jurado-Molina. 2000. A multispecies virtual population analysis of the eastern Bering Sea. *ICES Journal of Marine Science* 57: 294–299.

Loughlin, T.R., and A. York. 2000. An accounting of the sources of Steller sea lion, *Eumetopias jubatus,* mortality. *Marine Fisheries Review* 62: 40–45.

MacArthur, R.H., and R. Levins. 1967. The limiting similarity, convergence, and divergence of coexisting species. *American Naturalist* 101: 377–385.

Mace, P.M. 1997. Developing and sustaining world fisheries resources: The state of the science and management. In *Developing and sustaining world fisheries resources: Proceedings of the 2nd World Fisheries Congress,* ed. D.H. Hancock, D.C. Smith, A. Grant, and J.B. Beumer, 1–20. Collingwood, Australia: CSIRO Publishing.

Mackinson, S., J.L. Blanchard, J.K. Pinnegar, and R. Scott. 2003. Consequences of alternative functional response formations in models exploring whale-fishery interactions. *Marine Mammal Science* 19: 661–681.

MacLaren, A., S. Brault, J. Harwood, and D. Vardy. 2002. *Report of the eminent panel on seal management.* Ottawa: Department of Fisheries and Oceans.

Mitchell, E., and J.G. Mead. 1977. The history of the gray whale in the Atlantic Ocean. In *Proceedings of the Second Conference on the Biology of Marine Mammals,* 12. San Diego: Society of Marine Mammology.

Morisette, L., M.O. Hammill, and C. Savenkoff. Submitted for pub. The trophic role of marine mammals in the northern Gulf of St. Lawrence. *Marine Mammal Science*.

Mossner, S., and K. Ballschmiter. 1997. Marine mammals as global pollution indicators for organochlorines. *Chemosphere* 34: 1285–1296.

Munro, G., and U.R. Sumaila. 2002. The impact of subsidies upon fisheries management and sustainability: The case of the North Atlantic. *Fish and Fisheries* 3: 233–290.

Myers, R.A., and B. Worm. 2003. Rapid world-wide depletion of predatory fish communities. *Nature* 423: 280–283.

Naylor, R.L., J. Goldberg, J.H. Primavera, N. Kautsky, M.C.M. Beveridge, J. Clay, C. Folke, J. Lubchenco, H. Mooney, and M. Troell. 2000. Effect of aquaculture on world fish supplies. *Nature* 405: 1017–1024.

Neutel, A.-M., J.A.P. Heesterbeek, and P.C. de Ruiter. 2002. Stability in real food webs: Weak links in long loops. *Science* 269: 1120–1123.

Nilssen, K.T. 1995. Seasonal distribution, condition and feeding habits of Barents Sea harp seals (*Phoca groenlandica*). In *Whales, seals, fish and man: Proceedings of the International Symposium on the Biology of Marine Mammals in the North East Atlantic*, ed. A.S. Blix, L. Walløe, and Ø Ulltang, 241–254. Amsterdam: Elsevier.

Northridge, S. 2002. Effects of fishing industry. In *Encyclopedia of marine mammals*, ed. W.F. Perrin, B. Würsig, and J.G.M. Thewissen, 442–447. San Diego: Academic Press.

Northridge, S.P. 1984. *World review of interactions between marine mammals and fisheries*. 190. Rome: Food and Agricultural Organization of the United Nations.

———. 1991. An updated world review of interactions between marine mammals and fisheries. 58. Rome: Food and Agricultural Organisation of the United Nations.

Okey, T.A., S. Banks, A.R Born, R.H. Bustamante, M. Calvopina, G.J. Edgar, E. Espinoza, J.M. Farina, L.E. Garske, G.K. Reck, S. Salazar, S. Shepherd, V. Toral-Granda, and P. Wallem. 2004. A trophic model of a Galapagos subtidal rocky reef for evaluating fisheries and conservation strategies. *Ecological Modelling* 172: 383–401.

Palka, D. 2000. Effectiveness of gear modifications as a harbour porpoise by-catch reduction strategy off the Mid-Atlantic coast of the USA. (SC/52/SM24). In *International Whaling Commission—Scientific Committee Meeting*, Adelaide, Australia. Unpublished, 27.

Parsons, T.R. 1992. The removal of marine predators by fisheries and the impact of trophic structure. *Marine Pollution Bulletin* 25: 51–53.

Pauly, D., and V. Christensen. 1995. Primary production required to sustain global fisheries. *Nature* 374: 255–257.

Pauly, D., V. Christensen, and C. Walters. 2000. Ecopath, ecosim, and ecospace as tools for evaluating ecosystem impact of fisheries. *ICES Journal of Marine Science* 57: 697–706.

Pauly, D., V. Christensen, J. Dalsgaard, R. Froese, and F.J. Torres. 1998b. Fishing down marine food webs. *Science* 279: 860–863.

Pauly, D., A.W. Trites, E. Capuli, and V. Christensen. 1998a. Diet composition and trophic levels of marine mammals. *ICES Journal of Marine Science* 55: 467–481.

Pauly, D., J. Alder, E. Bennet, V. Christensen, P. Tyedmers, and R. Watson. 2003. The future of fisheries. *Science* 302: 1359–1360.

Pauly, D., V. Christensen, S. Guénette, T.J. Pitcher, U.R. Sumaila, C.J. Walters, R. Watson, and D. Zeller. 2002. Towards sustainability in world fisheries. *Nature* 418: 689–695.

Perry, S.L., D.P. DeMaster, and G.K. Silber. 1999. The great whales: History and status of six species listed as endangered under the U.S. Endangered Species Act of 1973. *Marine Fisheries Review* 61: 74.

Perryman, W.L., M.A. Donahue, P.C. Perkins, and S.B. Reilly. 2002. Gray whale calf production 1994–2000: Are observed fluctuations related to changes in seasonal ice cover? *Marine Mammal Science* 18: 121–144.

Piatkowski, U., G.J. Pierce, and M. Morais da Cunha. 2001. Impact of cephalopods on the food chain and their interaction with the environment and fisheries: An overview. *Fisheries Research* (Amsterdam) 52: 5–10.

Plagányi, É.E., and D.S. Butterworth. 2002. Competition with fisheries. In *Encyclopedia of marine mammals*, ed. W.F. Perrin, B. Wursig, and H.G.M. Thewissen, 268–273. San Diego: Academic Press.

Punt, A.E., and D.S. Butterworth. 2001. The effects of future consumption by Cape fur seal on catches and catch rates of the Cape hakes. 4. Modelling the biological interaction between Cape fur seals *Arctocephalus pusillus pusillus* and the Cape hake *Merluccius capensis* and *Merluccius paradoxus*. *South African Journal of Marine Science* 16: 255–285.

Ray, G.C. 1981. The role of large organisms. In *Analysis of marine ecosystems*, ed. A.R. Longhurst, 397–413. New York: Academic Press.

Read, A.J. 2000. *Potential mitigation measures for reducing the* bycatches of small cetaceans in ASCOBANS waters. Bonn, Germany: ASCOBANS.

Ridoux, V. 2001. Studies on fragmented and marginal seal populations in Europe: An introduction. Mammalia 65: 277–282.

Rodriguez, D., and R. Bastida. 1998. Four hundred years in the history of pinniped colonies around Mar del Plata, Argentina. Aquatic Conservation 8: 721–735.

Sigurjónsson, J., and G.A. Vikingsson. 1992. Investigations on the ecological role of cetaceans in Icelandic and adjacent waters. (CM 1992/N:24). In ICES–Marine Mammal Committee. Unpublished.

————. 1997. Seasonal abundance of and estimated food consumption by cetaceans in Icelandic and adjacent waters. Journal of Northwest Atlantic Fishery Science 22: 271–287.

Smith, S.J., S.J. Iverson, and W.D. Bowen. 1997. Fatty acid signatures and classification trees: New tools for investigating the foraging ecology of seals. Canadian Journal of Fisheries and Aquatic Sciences 54: 1377–1386.

Stenson, G.B., and E. Perry. 2001. Incorporation uncertainty into estimates of Atlantic cod (Gadus morhua), capelin (Mallotus villosus) and Arctic cod (Boreogadus saida) consumption by harp seals in NAFO Divisions 2J3KL. In Marine mammals: From feeding behaviour or stomach contents to annual consumption—What are the main uncertainties? NAMMCO—Scientific Council Meeting, Tromsø, Norway. Unpublished.

Tamura, T. 2001. Geographical and seasonal changes of prey species and prey consumption in the western North Pacific minke whales. (SC/9/EC/8). In International Whaling Commission—Scientific Committee Meeting 13. Norway. Unpublished.

————. Regional assessment of prey consumption and competi-tion by marine cetaceans in the world. 2003. In Responsible fisheries in marine ecosystems, ed. M. Sinclair and G. Valdimarsson, 143–170. Food and Agricultural Organization of the United Nations and CABI Publishing, Wallingford, England.

Thomson, R.B., D.S. Butterworth, I.L. Boyd, and J.P Croxall. 2000. Modeling the consequences of Antarctic krill harvesting on Antarctic fur seals. Ecological Applications 10: 1806–1819.

Tjelmeland, S. 2001. Consumption of capelin by harp seal in the Barents Sea: Data gaps. In Marine mammals: From feeding behaviour or stomach contents to annual consumption—What are the main uncertainties? NAMMCO—Scientific Council Meeting 8. Tromsø, Norway. Unpublished.

Tollit, D.J. M. Steward, P.M. Thompson, G.J. Pierce, M.B. Santos, and S. Hughes. 1997. Species and size differences in the digestion of otoliths and beaks; implications for estimates of pinniped diet composition. Canadian Journal of Fisheries and Aquatic Sciences 54: 105–119.

Tollit, D.J., M. Wong, A.J. Winship, D.A.S. Rosen, and A.W. Trites. 2003. Quantifying errors associated with using prey skeletal structures from fecal samples to determine the diet of Steller's sea lion (Eumetopias jubatus). Marine Mammal Science 19: 724–744.

Torres, D.N. 1987. Juan Fernandez fur seal, Arctocephalus philippii. In International symposium and workshop on the status, biology, and ecology of fur seals, 37–40. Cambridge: National Oceanic and Atmospheric Administration.

Trites, A.W., V. Christensen, and D. Pauly. 1997. Competition between fisheries and marine mammals for prey and primary production in the Pacific Ocean. Journal of Northwest Atlantic Fishery Science 22: 173–187.

Trites, A.W., P.A. Livingston, S. Mackinson, M.C. Vasconcellos, A.M. Springer, and D. Pauly. 1999. Ecosystem change and the decline of marine mammals in the eastern Bering Sea: Testing the ecosystem shift and commercial whaling hypotheses. Vancouver: Fisheries Centre, University of British Columbia.

United Nations Environment Programme (UNEP). 1999. Report of the scientific advisory committee of the marine mammals action plan.

van Zile, D. 2000. To whale or not to whale? National Fisherman: 88: 44–46.

Wade, P. 2002. A Bayesian stock assessment of the eastern Pacific gray whale using abundance and harvest data from 1967–1996. Journal of Cetacean Research and Management 4: 85–98.

Walters, C., and J.F. Kitchell. 2001. Cultivation/depensation effects on juvenile survival and recruitment: Implications for the theory of fishing. Canadian Journal of Fisheries and Aquatic Sciences 58: 1–12.

Ward, A.R., and D.J. Jeffries. 2000. A manual for assessing post-harvest fisheries losses. Chatham, England: Natural Resource Institute.

Watson, R., and D. Pauly, D. 2001. Systematic distortions in world fisheries catch trends. Nature 414: 534–536.

Watson, R., A. Kitchingman, A. Gelchu, and D. Pauly. 2004. Mapping global fisheries: Sharpening our focus. Fish and Fisheries 5, 168–177.

Weller, D.W., A.M. Burdin, B. Wuersig, B.L. Taylor, and R.L.J. Brownell. 2002a. The western gray whale: A review of past exploitation, current status, and potential threats. Journal of Cetacean Research and Management 4: 7–12.

Weller, D.W., S.R. Reeve, A.M. Burdin, B. Wuersig, and R.L.J. Brownell. 2002b. A note on the spatial distribution of western gray whales (*Eschrichtius robustus*) off Sakhalin Island, Russia in 1998. *Journal of Cetacean Research and Management* 4: 13–17.

Wickens, P., and A.E. York. 1997. Comparative population dynamics of fur seals. *Marine Mammal Science* 13: 241–292.

Wickens, P.A., D.W. Japp, P.A. Shelton, F. Kriel, P.C. Goosen, B. Rose, C.J. Augustyn, C.A.R. Bross, A.J. Penney, and R.G. Krohn. 1992. Seals and fisheries in South Africa: Competition and conflict. In *Benguela trophic functioning*, ed. A.I.L. Payne, K.H. Brink, K.H. Mann, and R. Hilborn. *South African Journal of Marine Science* 12: 773–789.

Yodzis, P. 1998. Local trophodynamics and the interaction of marine mammals and fisheries in the Benguela ecosystem. *Journal of Animal Ecology* 67: 635–658.

————. 2001. Must top predators be culled for the sake of fisheries? *Trends in Ecology and Evolution* 16: 78–83.

Zeppelin, T.K., D.J. Tollit, K.A. Call, T.J. Orchard, and C.J. Gudmundson. 2004. Sizes of walleye pollock (*Theragra chalcogramma*) and Atka mackerel (*Pleurogrammus monopterygius*) consumed by the western stock of Steller sea lions (*Eumetopias jubatus*) in Alaska from 1998–2000. *Fishery Bulletin* 102: 509–521.

Chimpanzees in Research: Past, Present, and Future

CHAPTER 9

Kathleen M. Conlee and Sarah T. Boysen

Introduction

Chimpanzees have been used in research in the United States since the 1920s (Brent 2004), with their breeding and use highlighted in the 1980s as a model for acquired immune deficiency syndrome (AIDS) research. However, the use of chimpanzees in harmful research has come to be questioned throughout the world, based on both ethical and scientific concerns. Public support for chimpanzee research has been declining over time (National Science Board 2002), costs of using chimpanzees in research have been rising, the number of chimpanzees in laboratories (including in the United States) has been declining, and legislation and policies prohibiting the use of great apes in research have been on the rise internationally. These trends may indicate an end to the use of chimpanzees in research in the United States and abroad in the near future. Other than increased attention to the use of chimpanzees in research, animal protection groups, conservationists, lawyers, and others are focusing on issues related to chimpanzees as well, including their use in entertainment, hunting of them in the wild for food (known as "bushmeat") and the pet trade, general

conservation issues, and pursuit of their legal rights (Cavalieri and Singer 1993; Wise 2000, 2002).

Why is there particular interest in the use of chimpanzees in research? They are the only apes (of both great and small) used in biomedical research and testing in the United States, and much has been learned about their emotional lives and intelligence over the last several decades.[1]

Although the welfare of chimpanzees encompasses many issues, this chapter addresses their use in research, including their historical and current use in the United States, ethical and scientific concerns, public opinion, international legislation, and future directions.

The Species Chimpanzee (*Pan troglodytes*)

Chimpanzees are members of the taxonomic order primates and the great ape family (*Pongidae*), which also includes gorillas (both lowland and mountain subspecies), orangutans, and bonobos (formerly referred to as pygmy chimpanzees). The natural habitat of the chimpanzee is a range of countries

across equatorial Africa, from Senegal, Mali, Sierra Leone, Côte d'Ivoire, Ghana, Nigeria, Cameroon, and Gabon in West Africa; the central African countries of Congo, Equatorial Guinea, the Central African Republic, the Democratic Republic of Congo, Uganda, and Burundi; and Tanzania in east Africa. Chimpanzee social structure has been observed to include nearly every type of relationship seen among different primate species, including multimale or multifemale groups, bachelor groups, male/female breeding pairs, a mother and her infant, or a female and her offspring of various ages.

In general, chimpanzee social organization is described as a fission-fusion society, with individuals or small groups leaving and then periodically rejoining the group. Like many primate species, chimpanzees give birth to a single infant, who may nurse for four to five years, so the offspring have an extended period of maturation and learning. Males remain in their natal group for their entire life, while females of reproductive age emigrate and take up residence in neighboring communities. These sex-related behavioral strategies thus serve as a natural incest taboo and help maintain genetic diversity within and among different chimpanzee groups in a given area. Male chimpanzees maintain order and position in their groups through a dominance hierarchy and often form coalitions of two to three males who co-rule the group. Females, however, are not as social with other females as males are with males, although a dominance structure does exist among them. Exceptions have been observed, even to the point of a female who participated in cooperative hunting with the males of her group, although most of such opportunistic predation on small mammals (including monkeys such as the red colobus) has typically occurred among all-male groups.

Like many nonhuman primates whose habitats are being encroached upon, the chimpanzee is listed as "endangered" in the wild under the U.S. Endangered Species Act. Some estimates are that only 110,000 animals remain across Africa. However, unlike any other species on the list, the chimpanzee is the only species that is cross-listed as "threatened" in captivity, thereby given less protection from certain types of biomedical and invasive research. Consequently, the "threatened" status of the captive population permits procedures and other activities that are not legally permitted with wild chimpanzees. If chimpanzees were listed solely as endangered, the types of research that are currently allowable could simply not be done. Currently, only a few countries other than the United States, including Gabon, Liberia, and Japan (although a ban is in preparation there), permit biomedical research on chimpanzees. Chimpanzee research is not permitted in the United Kingdom, Sweden, Australia, New Zealand, or the Netherlands (although not formally declared by each country, no European Union countries conduct research on chimpanzees).

Chimpanzee Intelligence

Cognitive and behavioral research with chimpanzees, including both field studies and captive work over the past forty years in particular, have taught us much about the remarkable capabilities chimpanzees share with humans. These include:

- An extensive list of some thirty-nine-plus types of tool use in the wild (e.g., Goodall 1968; McGrew 1992; Whiten et al. 1999)
- Complex processing capacities for acquiring concepts such as "same vs. different" (e.g., Premack and Premack 1983)
- Numerical skills, including counting abilities, that are comparable in chimpanzees' development as they are in young children (e.g., Boysen and Berntson 1989; Matsuzawa 1985a)
- Productive use and comprehension of symbolic language-like systems of several types, including signed English based on American Sign Language, visual symbol systems such as plastic shapes that stand for words, or graphic symbols that are computer-interfaced to display the word-like symbols chosen and the order in which they have been selected (e.g., Matsuzawa 1985b; Premack 1986; Savage-Rumbaugh 1986; Gardner, Gardner, and van Cantfort 1989)
- Extensive skills with problem solving of all kinds observed in both the wild and under experimental conditions in captivity (e.g., Matsuzawa 1985b; Limongelli, Boysen, and Visalberghi 1995; Kuhlmeier and Boysen 2002)
- Recognition of kin relationships based on comparing photographs alone of chimpanzees and their offspring (Parr and de Waal 1999a)
- Studies that suggest chimpanzees, like humans, understand that other chimpanzees may have the same or different set of beliefs, desires, and knowledge from their own, a capacity formerly believed to be unique to humans (e.g., Hare, Call, and Tomasello 2001; Tomasello and Call 1997).

Clearly, the evidence demonstrates that the chimpanzee is a species whose genetic, morphological, anatomical, neurological, biochemical, behavioral, and cognitive similarity to humans is unique among all other species living today.

Chimpanzee Emotions and Motivation

During the past several decades, much has been learned about the chimpanzee's motivation and capacity for emotional expression. Empirical studies under controlled conditions in captivity have documented that the emotional range of chimpanzees is quite comparable to that observed in humans, with considerable overlap in facial expressions (Parr, Dove, and Hopkins 1998; Parr 2001, 2003). These include expressions exhibited during laughter; under conditions of fear, anger, or sadness; and a range of grimaces observed in human neonates, such as disgust or pleasure in response to odors and/or taste.

Observations in both wild and captive settings suggest that chimpanzees are subject to some of the same types of behavioral and emotional pathologies as have been observed in humans, including depression, various neuroses, anxiety, and even grief to the point of death (Goodall 1986). It is typically easy, especially for young children, to watch chimpanzees in a zoo or sanctuary and recognize that the animals are playing tag or play-fighting or that a disagreement has occurred between animals, with resultant real fighting. The overlap among behavioral and emotional expressions between humans and chimpanzees is quite dramatic, such that even very young children are able to interpret often complex social interactions among chimpanzees quite accurately. (There are notable exceptions, however, such as differences in the two species' respective "smiles"—a chimpanzee "smiling" with upper and lower teeth showing is expressing fear, for example.)

The History of U.S. Chimpanzee Research: 1920–1979

Chimpanzee research began with the work of Robert M. Yerkes of Yale University, who established a laboratory at his rural home in the early 1920s with two purchased chimpanzees (Yerkes and Learned 1925). His early writing about these animals, a male and a female, explored a wide range of behavioral and intellectual capacities observed both directly and indirectly as the young chimpanzees developed. He was particularly interested in and wrote fairly extensively about the differences he noted between the two animals and, at the time, attributed such to sex differences. However, it was later confirmed that Yerkes actually had one chimpanzee (Pan troglodytes) and one bonobo (Pan paniscus), so many of the differences he attributed to sex may actually have been species differences. This was particularly notable with respect to differences in vocalizations, although many other behavioral traits were also confounded by reporting them as sex rather than species differences (Yerkes and Learned 1925). Despite this misguided start, Yerkes and his wife contributed several of the first descriptions of chim-

panzee behavior, including a range of observations that included social interaction, play, sexual activity, diet, morphology, anatomy, emotional states, facial expressions, vocalizations, and intelligence.

Yerkes's work was critical to the emergence of primate studies in the United States. His burgeoning laboratory moved first to Orange Park, Florida, in 1930 and then to Emory University in Atlanta, Georgia, in 1965 where, as the Yerkes National Primate Research Center, it remains today (Yerkes National Primate Research Center n.d.). In addition to his numerous books on apes, including chimpanzees, Yerkes contributed a wealth of scientific papers to the emerging literature. Yerkes's books and journal articles remain an important source for researchers, particularly for those whose interests are in chimpanzee cognition and behavior. He was the first to study many phenomena in chimpanzees of great importance to the field of primatology and is considered to be one of the fathers of primatology in the United States.

In the 1940s the focus at Yerkes National Primate Research Center shifted from the study of behavior to the study of infectious disease (Committee on Animal Models in Biomedical Research 1995). The use of chimpanzees for the study of infectious disease has increased ever since, particularly in hepatitis and human immunodeficiency virus (HIV), and continues at a number of facilities (Table 1).

In the 1950s the U.S. Air Force created a research and breeding program with sixty-five wild-caught chimpanzees to determine the effects of space flight on humans (Brent 2004; Save the Chimps n.d.). The aeronautics research involved subjecting chimpanzees to a number of stressors during training as well as the obvious stressors associated with being launched into space. These stressors included exposure to G forces, loss of consciousness in decompression cham-

bers, spinning in giant centrifuges, and use of shock as punishment while training (Save the Chimps n.d.). In January 1961 a chimpanzee named Ham was placed on a ballistic trajectory flight and forced to perform a motor task throughout the flight for which he had been trained. In November 1961 a second chimpanzee, Enos, orbited the earth twice and was forced to perform a more complex task (NASA 2004). Unfortunately, through a malfunction in equipment, Enos received a shock for every correct maneuver he made, which contradicted the 1,263 hours of training he had undergone (NASA 2004; Save the Chimps n.d.); despite the shocks, Enos continued to complete the task correctly.

After some Air Force chimpanzees were sent into space, they were reassigned to other projects, such as testing seat belts. In the 1970s the Air Force no longer used chimpanzees but did lease them out for biomedical research studies (Save the Chimps n.d.). In 1975 the Convention on International Trade in Endangered Species (CITES) was adopted, which greatly restricted importation of chimpanzees from the wild. This prompted a captive-breeding effort within the United States, which has been federally funded since 1986 (Brent 2004).

Chimpanzee Research: 1980 to the Present

AIDS Research in the 1980s

During the 1980s there was a drastic increase in chimpanzee research, primarily prompted by the human AIDS epidemic. A massive breeding effort was launched in 1986 (National Research Council 1997), and in 1992 scientists representing animal welfare and AIDS research interests met to discuss

Table 1
U.S. Facilities Housing Chimpanzees:
Types of Research and Numbers of Animals

Facility*	Location	Type of Research	Total Number of Chimpanzees	Number of NCRR-Supported Chimpanzees[3]
New Iberia Research Center	New Iberia, La.	Breeding, vaccine research, drug efficacy	350[1]	130
Alamogordo Primate Facility	Alamogordo, N.M.	Behavioral	275[1]	270
Southwest National Primate Research Center	San Antonio, Tex.	Vaccine and drug testing, hepatitis, Alzheimer's, HIV	250[1]	15
Yerkes National Primate Research Center	Atlanta, Ga.	HIV, behavioral, neuroscience, reproduction	197[1]	75
M.D. Anderson Cancer Center	Bastrop, Tex.	Breeding colony, hepatitis, infectious disease	154[1]	105
Primate Foundation of Arizona	Mesa, Ariz.	Behavioral, reproductive, research supply	75[1]	74
Bioqual	Rockville, Md.	Hepatitis, respiratory viruses	63[2]	Not mentioned
Centers for Disease Control and Prevention	Atlanta, Ga.	Hepatitis	14[2]	Not mentioned
Food and Drug Administration	Rockville, Md.		11[2]	Not mentioned
Ohio State University	Columbus, Ohio	Behavioral, cognitive (noninvasive)	11[1]	0
Language Research Center, Georgia State University	Decatur, Ga.	Behavioral (noninvasive)	4[2]	Not mentioned
Chimpanzee and Human Communication Institute, Central Washington University	Ellensburg, Wash.	Behavioral (noninvasive)	4[2]	Not mentioned

*This is not meant to be an exhaustive list of the types of research being conducted at each facility.

[1] According to the *International Directory of Primatology*.

[2] According to Goodall et al. 2003.

[3] According to a presentation given by J. Strandberg at the American Association of Laboratory Animal Science (AALAS) conference in 2003. The remaining chimpanzees are not federally owned, but the facilities may still receive federal funding for research.

the use of chimpanzees in human immunodeficiency virus (HIV) research (van Akker et al. 1993). At that time, the group acknowledged there were some areas of HIV research for which chimpanzees were not necessary, such as prevention of maternal-infant transmission and physiological safety tests for vaccine development. The group advocated for alternatives, such as using monkeys, but it emphasized that some of the suggested approaches engendered animal welfare concerns as well. The group considered other factors related to HIV research on chimpanzees, such as housing conditions, and concluded that not allowing chimpanzees in HIV research to interact socially with other chimpanzees or humans "is both unnecessary and unethical" (van Akker et al. 1993). The group advocated the use of environmental enrichment (innovative ways to enrich the lives of chimpanzees that promote natural behavior) and housing that allows the chimpanzees to express natural locomotor behaviors.

It is not known whether HIV survives in chimpanzees, but we do know that the animals do not develop the AIDS-related complex seen in humans (Balls 1995; Nath, Schumann, and Boyer 2000). There is, however, a specific strain that is pathogenic in chimpanzees and typically takes up to ten years to progress to AIDS-like symptoms. Great controversy has arisen over whether chimpanzees should, in fact, be challenged with that particular strain (Nath Schumann, and Boyer 2000). Some members of the research community have strongly opposed the idea, some publicly (Prince et al. 1999). Over time, however, it has been determined that the chimpanzee is a poor model for HIV research, and some researchers argue that the use of chimpanzees is not likely to lead to a cure for AIDS (Reynolds 1995). Despite this, HIV-related research in chimpanzees continues.

The Humane Society of the United States (HSUS) examined U.S. Public Health Service (PHS)-funded grants that involved captive chimpanzees in HIV research in some way (including breeding for HIV research), beginning in 1980.

Some grants extended over as many as twenty-five years; therefore, data for each year reflect both ongoing research and newly funded projects. In 1980 three PHS-funded studies involved the use of chimpanzees in HIV-related research.

Table 2
Public Health Service-Funded Grants: HIV Research Involving Captive Chimpanzees

Year	Number of Grants	Types of HIV Research
1980	3	Receptors Vaccine safety Chimpanzee housing
1984	5	Receptors Vaccine safety Chimpanzee housing Transmission of HIV
1988	17	Receptors Vaccine safety Chimpanzee housing Transmission of HIV Vaccine efficacy Chimpanzee breeding/management
1992	18	Receptors Vaccine safety Chimpanzee housing Transmission of HIV Vaccine efficacy Chimpanzee breeding/management Immune response
1996	20	Receptors Vaccine safety Chimpanzee housing Transmission of HIV Vaccine efficacy Chimpanzee breeding/management Immune response HIV progression and pathogenesis Genetic inoculation
2000	23	Receptors Vaccine safety Chimpanzee housing Transmission of HIV Vaccine efficacy Chimpanzee breeding/management HIV progression in young chimpanzees Infection with strain most virulent in chimpanzees Cell-based immunotherapy
2004	7	Chimpanzee breeding/management Gene expression in infected chimpanzees Vaccine development

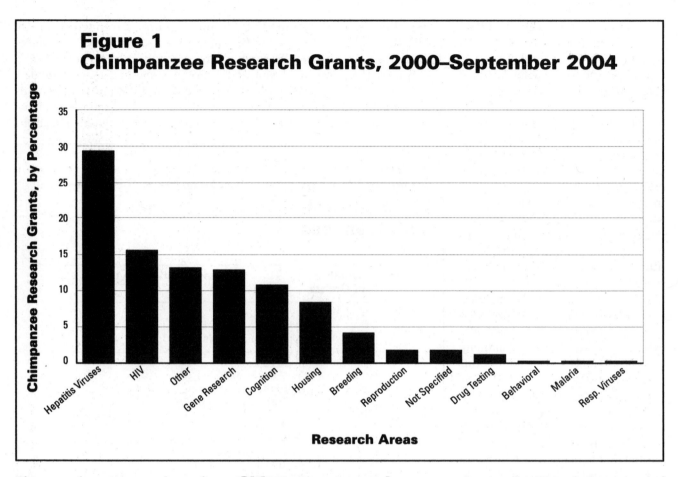

Figure 1
Chimpanzee Research Grants, 2000–September 2004

Chimpanzee Research Grants, by Percentage (y-axis: 0, 5, 10, 15, 20, 25, 30, 35)

Research Areas (x-axis): Hepatitis Viruses, HIV, Other, Gene Research, Cognition, Housing, Breeding, Reproduction, Not Specified, Drug Testing, Behavioral, Malaria, Resp. Viruses

This number increased to five grants in 1984 and jumped to seventeen in 1988. The next few years resulted in an increase in these grants, to twenty-three in 2000, but this number fell to seven grants in 2004 (Table 2). As of 2001 150 chimpanzees had been infected with various strains of HIV, but only four had had evidence of "progressive HIV infection," and one of the four had progressed to AIDS (Muchmore 2001). AIDS research on chimpanzees (including colony maintenance) has been conducted primarily at Yerkes National Primate Research Center (Atlanta, Georgia), Southwest National Primate Research Center (San Antonio, Texas), New Iberia Primate Research Center (New Iberia, Louisiana), and the M.D. Anderson Cancer Center Science Park (Bastrop, Texas) (Table 2).

Chimpanzees and Research Facilities in the United States

According to Stephens (1995), there were approximately 1,800 chimpanzees in fourteen biomedical and behavioral research facilities in the United States in 1993. In 2001 a National Institutes of Health (NIH) report to Congress identified 1,584 chimpanzees, including 614 who were government owned, who may have been used in federally supported or conducted research and were housed in thirteen biomedical and behavioral research facilities in the United States (National Center for Research Resources 2001). Since that time approximately 266 chimpanzees formerly owned by a biomedical research facility in Alamogordo, New Mexico, were transferred and are now being cared for by a sanctuary organization based in Florida. It was estimated that there were approximately 1,300 chimpanzees in twelve facili-

ties in the United States as of 2005. Table 1 provides a list of research facilities that as of 2005 housed chimpanzees, some areas of research conducted at each facility, and the number of chimpanzees (if known) at each facility. The majority of captive research chimpanzees are housed at six biomedical facilities. Information regarding the number of chimpanzees and chimpanzee research facilities in the United States was also supported by a census conducted and reported by the Great Ape Project (Goodall et al. 2003).

A review of the literature published during 2001 and included in the National Library of Medicine and PrimateLit databases revealed that of the 4,411 studies worldwide involving nonhuman primate research, nine involved the use of apes (Carlsson et al. 2004). Overall, it was estimated that 41,000 primates were used, although the specific number of great apes represented by these studies is unknown, particularly because not all publications specify the number of animals used (Carlsson et al. 2004). Some studies, particularly those from private-sector organizations such as pharmaceutical companies, are not published (Carlsson et al. 2004) at all. These data suggest that a review of the published literature may not produce reliable information about the actual number of chimpanzees used in research, consequently requiring reliance on other sources of information.

Research in Which Chimpanzees Are Used

Chimpanzees are most commonly used for hepatitis (particularly hepatitis C) and HIV/AIDS research. A total of 334 federally funded grants between 2000 and 2004 involved the use of live chimpanzees, with approximately 29 percent related to hepatitis research and 16 percent related to HIV/AIDS research. Stephens (1995) reported that approximately 80 percent of research conducted on chimpanzees in the early '90s was related to hepatitis and HIV/AIDS. Therefore, these types of biomedical research with chimpanzees are not as prevalent as they are in the recent past, although such invasive studies continue.

Other areas of research for which chimpanzees are currently used include cognitive and behavioral studies, as models for human reproduction, malaria, gene therapy, respiratory viruses, Crohn's disease, drug and vaccine testing, and a variety of other infectious diseases (Figure 1). Experiments in some of these areas, such as studies of certain strains of HIV, can lead to severe appetite and weight loss, lethargy, diarrhea, severe illness, infections, and/or eventual death. Procedures such as major surgery, liver biopsies (required for some protocols in hepatitis research and involving multiple biopsies), frequent blood sampling, and restraint can also cause pain and distress. Invasive research, in general, raises particular concerns regarding chimpanzee welfare in captivity.

Chimpanzee Housing and Care

Individuals who have worked closely with chimpanzees in research report that those used in many invasive protocols are typically housed alone in cages required by USDA standards to be only five feet by five feet by seven feet, with twenty-five square feet of floor space. This can be compared to the interior of an elevator (Figure 2). Cages are typically constructed from steel and, in some cases, include a perch for resting or sleeping. Many cages also have a "squeeze back," a moveable interior wall that can be pulled from the back of the cage toward the front and can press or hold a chimpanzee closer to the front of the cage so that a technician, veterinarian, or researcher can administer injections or perform other procedures without anesthetizing the chimp. Under some conditions, housing areas do not have any natural light, and the animals live under artificial lighting (light/dark) cycles at all times.

In the wild, chimpanzees are very social and live in complex groups of varying sizes. Therefore, social housing is almost certainly the single most important factor for chimpanzee psychological well-being (National Research Council 1997). Individual housing can lead to profound depression, increased aggression, psychological withdrawal, extreme frustration, and self-mutilation, such as physical wounding, hair plucking, rocking, and other psychotic-like behaviors. Chimpanzees who are not being used in active research protocols typically are housed in pairs or social groups. The physical environment for social housing can range from a cage that is slightly larger than the individual cage depicted in Figure 2 to large outdoor enclosures where the ani-

mals live in large social groups of eight to 20 individuals. The type of housing used depends on the particular institution and the type of research being conducted. Chimpanzees who live in groups also can be separated for a period and placed on research protocols that involve single housing. The likelihood of this depends on several factors, including the specific institution, the type of research conducted there (whether study animals could infect others if they were housed together), and precedents within the institution that may not be necessary for the specific study but instead reflect the culture of the institution.

An analysis of chimpanzee research for the years 2000 to mid-2002 conducted by The HSUS revealed that information about the types of housing provided in publications or in federal grant abstracts was lacking (Conlee, Hoffeld, and Stephens 2004). Among 189 publications 24 percent mentioned social housing and 76 percent did not mention any specific housing type. Overall, information regarding the specific number of chimpanzees maintained in each type of housing (individual vs. social) was not readily available. Housing and environmental conditions, however, can have significant effects on research

Figure 2.
A typical laboratory cage for individually housed chimpanzees.

results, so such information should be included in all publications. Regardless of whether housing information is available, Balls (1995) raises an important point: it may be impossible to provide housing in laboratories that truly meets the physiological and behavioral needs of chimpanzees under captive conditions.

Funding for Research

The HSUS analysis of federally funded great ape research found that $20 million to $25 million dollars of federal funding per year is devoted to chimpanzee research and care (Conlee, Hoffeld, and Stephens 2004) (Figure 3). Hepatitis research accounts for $4.2 million of this funding each year, and HIV research accounts for approximately $500,000. The amount of private-sector funding for chimpanzee research is not available to the public; however, the use of chimpanzees by the private sector may be on the rise. A chimpanzee researcher sitting on a panel at the 2003 American Association of Laboratory Animal Science conference indicated that 75 percent of private-sector growth (particularly pharmaceutical companies) at the New Iberia Research Center was due to requests for chimpanzee use.

It is estimated that it costs $20–$30 a day to care for a chimpanzee in the laboratory and $15 a day to care for one—better—in a sanctuary. Compare the $9.5–$14.2 million a year to care for the United States' 1,300 chimpanzees in a laboratory to the $7.1-million-a-year cost of sanctuary care. It is important to emphasize that the sanctuary setting not only costs less per chimpanzee per day, but also can provide a much more naturalistic and stimulating environment.

Ethical Questions and Responsibilities

The United States currently uses more chimpanzees in biomedical research than any other country in the world. The U.S. government provides more funding for the study of chimpanzee cognition and behavior than does any other country. Results from studies over the past four decades in particular have provided a wealth of scientific evidence showing that chimpanzees and humans bear striking similarities. While we have known for up to two hundred years that the anatomy, physiology, morphology, biochemistry, and genetic overlap between chimpanzees and humans is overwhelming, it has only been within the last forty years that demonstrations of chimpanzee cognitive abilities and behavior, including a wide range of emotions evoked by chimpanzees and human beings in similar situations, have been reported from field studies (e.g., Goodall 1968) and captive work (e.g., Washburn and Rumbaugh 1992; Brown and Boysen 2000). Recent technological advances have allowed direct comparisons at the neuroanatomical level between the two species, with notable correspondence between a significant number of neuroanatomical structures that likely support the same functions (e.g., Cantalupo, Pilcher, and Hopkins 2003; Hopkins and Cantalupo 2004).

With more than thirty years of direct interactions with chimpanzees as part of a comparative cognition project, one author (S.B.) (2000) reports that her chimps have shown a number of behaviors suggesting that they were responding to natural events such as wind or thunderstorms with great fear. A similar response was likely felt by early humans, who subsequently created myths and legends to explain these phenomena. When a chimpanzee lost a

tooth and the chimp's loud alarm calls drew the other chimps to the scene, the group's response—raucous calls and all members peering at the tiny white tooth on the ground—clearly suggested that the group interpreted the pain and blood loss as caused by the tooth itself as an animate object.

One author (S.B.) and her students have observed their subjects readily sharing food with younger chimps, assisting older animals having difficulty moving from place to place in the facility, and responding with "reverence" to the body of a group member who had died of natural causes. In the last instance, the dead chimp's cage mate picked up a blanket, covered the dead chimp's head, and then placed a second blanket over her body. A videotaped record of these events leads an observer to the conclusion that the "friend's" response was intentional and empathetic (S.B., personal observation 2003). Goodall (1968) reports similar behaviors to those described above among wild chimps, suggesting that captive chimpanzees are not acquiring behaviors unseen in the wild. Long-term observations of chimps in the field and captivity have increasingly complemented and confirmed a range of comparable behaviors that are seen in humans as well as in the chimpanzee. Observations of behaviors of this level of sophistication and complexity raise difficult ethical and moral questions about the types of research on chimpanzees that are permitted in the United States.

More detailed studies of the similarities between human and chimpanzee behavioral and emotional responses are even more telling. Parr and de Waal (1999b) provided captive chimpanzees with photographs of chimpanzees they didn't know and found that the chimpanzees were not only able to match two different photographs of the same individual, but also to match mothers and sons. This demonstrates that chimpanzees are capable of identifying similarities in the faces of related individuals who were unfamiliar to them.

In another test by Parr and De Waal, chimpanzees were presented with sample head-shot photographs of chimpanzees. The subjects recognized the emotional expressions of the chimpanzees in the sample photographs and matched them to photographs of novel chimpanzees showing facial expressions that depicted the same emotional state. The subjects chose the photograph that best matched the sample chimpanzee's picture, based on the underlying meaning of the facial features and configuration, since the perceptual and physical features were not precisely the same.

Such trials underscore chimpanzees' capacity for empathetic responses. Such responses, coupled with the cognitive capacities humans demonstrably share with chimps, indicate that, under circumstances in which a human being might experience emotional distress or trauma, chimpanzees respond similarly under comparable conditions. One example would be for a chimpanzee to be housed in isolation, with no physical or social contact with other chimpanzees, as well as with only minimal daily contact with caregivers. There is a reason that similar housing conditions in our nation's prisons, that is, solitary confinement, are considered to be the worst conditions for inmates to endure. (Indeed, solitary confinement of human prisoners is considered by some to be "cruel and unusual punishment.")

These findings suggest that the range and nature of invasive research in the United States represents unethical and, indeed, immoral actions. In its 1997 report, the National Research Council that examined the status of chimpanzees in research facilities in the United States noted the ethical and moral responsibilities to chimps (National Research Council 1997). Unlike humans who participate in biomedical research, chimpanzees are incapable of giving informed consent. Therefore, it is clearly time for society to reappraise the status of humankind's closest primate relative.

Public Opinion: Driving Change

Increasing public concern has largely driven international efforts to end the use of chimpanzees in research. According to a recent opinion poll conducted by Zogby International for the Doris Day Animal League in 2001 (in Conlee 2003), 90 percent of Americans believe it is unacceptable to confine chimpanzees in government-approved cages (Figure 2), 54 percent believe it is unacceptable for chimpanzees to "undergo research which causes them to suffer for human benefit," and 65 percent say it is unacceptable to kill them for research.

A 2002 opinion poll by Penn, Schoen, and Berland Associates for The Humane Society of the United States (HSUS n.d.) found that 79 percent of the U.S. public supports creation of a government-sponsored sanctuary system to provide lifetime care to chimpanzees no longer used in research. This and other survey findings indicate that not only does the public oppose the suffering of chimpanzees in research, but it also is willing to financially support a significant commitment to chimpanzees, who can live to be sixty years old in captivity.

The National Science Board, which conducts surveys of public attitudes toward scientific research every three years, included the following statement in its 1985 survey: "Scientists should be allowed to do research that causes pain and injury to animals like dogs and chimpanzees if it produces new information about human health problems." In 2002 (the most recent survey results available as of 2005), 52 percent of adults opposed or strongly opposed this statement. When the same statement was used in a 1985 survey, only 30 percent of adults voiced opposition (National Science Board 2002) (Table 3).

U.S. Overview

Recent Issues

Over the last twenty years, major changes in the use of chimpanzees in research have taken place. The rush to increase breeding for HIV research in the 1980s was followed by a significant decrease in the number of facilities housing chimpanzees as well as in the number of chimpanzees at each facility in subsequent years. Three large chimpanzee research laboratories have closed since 1995, and many of their chimpanzees are now permanently retired at sanctuaries throughout the United States. In 1995 New York University decided to close its Laboratory of Experimental Medicine and Surgery in Primates (LEMSIP). Approximately half of the LEMSIP chimpanzees were sent to various retirement facilities, but the other half were sent to the Coulston Foundation, Alamagordo, New Mexico, the largest chimpanzee colony in the world at that time, which had a poor record of compliance with the Animal Welfare Act (AWA).

The second large closure was that of the chimpanzee colony at the Holloman Air Force base, also in New Mexico, in 1997. This colony of 141 chimpanzees who were used by the space program was released from the Air Force. In a controversial decision, all but thirty chimpanzees were sent to the Coulston Foundation instead of to sanctuaries that had volunteered to take in a number of them. (Those requests had been denied by the Air Force.) One of those sanctuaries was the Center for Captive Chimpanzee

Table 3
Public Opinion on Using Chimpanzees and Dogs in Painful and Injurious Research

Survey Statement: Scientists should be allowed to do research that causes pain and injury to animals like dogs and chimpanzees if it produces new information.

Year	Supporting/Strongly Supporting Animal Research	Opposing/Strongly Opposing Animal Research
1985	63	30
1988	53	42
1990	50	44
1992	53	42
1995	50	46
1997	46	51
1999	50	47
2001	44	52

Source: National Science Board 1985–2001.
Number of adults surveyed varied per year and ranged from 904 to 2,041.

Care (the CCCC—now known as Save the Chimps), an organization that ultimately sued to obtain custody of twenty-one of the chimpanzees. The CCCC entered into an agreement with the Coulston Foundation in October 1999 that brought those chimpanzees to live at the Save the Chimps' sanctuary in Florida.

The most recent laboratory closing was that of the Coulston Foundation in 2002. Approximately one year before closing, Coulston transferred three hundred chimpanzees to the Alamogordo Primate Facility, currently run under contract by Charles River Laboratories, to settle violations of the AWA. The chimpanzees at the Alamogordo Primate Facility were not being used for research at that facility as of mid-2005, but they could be transferred elsewhere for research (Brent 2004). In 2001 the National Institutes of Health stopped funding the Coulston Foundation (Brent 2004).

By 2002 the company had collapsed financially and divested itself of 266 chimpanzees, selling them to Save the Chimps, which purchased the land and facilities from the company.

Despite the decrease in the number of chimpanzee laboratories and the retirement of a significant number of chimpanzees, there are signs that some aspects of chimpanzee research have been growing. In addition to 75 percent of private-sector growth at the New Iberia Research Center coming from requests for use of chimpanzees in research, New Iberia and the Southwest National Primate Research Center have each received funds from the National Institutes of Health to expand their chimpanzee-holding facilities. The abstract of the grant for New Iberia specifies that such a facility will allow other laboratories to hold their chimpanzees within the biomedical research community with-

out retiring them under the CHIMP Act (see below). This is an unfortunate development.

U.S. CHIMP Act

The large chimpanzee breeding effort launched in the United States in 1986 exceeded expectations at the same time it was determined that the chimpanzee was not a critical model for HIV research after all. This created a "surplus" of chimpanzees for research. As a result, the National Institutes of Health called on the National Research Council (NRC) to provide input on key issues, including the number of chimpanzees required to support research needs and how to address the long-term needs of the animals who had been produced. The NRC found (1) that euthanasia is not considered by the public to be an acceptable means of addressing the surplus issue (as previously noted); (2) a five-year breeding moratorium should be adopted; and (3) sanctuaries should be established for the long-term care of retired chimpanzees (National Research Council 1997).

Following the NRC report, lobbying efforts began for the creation of a national chimpanzee sanctuary system through what became known as the Chimpanzee Health Improvement, Maintenance and Protection Act (CHIMP Act). The animal protection coalition devoted to passage of the CHIMP Act was known as the National Chimpanzee Research Retirement Task Force (NCRRTF). It consisted of The HSUS, the American Anti-Vivisection Society, the American Society for the Prevention of Cruelty to Animals, the Society for Animal Protective Legislation, and the National Anti-Vivisection Society, with the support of an advisory board of numerous primatologists. The CHIMP Act was sponsored and introduced in the House of Representatives (H.R. 3514) by Rep. James Greenwood (R-PA) on

November 22, 1999; a companion bill, sponsored by Sens. Richard Durbin (D-IL) and Bob Smith (R-NH), was introduced in the Senate (S. 2725) on June 13, 2000. A legislative hearing was held on May 18, 2000, with key individuals testifying, including Jane Goodall of the Jane Goodall Institute. (John Strandberg of the National Center for Research Resources, National Institutes of Health [NIH], provided the only oral testimony against the bill).

The CHIMP Act incited a fair amount of controversy when then-House Commerce Committee Chairman Thomas Bliley (R-VA) proposed amendments that would have provided the research community with limited access to chimpanzees after they were sent into the sanctuary system. When this amendment was proposed, the animal protection community, including NCRRTF, became divided, and its support for the legislation declined. Some groups decided to continue work on the legislation to ensure that any opportunity to remove chimpanzees from the sanctuary system was as narrow and difficult as possible, fearing that the bill ultimately would allow the research community to have easy access to chimpanzees

while holding them in less expensive housing in the interim.

The final legislative language specified that various requirements be met before any individual chimpanzee could be removed from the system, thereby greatly reducing the chances that animals would be moved back into the laboratory. These requirements included:

- Researchers could subject the chimpanzee and his or her social group to only minimal pain, distress, and disturbance (as determined by the board of directors of the sanctuary).
- Special circumstances related to the particular chimpanzee's medical history might make him or her uniquely needed for research.
- The technology to be used was not available when the chimpanzee entered the sanctuary system.
- The research is essential to address an important public health need, and that the applicant has not violated the AWA.
- The proposal is subject to public scrutiny through a sixty-day formal notice and comment process.

The CHIMP Act (P.L. 106–551) was signed into law on December

20, 2000, by President Bill Clinton. Some pro-animal groups pursued a repeal of the CHIMP Act, but they were unsuccessful. One important and positive result of the CHIMP Act was a shift in thinking and policy related to the use of chimpanzees in research.

Since passage of the legislation, various efforts have been underway to create the national sanctuary system. The NIH published a "sources sought" notice in 2001 (*Federal Register,* April 19, 2001) and, on September 30, 2002, granted the nonprofit Chimp Haven, in Shreveport, Louisiana, the contract to run the entire system. Chimp Haven's mission is to provide lifetime care to chimpanzees previously used in research, as pets, or for entertainment (Brent 2004).

The sanctuary contract stipulates that the federal government will provide $19 million for the care of an initial two hundred chimpanzees for ten years, with Chimp Haven providing matching funds of $4 million (Brent 2004). The government will also provide $10 million in construction costs, and Chimp Haven is expected to match 10 percent of those funds (Brent 2004).

The Chimp Haven facility in Shreveport will house two hundred chimpanzees at the outset and eventually expand to house a total of three hundred. At least two other sites will hold groups of seventy-five or more. Chimp Haven can also contract care out to other facilities, but it will ultimately be responsible for all of the chimpanzees in the system—a maximum of nine hundred individuals (Brent 2004). The first phase of construction at Chimp Haven has been completed, and chimpanzees began to arrive on April 1, 2005 (personal communication, Chimp Haven representative, with S.B., April 22, 2005).

The U.S. government has asked laboratories and government entities holding chimpanzees to prepare lists of animals no longer

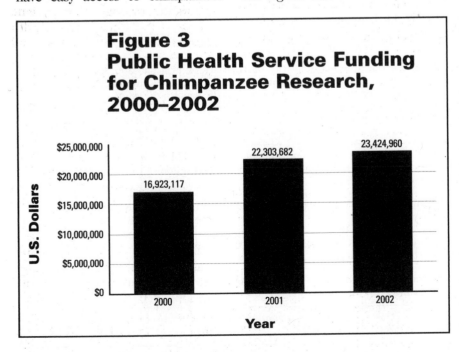

Figure 3
Public Health Service Funding for Chimpanzee Research, 2000–2002

needed for research. These lists will be shared among the facilities so that laboratories can share and undertake research on chimpanzees if desired, but the lists had not been made available to the public as of mid-2005. Table 4 provides a timeline of events related to the creation of the national sanctuary system.

International Activities

Some countries already prohibit or strongly restrict the use of chimpanzees in research. In 1997 the United Kingdom announced that licenses to conduct research on great apes would no longer be granted, although great apes have not been used in research in the United Kingdom since 1986 (U.K. Animal Procedures Committee 1998, 2001).

In 2000 New Zealand placed stringent restrictions on the use of non-human hominids (nonhuman great apes—which include chimpanzees, bonobos, gorillas, and orangutans) within its Animal Welfare Act (*www.maf.govt.nz/biosecurity/ legislation/animal-welfare-act/*

Table 4
National Chimpanzee Sanctuary System: Timeline of Events

Date	Action
April 15, 1999	A coalition that includes representatives from the research, animal-protection, zoo, and sanctuary communities writes a letter regarding the issue of chimpanzee "retirement" and submits it to U.S. Rep. J.E. Porter (R-IL) and U.S. Sen. A. Specter (R-PA).
November 22, 1999	H.R. 3514, the Chimpanzee Health Improvement, Maintenance, and Protection (CHIMP) Act, is introduced in the U.S. House of Representatives by Rep. J. Greenwood (R-PA). This bill will require the federal government to provide for permanent "retirement" of chimpanzees who are identified as no longer needed for research.
May 18, 2000	The House Committee on Commerce holds a hearing on H.R. 3514. Those presenting testimony include J. Goodall (Jane Goodall Institute), J. Strandberg (NIH), T. Nelson (National Chimpanzee Research Retirement Task Force), and A. Prince (New York Blood Center).
June 14, 2000	S. 2725, the Chimpanzee Health Improvement Maintenance and Protection (CHIMP) Act, is introduced in the U.S. Senate by Sens. R. Smith (R-NH) and R. Durbin (D-IL).
September 20, 2000	S. 2725 gains approval by the Senate Health, Education, Labor, and Pensions Committee.
October 24, 2000	The House passes H.R. 3514 with the Bliley amendments (see section, entitled *Legislation: United States and International*).
December 6, 2000	The Senate passes S. 2725 unanimously.
December 20, 2000	President Clinton signs the CHIMP Act into public law (P.L. 106–551).
April 16, 2001	The National Center for Research Resources (NCRR), part of NIH, publishes a "sources sought" notice to determine whether there is an existing nonprofit that fulfills the requirements of the CHIMP Act and is interested in serving as the "contractor" of the sanctuary system.
September 28, 2001	NIH publishes a Request for Proposal for an entity to operate and maintain a sanctuary system via the CHIMP Act.
December 20, 2001	The departments of Labor, Education, Health and Human Services and related agencies' 2002 Appropriations Act (H.R. 3061) allocates $5 million to begin construction of the national chimpanzee sanctuary facilities.
January 10, 2002	President G.W. Bush signs H.R. 3061 into public law, including $5 million toward construction of the national sanctuary system.
September 30, 2002	NIH announces the award of a contract to Chimp Haven to establish and operate a chimpanzee sanctuary, pursuant to the CHIMP Act.
May 1, 2003	Chimp Haven, the contractor of the national chimpanzee sanctuary system, breaks ground on its Shreveport, La., facility.
January 11, 2005	NIH publishes a notice of proposed rule making regarding standards of care for chimpanzees held in the national chimpanzee sanctuary system.

guide/awguide.pdf, 24). The country's director-general can approve the use of nonhuman hominids, but he or she must first consult the National Animal Ethics Advisory Committee; the use of these species must be in the best interest of the individual animal or the species; and the benefit must outweigh the harm. At the time this ban was implemented, no great apes were being used in research, but the action sent a strong message about the ethics of such use.

When the Netherlands finalized an amendment to the Dutch Law on Animal Experiments in 2002 that prohibits the use of great apes in biomedical experiments (Conlee, Hoffeld, and Stephens 2004), six chimpanzees being used in hepatitis research already underway were exempted from the ban. At the time of the amendment, the only chimpanzees in the European Union were located at the Biomedical Primate Research Centre (BPRC) in the Netherlands. In October 2002 the Dutch minister of education and the director of the BPRC signed an agreement for the transfer of ownership of fifty-nine chimpanzees to the AAP Sanctuary for Primates and other Exotic Animals (Anonymous 2003). AAP suffered various delays but had secured a site for the sanctuary and expected construction to begin in mid-2005 (AAP Sanctuary for Exotic Animals 2005).

In June 2003 Sweden's National Board for Laboratory Animals established new regulations that ban the use of apes (great apes and gibbons) in research (Anonymous 2003). The only exception is for the conduct of noninvasive behavioral studies. As was the case in New Zealand, great apes were not being used in research in Sweden when these regulations were being implemented, but the rules would prohibit any such use in the future.

Japan has also taken steps by banning invasive research on great apes (Goodman and Check

Table 5
International Legislation, Policies, and Regulations Related to Chimpanzees in Research

Country	Type of Action	Year Enacted	Comments
United Kingdom	Policy	1997*	Licenses to conduct research on nonhuman great apes will no longer be granted
New Zealand	Legislation	2000	Stringent restrictions on the use of nonhuman great apes in research
United States	Legislation (P.L. 106-551)	2000	Chimpanzees determined no longer needed in research are transferred to a national sanctuary system
Netherlands	Legislation: an amendment to the Dutch Law on Animal Experiments	2002	The use of great apes in biomedical experiments is prohibited
Sweden	Regulations	2003	The use of apes in research is prohibited
Japan	Unknown	Unknown	Invasive research on great apes is prohibited (Goodman and Check 2002)

*Although the United Kingdom has had its policy in place since 1997, great apes have not been used in research in that country since 1986.

2002), but it appears that noninvasive research is still allowed. Table 5 provides a summary of international legislation, regulations, and policies.

The Future of Chimpanzee Research

Trends in international legislation strongly suggest that additional countries will adopt legislation to restrict or end the use of chimpanzees (and other apes) in biomedical research and testing. The U.S. CHIMP Act of 2000 acknowledged the special status of chimpanzees and human responsibility for their lifetime care. There are current efforts, including by The

HSUS, to end invasive research on chimpanzees in the United States in the coming years.

Regardless of legislative efforts, the drastic decline in chimpanzee research in the United States over the past twenty years is the result of various factors, including the high cost of keeping chimpanzees in laboratories, public pressure, and evidence of the physical and psychological similarities between chimpanzees and humans. Trends suggest that the use of chimpanzees in research in the United States will continue to decline. Additional efforts to protect chimpanzees, such as legislation to prevent private ownership of chimpanzees, legal work to gain personhood for chimpanzees, and inclusion of chimpanzees and humans in the same genus, are likely continue or expand. In the meantime, the likelihood of primatologists providing even more evidence of the intelligence and emotional capabilities of chimpanzees will further support the argument that their use in biomedical research and testing should come to an end.

The authors thank Jennifer Ball, Leah Nickle, and Stephany Harris for research assistance for this chapter.

Note
[1] Other apes, including gorillas, orangutans, and gibbons, were used in the research laboratory at one time, but chimps successfully breed in captivity and as adults are smaller and easier to handle than either gorillas or orangutans.

Literature Cited

AAP Sanctuary for Exotic Animals. 2005. Breakthrough in Spain: Villena Town Council says yes to establishment of Primadomus. Electronic newsletter of AAP Sanctuary for Exotic Animals. March 9.

Anonymous. 2003. Last European research chimps to retire. *Laboratory Primate Newsletter* 42(1): 26. January.

Balls, M. 1995. Chimpanzee medical experiments: Moral, legal, and scientific concerns. *Alternatives to Laboratory Animals* 23: 607–614.

Boysen, S.T. 2000. The tooth monster. In *The smile of the dolphin*, ed. M. Bekoff, 82–83. New York: Discovery Books.

Boysen, S.T., and G.G. Berntson. 1989. Numerical competence in a chimpanzee *(Pan troglodytes). Journal of Comparative Psychology* 103: 23–31.

Brent, L. 2004. Solutions for research chimpanzees. *Lab Animal* 33(1): 37–43.

Brown, D.A., and S.T. Boysen. 2000. Spontaneous discrimination of natural stimuli by chimpanzees *(Pan troglodytes). Journal of Comparative Psychology* 114: 392–400.

Cantalupo, C., D. Pilcher, and W.D. Hopkins. 2003. Are asymmetries in sylvian fissure length associated with the planum temporale? *Neuropsychologia* 41: 1975–1981.

Carlsson, H., S.J. Schapiro, I. Farah, and J. Hau. 2004. Use of primates: A global overview. *American Journal of Primatology* 63: 225–237.

Cavalieri, P., and P. Singer, eds. 1993. *The Great Ape Project: Equality beyond humanity.* London: Fourth Estate Limited.

Committee on Animal Models in Biomedical Research. 1995. *Aping science: A critical analysis of research at the Yerkes Regional Primate Research Center.* New York: Medical Research Modernization Committee.

Conlee, K.M. 2003. Great ape research: Exposing the hard facts and pursuing a ban. *AV Magazine* 111: 12–14.

Conlee, K.M., E.H. Hoffeld, and M.L. Stephens. 2004. A demographic analysis of primate research in the United States. *Alternatives to Laboratory Animals* 32 (Supplement 1): 315–322.

Gardner, R.A., B.T. Gardner, and T.E. van Cantfort. 1989. *Teaching sign language to chimpanzees.* Albany: State University of New York Press.

Goodall, J. 1968. The behaviour of free-living chimpanzees in the Gombe Stream Reserve. *Animal Behaviour Monographs* 1: 161–311.

———. 1986. *The chimpanzees of Gombe: Patterns of behavior.* Cambridge, Mass.: Belknap, Harvard University Press.

Goodall, J., R. Fouts, F. Patterson, E. Katz, M. Bekoff, and B. Galdikas. 2003. *The Great Ape Project census.* Portland, Ore.: Great Ape Project Books.

Goodman, S., and E. Check. 2002. The great primate debate. *Nature* 417: 684–687.

Hare, B., J. Call, and M. Tomasello. 2001. Do chimpanzees know what conspecifics know? *Animal Behaviour* 61: 139–151.

Hopkins, W.D., and C. Cantalupo. 2004. Handedness in chimpanzees is associated with asymmetries in the primary motor but not with homologous language areas. *Behavioral Neuroscience* 118: 1176–1183.

Kuhlmeier, V.A., and S.T. Boysen. 2002. Chimpanzees *(Pan troglodytes)* recognize spatial and object correspondences between a scale model and its referent. *Psychological Science,* January: 60–63.

Limongelli, L., S.T. Boysen, and E. Visalberghi. 1995. Comprehension of cause-effect relations in a tool-using task by chimpanzees *(Pan troglodytes). Journal of Comparative Psychology* 109: 18–26.

Matsuzawa, T. 1985a. Use of numbers by a chimpanzee. *Nature* 315: 57–59.

———. 1985b. Color naming and classification in a chimpanzee *(Pan troglodytes). Journal of Human Evolution* 14: 283–291.

McGrew, W.C. 1992. *Material culture in chimpanzees.* Cambridge: Cambridge University Press.

Muchmore, E. 2001. Chimpanzee models for human disease and immunobiology. *Immunological Reviews* 183: 86–93.

National Aeronautics and Space Administration (NASA). 2004. Project Mercury Ballistic and Orbital Chimpanzee Flights (CHIMP). *http://lsda.jsc.nasa.gov/scripts/cf/exper.cfm?exp_index=907.*

Nath, B.M., K.E. Schumann, and J.D. Boyer. 2000. The chimpanzee and other non-human primate models in HIV-1 vaccine research. *Trends in Microbiology* 8(9): 426–431.

National Center for Research Resources (NCRR). 2001. Report to Congress regarding number of chimpanzees and funding for care of chimpanzees, Public Law 106-551, Chimpanzees Health Improvement, Maintenance, and Protection Act. Bethesda, Md.: NCRR.

National Research Council. 1997. *Chimpanzees in research: Strategies for their ethical care, management, and use.* Washington, D.C.: National Academy Press.

National Science Board 2002. *Science and engineering indicators 2002: Appendix table 7–27.*

Parr, L.A. 2001. Cognitive and physiological markers of emotional awareness in chimpanzees (*Pan troglodytes*). *Animal Cognition* 4: 223–229.

———. 2003. The discrimination of faces and their emotional content by chimpanzees (*Pan troglodytes*). *Annals of the New York Academy of Sciences* 1000: 56–78.

Parr, L.A., and F.B.M. de Waal. 1999a. Like mother—like son: Visual kin recognition in chimpanzees. *American Journal of Primatology* 49: 84–85.

———. 1999b. Visual kin recognition in chimpanzees. *Nature* 399: 647–648.

Parr, L.A., T. Dove, and W.D. Hopkins. 1998. Why faces may be special: Evidence of the inversion effect in chimpanzees. *Journal of Cognitive Neuroscience* 10: 615–622.

Premack, D. 1986. *Gavagai! or the future history of the animal language controversy.* Cambridge, Mass.: MIT Press.

Premack, D., and A. Premack. 1983. *The mind of an ape.* New York: Norton.

Prince, A.M., J. Allan, L. Andrus, B. Brotman, J. Eichber, R. Fouts, J. Goodall, P. Marx, K.K. Murthy, S. McGreal, C. Noon. 1999. Virulent HIV strains, chimpanzees, and trial vaccines. *Science* 283 (5405): 1117–1118.

Reynolds, V. 1995. Moral issues in relation to chimpanzee field studies and experiments. *Alternatives to Laboratory Animals* 23: 621–625.

Savage-Rumbaugh, E.S. 1986. *Ape language: From conditioned response to symbol.* New York: Columbia University Press.

Save the Chimps n.d. History: Saving space chimps. *http://www.savethechimps.org/about_history.asp.*

Stephens, M. 1995. Chimpanzees in laboratories: Distribution and types of research. *Alternatives to Laboratory Animals* 23: 579–583.

The Humane Society of the United States (HSUS). n.d. Statement of The HSUS on ending biomedical research on nonhuman apes. *http://www.hsus.org/animals_in_research/monkeys_and_apes_in_research/ending_biomedical_research_on_nonhuman_apes/statement_of_the_hsus_on_ending_biomedical_research_on_nonhuman_apes.html.*

Tomasello, M., and J. Call. 1997. *Primate cognition.* New York: Oxford University Press.

United Kingdom Animal Procedures Committee. 1998. Government announces end to cosmetic testing on animals. Press release *http://www.apc.gov.uk/press_releases/981126b.htm.*

———. 2001. *Report of the Animal Procedures Committee for 2001.* London: The Stationary Office. *http://www.apc.gov.uk/reference/annrep2001.pdf.*

van Akker, R., M. Balls, J.W. Eichberg, J. Goodall, J.L. Heeney, A.D.M.E. Osterhaus, A.M. Prince, and I. Spruit. 1993. Chimpanzees in AIDS research: A biomedical and bioethical perspective. *Journal of Medical Primatology* 22: 330–392.

Washburn, D.A., and D.M. Rumbaugh. 1992. Comparative assessment of psychomotor performance: Target prediction by humans and macaques (*Macaca mulatta*). *Journal of Experimental Psychology: General* 121: 305–312.

Whiten, A., J. Goodall, W.C. McGrew, T. Nishida, V. Reynolds, Sugiyama, Y., Tutin, C.E.G., Wrangham, R.W., and Boesch, C. 1999. Culture in chimpanzees. *Nature* 399: 682–685.

Wise, S. 2000. *Rattling the cage.* Cambridge, Mass.: Perseus Books Group.

———. 2002. *Drawing the line: Science and the case for animal rights.* Cambridge, Mass.: Perseus Books Group.

Yerkes, R.M., and B.W. Learned. 1925. *Chimpanzee intelligence and its vocal expressions.* Baltimore: Williams and Wilkins Co.

Yerkes National Primate Research Center. n.d. Innovation and science: The history of Yerkes. *http://www.yerkes.emory.edu/about_history.html.*

About the Contributors

Sarah Boysen received her Ph.D. in 1984 from The Ohio State University. Her current research interests are animal cognition, particularly the acquisition of counting abilities and numerical competence in nonhuman primates; cognitive development in the great apes, including attribution, self-recognition, and intentional behavior; and social behavior and tool use in captive lowland gorillas. She is currently consulting editor for the *Journal of Comparative Psychology*.

Kathleen Conlee is director of program management, Animal Research Issues, at The HSUS and is responsible for the organization's work related to nonhuman primates in research, the use of animals in education, and the HSUS Pain and Distress campaign. She previously worked for seven years at a large nonhuman primate breeding facility and a year and a half at a chimpanzee and orangutan sanctuary.

Jennifer M. Felt graduated from the University of Vermont in 1999 and served for two and a half years in the Peace Corps in Honduras. She was program manager for Latin America and the Caribbean for Humane Society International (HSI), the international arm of The HSUS, until June 2004, when she became deputy director for trade capacity building at The HSUS.

Stephanie Edwards is a 2003 graduate of the University of Maryland and program assistant and Web content manager for HSI.

Katherine C. (Kasey) Grier is associate professor in the Department of History, University of South Carolina. She is the author of *Culture and Comfort: Parlor Making and Middle Class Identity* and the forthcoming *Pets in America: A History*. Her current research focuses on the history of animal-human interaction. She serves as guest curator for an exhibition on the history of pet keeping in the United States originating at McKissick Museum, the University of South Carolina, in 2005 and traveling for three years thereafter.

Kristin Kaschner received her M.Sc. from Albert-Ludwigs-Universität of Freiburg, Germany, in 1997. Based at the Underwater Acoustics Group at Loughborough University, Leicestershire, England, she developed an acoustic analysis technique to study the behavior of small cetaceans around midwater trawl nets. She joined the Marine Mammal Research Unit at the Fisheries Centre at the University of British Columbia (UBC) in 1998 and has been a member of the Sea Around Us Project, based at UBC and devoted to studying the impact of fisheries on the world's marine ecosystems, since 1999. Ms. Kaschner was an invited participant at the International Whaling Commission Scientific Committee workshop on bycatch mitigation and acoustic deterrents in 1999 and is a member of the Cetacean Bycatch Task Force. She has been a FishBase collaborator since 2000, compiling information about the acoustical behavior of fish.

Randall Lockwood received his Ph.D. from Washington University in St. Louis. He is senior vice president for anti-cruelty initiatives and training for the American Society for the Prevention of Cruelty to Animals and former vice president/Research and Educational Outreach for The HSUS. He is the co-editor of *Cruelty to Animals and Interpersonal Violence* and co-author (with Frank Ascione) of "Cruelty to Animals: Changing Psychological, Social, and Legislative Perspectives," which appeared in *The State of the Animals: 2001*.

Kelly O'Meara is program manager, Africa and Asia, for HSI. She has promoted humane slaughter practices to government representatives in Indonesia and Vietnam; initiated and organized first-of-their-kind workshops on stray dog/street animal control in Moscow and St. Petersburg; and managed a two-year street dog control program on the island of Abaco in the Bahamas. A graduate of the University of Massachusetts, she holds certificates from the Royal Society for the Prevention of Cruelty to Animals (RSPCA) in large-animal euthanasia and from Bristol University, England, for animal welfare officer training. She is co-author of the HSI report *Dogs on Abaco Island, the Bahamas: A Case Study*.

Daniel Pauly acquired his doctorate in fisheries biology in 1979 from the University of Kiel in Germany. He is a former division director of the International Center for Living Aquatic Resources Management (ICLARM) in Manila and taught fisheries sciences at the University of the Philippines. In 1994 he joined the Fisheries Centre, University of British Columbia, while remaining ICLARM's principal science advisor until 1997 and the science advisor of its FishBase project until 2000. Since 1999 he has been principal investigator for the Sea Around Us Project. In 2001 he received the Murray Newman Award for Excellence in Marine Conservation Research and the Oscar E. Sette Award of the Marine Fisheries Section, American Fisheries Society. He was named an honorary professor at Kiel University in 2002 and elected a Fellow of the Royal Society of Canada (Academy of Science) in 2003.

Nancy Peterson, a registered veterinary technician, is an issues specialist in the Companion Animals section of The HSUS and coordinator of the Pets for Life Training Centers. Before joining The HSUS, Ms. Peterson worked in small-animal veterinary hospitals and as a trainer of dogs for people with disabilities. Her articles promoting pet-friendly rental housing have been published in numerous housing magazines. She was a member of the HSUS staff who collaborated on *The Humane Society of the United States Complete Guide to Cat Care* (co-authored with Wendy Christensen).

J.F. Reece received his B.Sc.(Hons.) in biology from University of York and was qualified (B.V.Sc.) from Liverpool University Veterinary School in 1994. He worked for more than three years in rural, large-animal veterinary practice in Devon, England. Since 1998 he has been associated with the work of Help in Suffering, an animal welfare charity in Jaipur, India, as a volunteer veterinary surgeon. Since 2002 he has been in charge of the ongoing ABC Extension Project, sponsored by HSI, at Help in Suffering Jaipur.

Beth Rosen has worked in the HSUS Government Affairs and Evaluation and Planning departments since 2001. She received her master's degree in public administration from New York University.

Andrew N. Rowan is executive vice president, operations, for The HSUS. He is the author of *Of Mice, Models, and Men*; co-author of *The Animal Research Controversy: Protest, Process, and Public Policy*; and coeditor of Humane Society Press's State of the Animals series.

Stephanie Shain is director of companion animal outreach for The HSUS and one of the organization's leading spokespeople on pet-related topics. From 1995 to 2000 she worked as assistant director of programs for the American Anti-Vivisection Society.

Margaret R. Slater is a veterinarian and associate professor of epidemiology in the departments of Veterinary Anatomy and Public Health and Small Animal Medicine and Surgery in the College of Veterinary Medicine at Texas A&M University in College Station, Texas. The author of *Community Approaches to Feral Cats: Problems, Alternatives, and Recommendations*, she is frequently invited to speak on feral cat issues at professional conferences nationwide.

Neil Trent is executive director of HSI. A graduate of the law enforcement division of the RSPCA, he worked in a number of capacities for the RSPCA in England, the Bahamas, and Australia. He is a former field officer and field services director for the World Society for the Protection of Animals. He is co-author of "The State of Meat Production in Developing Countries: 2002," which appeared in *The State of the Animals II: 2003*.

Index

meat sold to U.S., humane methods required, 81
nonambulatory livestock in slaughterhouses, 82
poultry inclusion in humane standards, 83
preslaughter handling of animals used for
food, 81
religious slaughter not covered, 83
slaughterhouse reform publicity and support, 81
28-Hour Law, 81
Humane slaughter laws, 68, 72, 75
The Humane Society of the United States (HSUS)
passage of CHIMP Act, 128
policy statements on free-roaming cats, 45
reviews cases of animal abuse, 20
split from the American Humane Association, 81
Human immunodeficiency virus (HIV)
chimpanzees and AIDS-related symptoms, 123
specific strain of virus in chimpanzees, 123
Yerkes National Primate Research Center, 121
Human-like tone of cries of cats in pain
"cat organs," 19
tormenting during rituals, 19
Hunting licenses, 3

I

IFAW. *See* International Fund for Animal Welfare
(IFAW)
Impact of feral cats on shelters, 51
Improvements in declawing surgical techniques
and analgesics, 35
Inappropriate elimination linked to declawing, 37
Income as support for declawing, 36
Income breakdown of surveys, 7
Increase in animal protection organizations, *74*
India
Animal Welfare Board of India, 74
Assam Rhinoceros Preservation Act of 1954, 74
British origin of animal protection laws, 74
enforcement nonexistent, 74
Prevention of Cruelty to Animals Act of 1960, 74
Rajasthan Animals and Birds Sacrifice
(Prohibition) Act 1975, 74
Infectious disease research involving chimpanzees
cognitive and behavioral studies, 120, 121,
123, 125
Crohn's disease, 125
drug and vaccine testing, 125
gene therapy, 125
HIV/AIDS, 123, 125
malaria, 125
Inhumane methods of catching stray dogs, 58–59
Innocent VIII, Pope
issued order to persecute witches and kill
all cats, 16
Inspectors of slaughterhouses
paychecks and, 83

Institutionalized cat abuse, 16
Integration of cats into ecosystems, 46–47
Intentional cruelty toward cats and dogs, 20
International disfavor for declawing, 36
International Fund for Animal Welfare (IFAW), 68
International policies related to chimpanzees
in research, *131*
International restrictions on use of chimpanzees
in research
exception in Sweden for noninvasive behavioral
studies, 131
Japan allows noninvasive research, 131
Netherlands prohibits great apes in biomedical
experiments, 131
New Zealand restricts use of non-human
hominids, 130
New Zealand's National Animal Ethics Advisory
Committee, 131
Sweden bans use of apes, 131
United Kingdom prohibits use of great apes, 130
Internet listserv to communicate with campus
programs, 44
Internet survey methods, 5–6
Interrelation of feral cat management with
communities, 51–52
Interstate transportation of animals, 83–84
Interstate transportation of birds for fighting
purposes, 84
Iowa shelter case
youths break into shelter and kill cats, 87
Irwin, Paul G.
evaluates position of animals, 1, 2
Islamic religious practices of slaughtering, 75

J

Jaipur ABC program to control dog populations,
61–63
benefits to health of dogs, 63
data collection and dog censuses, 62
governmental lack of interest in animal
welfare, 63
human rabies data collection, 63
methods of catching and sterilizing dogs, 62
Jesperson, Keith
childhood killing of animals, 19–20
*Journal of the American Veterinary Medical
Association,* 52

K

Keeping cats indoors, owner routines, *31*
Kenya
Animal Transportation Act, 75
British origin of animal law, 75
camel shipping from Arab states, 75
halal method of slaughter, 75